Women and Christian Mission

Missional Church, Public Theology, World Christianity

Stephen Bevans, Paul S. Chung, Veli-Matti Kärkkäinen
and Craig L. Nessan, Series Editors

IN THE MIDST OF globalization there is crisis as well as opportunity. A model of God's mission is of special significance for ecclesiology and public theology when explored in diverse perspectives and frameworks in the postcolonial context of World Christianity. In the face of the new, complex global civilization characterized by the Second Axial Age, the theology of mission, missional ecclesiology, and public ethics endeavor to provide a larger framework for missiology. It does so in interaction with our social, multicultural, political, economic, and intercivilizational situation. These fields create ways to refurbish mission as constructive theology in critical and creative engagement with cultural anthropology, world religions, prophetic theology, postcolonial hermeneutics, and contextual theologies of World Christianity. Such endeavors play a critical role in generating theological, missional, social-ethical alternatives to the reality of Empire—a reality characterized by civilizational conflict, and by the complex system of a colonized lifeworld that is embedded within practices of greed, dominion, and ecological devastation. This series—Missional Church, Public Theology, World Christianity—invites scholars to promote alternative church practices for life-enhancing culture and for evangelization as telling the truth in the public sphere, especially in solidarity with those on the margins and in ecological stewardship for the lifeworld.

Women and Christian Mission
Ways of Knowing and Doing Theology

Frances S. Adeney

PICKWICK *Publications* · Eugene, Oregon

WOMEN AND CHRISTIAN MISSION
Ways of Knowing and Doing Theology

Missional Church, Public Theology, World Christianity 6

Pickwick Publications
An Imprint of Wipf and Stock Publishers
199 W. 8th Ave., Suite 3
Eugene, OR 97401

www.wipfandstock.com

ISBN 13: 978-1-4982-1719-4

Cataloguing-in-Publication Data

Adeney, Frances S.

Women and Christian mission : ways of knowing and doing theology / Frances S. Adeney.

xvi + 300 p. ; 23 cm. Includes bibliographical references.

Missional Church, Public Theology, World Christianity 6

ISBN 13: 978-1-4982-1719-4

1. Women in missionary work. 2. Women missionaries. I. Series. II. Title.

BV2610 .A34 2015

Manufactured in the U.S.A.   11/02/2015

This book is dedicated to my granddaughters Isobel, Addison, and Harper Mae with the prayer that each of you will find your place in God's mission in your world.

Contents

Preface

THIS BOOK DESCRIBES THE creative work of women in Christian mission designed and practiced in diverse contexts around the globe. Although often not named or self-identified as theologians, women in mission are doing creative mission theology that cuts across lines of received theologies of their traditions. Drawing from their experiences and relationships, women develop mission theologies out of their contexts and practices.

Despite differences in those contexts, women face common obstacles in that task. Their voices get muffled and their sense of belonging challenged. This book describes those ideas and challenges in the words of women practicing and teaching Christian mission. Based on ninety interviews over seven years, the literature of published women missiologists, lectures and countless conversations with women in mission, this study searches out the common threads of content, values, and methods of women doing mission theology today.

Interviews reveal themes that cut across lines of traditional theologies—the centrality of relationships, the equality of all people, the priority of needs, common qualities of character, methods of collaboration, and the use of emotions in doing theology. Women in Europe, missionaries in South America, theologians in South East Asia, and my own experiences as a missionary and theologian echoed some of those themes. There is much diversity in women's mission theologies as women come from diverse traditions. But the common concerns, values, and methods that arose during this study amazed me.

This book emphasizes those common themes avoiding comparison to specific traditions or gender-based theories as much as possible. That difficult task reveals the creative voices of Christian women in mission.

The content of their mission theologies, their sources of authority, their methods, their values, and the spiritual practices that nurture them contribute to mission theology, filling a lacuna in mission studies and crafting new directions based on experiential and contextual sources.

Acknowledgments

MANY INDIVIDUALS AND COMMUNITIES contributed to this project in significant ways. First thanks go to the women narrators who took the time to reflect on their journeys and thoughts about Christian mission. I appreciate their candor and willingness to share with me the place that mission holds in their lives. I want to thank the women authors that have written about women in mission, both past and present. Special thanks go to the women theologians of the American Society of Missiology for their enthusiastic support. My thanks also goes to Louisville Presbyterian Theological Seminary where I have taught evangelism and mission since 1999. Administrative support of this project includes time and support for two sabbaticals, the opportunity to teach courses on women doing mission theology, and time for travel to conferences and mission sites around the world. Individual faculty have been generous with their time and ideas. Students have shared their visions of Christian mission. Faculty secretary Laura March patiently pursued the myriad details such a project requires. Thanks too go to the Lilly Foundation and the Association of Theological Schools for their generous support of time and funds in granting me a Faculty Fellowship during the fall semester of 2012. Without the practical support of extended time to read, analyze interviews, and write, this project could not have been completed. I also want to thank Kim Okesson for volunteering her time and connections with women missionaries around the world to aid in the interview process. My friends "up North" encouraged me during the solitary task of writing. Finally, thanks go to my family— mother, daughters and sons, in-laws, and especially to my husband Terry Muck for his encouragement at every stage of the project.

Introduction

Beginnings

THIS PROJECT BEGAN IN 2005 at the women's luncheon of the annual American Society of Missiologists meeting. It was an inauspicious beginning. I first noted the enthusiasm of the twenty-odd women as each introduced herself and spoke of the projects they were currently involved in. Some were missiologists. Some were wives of missiologists. Some were mission workers. Some were students. All had theological reasons for what they were doing. All focused not on articulating those ideas but on the work itself. I was fascinated. Here were women actually doing theology instead of talking about it. An interesting dynamic at a conference of missiologists.

Later that summer I did my first interview with Dr. Bonnie Sue Lewis, missiologist at the Presbyterian seminary in Dubuque Iowa. She came up to our cabin in Wisconsin for a short visit. We spoke about women and mission theology. My husband Terry encouraged me to interview her for a new project on women and missiology. I was hooked.

In that first interview I learned some things that occurred repeatedly in the next ninety interviews that I did over the next seven years. Bonnie didn't consider herself a theologian but an educator. She was very modest about making theological claims. Although she spent a great deal of time mentoring Native American students and studying the history of the Native American church in the U.S.A., she expressed the view that her influence in those areas was quite minimal. Over and over through other interviews I found the same themes among highly educated women doing mission theology. They usually didn't consider themselves theologians.

They didn't articulate theological themes very often although their work showed strong theological commitments. They were modest about their influence—sometimes too modest.

I became more and more interested in the question of how to translate the *doing* of theology revealed by women narrators in the interviews with mission theology articulated in *language*, either written or spoken. That question is at the heart of this study.

In order to pursue that question I had to discover methods that would uncover women's theologies without changing the active forms in which they were presented. I was greatly helped by the interpretive theory of knowledge of Hans Georg Gadamer and the way that Juergen Habermas used grounded theory to discover hidden meanings of the classic sociologists of religion Max Weber, Emile Durkheim, and Karl Marx. Charles Taylor's *Philosophical Papers Vol. 2* helped me to see knowledge in a field, by someone, for someone. Knowledge didn't just exist in the realm of ideas but in the social world. My own teacher Robert Bellah stressed those same ideas as he outlined his views of religion and did his cooperative studies especially *Habits of the Heart*.

In the theological realm, Charles McCoy was ahead of his time when he published the postmodern book, *When Gods Change: Hope for Theology* in the early 1980s. Studying with McCoy steeped me in the milieu of contexts and perspectives, partial knowing and constant change. Through John Coleman's (SJ) patient teaching I discovered the difference between epistemological humility and ontological faith. And Marti Stortz encouraged my creativity and affirmed my enthusiasm for academic discovery.

As I brought those influence into this research project. I kept focusing on what I didn't know, a technique espoused scientist and philosopher by Michael Polanyi. What was it that women were doing in mission theology? How did they understand mission? What common themes did they exhibit despite coming from evangelical, Catholic, mainline Protestant, African American churches, Pentecostal backgrounds as well as different cultures from around the world. Were there common themes at all?

Those questions drove me to interview women about mission theology wherever I went—to academic meetings, to church gatherings, to the offices of the World Council and the Reformed Churches in Geneva Switzerland, to mission training sessions in Brazil, and to my own colleagues and students at Louisville Seminary.

My work on Christian women in Indonesia formed a base line for this broader study. Interviews and participant observations over the course of six years in Indonesia resulted in a discovery of practices that women used to sustain them as they sought to become leaders in the Indonesian church. I did not intentionally transfer the specific practices discovered in that work: forming relationships, honoring leaders, and creating beauty to this study. Interestingly, however, some of those themes did turn up in many of the interviews.

The first section of the book describes the journeys of women in mission, their theologies and some contemporary voices. Chapter 1 begins by documenting the journeys of women in Christian mission, using their own categories and quotes to illustrate the ways women enter the study and practice of Christian mission. Chapter 2, 3, and 4 follow by describing the sources of authority women use to think about and practice mission, along with common themes and diverging theologies of women in mission. Chapter 5 summarizes some theological themes articulated by contemporary missiologists, historians, and theologians. Those academic voices are set in a global context that is informed and indeed shaped by the history of women's interaction with the church and societies.

The next section of the book analyzes findings, documenting the themes, identity issues, obstacles and leadership styles of women in mission. Chapter 6 discovers themes of women in mission today focusing on ideas, values, and practices. In Chapter 7, women discuss identity, showing how various parts of their lives intersect and what kinds of crises they encounter as they work in many arenas of Christian mission. Chapter 8 presents Dorothy Day as an exemplar of contemporary Christian mission. Chapter 9 describes obstacles that face women in doing mission theology and what strategies they use to overcome those obstacles. Chapter 10 analyzes leadership styles of women, showing how they put into practice their mission theologies. A case study follows in Chapter 11, graphically illustrating some obstacles faced by women in mission and describing in their own language how they worked to overcome them. Summarizing the roadblocks women have faced and continue to face in mission places the accomplishments of women doing mission theology in perspective.

Chapter 12 shows how women use art, beauty, and a love of nature in their approaches to mission and theology. Part 3 begins with Chapter 13 taking the reader back into a brief overview of women in mission through the centuries beginning with the early church. A thumbnail sketch of this fascinating subject highlights the times of openness to women's leadership in the church.

Contributions of women to mission theology comprise Chapters 14 and 15. Mission theology and mission theory can both be enhanced by attending to women's voices. Listening to women's voices in Christian mission can make huge, direction-altering contributions to the fields of missiology, ethics, and theology. Approaches to mission and the impact of Christian mission in the world can also be understood more fully as women's mission practices and the values that source those practices enter the discourse in the sociological study of Christian mission.

An Appendix on Method concludes this book, documenting details of the study and placing those methods into a larger interpretive framework. This study is intended to be more a sociological than a theological work. I am gathering, collating, and reporting women's practices and views of mission theology—ways of knowing and doing theology. I am not advocating any one theological viewpoint. I am not creating a new theology of mission. Rather I am bringing to voice the ways that women are doing mission theology in our contemporary world.

Yet, my methodology does not attempt to be value-free. I do bring values to this study, specifically values of human worth and gender equality. The values of Christianity and responsible sociology also inform this work. Perhaps, like so many of the narrators in this study, I too am doing theology.

By articulating mission theologies of women, I hope this book will become a source for women and men doing mission to help identify the mission theologies they are already practicing and be more clear in stating those theologies. I hope this work will influence the field of missiology to pay more attention to women's theologies and to the contributions that women's ideas, values, and mission practices bring to mission theology.

PART I

1

The Journey

"But certain flowers grow near as deep as trees. . . . Then let me grow within
my wayside hedge, and pass your way!"

—ELIZABETH BARRETT BROWNING[1]

JANE FELT UNCOMFORTABLE IN Brazil.[2] She didn't belong there. Her children were in the United States. She described her sense of dislocation: "I know I shouldn't be here. I'm not called to be a missionary. But what can I do about that? My husband is a leader here. He brought me. I feel out of place." Jane had been following her husband to academic and mission organization posts for years. She struggled with the meaning of her accompanying him and the reasons that she needed to be so mobile, so much in the wake of decisions of her husband. Where should she be? With children in college, Jane felt she should be near them, at least in the United States. Yet here she was, in Brazil, facing two weeks as wife of a missionary leader with little to do since she held no position in the organization itself.

Jane responded in two ways. She did not let go of the idea of a call from God, something highly prized in Protestant mission circles. She said that her calling was to relationships. She developed friendships with women in whatever context she found herself as wife of a mission leader. She found fulfillment in mentoring younger women, sharing her culinary

1. "Aurora Leigh," lines 846–50, in Bolton and Holloway, *Aurora Leigh*, 56.

2. Pseudonym used here to protect the privacy of the narrator. I use the term narrator rather than interviewee to show the value and status of the women interviewed. They are narrating their own story rather than simply answering questions.

skills, and learning from her new friends about their cultures. She had a life-long love of cultures, finding them intriguing as a child and no less stimulating as an adult. Jane also quietly refused to be pushed into a traditional role as missionary wife. She did not help with childcare, she did not cook during the conference, nor did she lead music or coordinate free time activities. Jane felt out of place, but she maintained a sense of her identity as she made choices about what she would and wouldn't do at the site of her dislocation.

In this and coming chapters, we look at women's journeys into Christian mission. We explore childhood experiences and the beginnings of a sense of call to service in the Church, in academic institutions, or as a missionary in their home country or somewhere else. Ideas of place and call intertwine with one another. What is God asking me to do? Where should I be—in mission? In theology? In my home country? Somewhere else? Should I become a leader, ordained or not? How does my calling intersect with my relationships—with my husband, children, parents, and friends?

As narrators addressed those questions, their comments are inserted in the text using indentations to mark actual quotes.

Experiences

Narrators spoke of early experiences that prepared them for doing mission and theological reflection on mission. Some had a spiritual experience, either in a worship setting or when alone. That experience might be related to the church, to a missionary sharing their work, to reading about Christian mission, to a conversion experience, to a parent's encouragement or to a range of other social and religious events. The commonality is that an early experience or series of experiences set the woman on a course that led her into doing mission and mission theology.

Narrators that worked in traditional Protestant missions spoke of early experiences:

> I wanted to be a missionary from the time I was about 8 years old.

> My parents often had missionaries stay in our house and I know they supported missionaries. We had a world map with prayer cards and strings to their countries just above the breakfast table. I thought it was great for other people but I wasn't interested

in being a missionary. I wanted a very nice, comfortable life in the U.S.

I was always very fascinated with other cultures and languages. I applied to be part of Children's International Village.

I was not attracted as a child— "mission meant old people going to far away, scary places for the rest of their lives—except for furloughs."

I remember one of our zealous Sunday school teachers teaching us a song that plays in my head still today and that has ministered to me in tough financial times, or when I feel like a person without a country or home. "He owns the cattle on a thousand hills, the wealth in every mine. . . . He is my Father so they're mine as well." I'm sure that teacher had no idea that God would use that funny little song to me as a missionary serving in Africa and Europe.

At age thirteen, before I knew Christ personally or had any contact with missionaries, I used to tell my best friend that in the future I would join the Peace Corps and go to a third-world country. Was God preparing my heart even before I came to faith?

After my parents converted to Christianity when I was six years old, I also had an early conversion experience at age seven.

Narrators that came from other Christian backgrounds also spoke of early experiences that formed their views of mission—experiences that seemed at odds with their tradition. Reverend Nyambura Njoroge, a Presbyterian who became the first woman pastor in Ghana felt that she wanted to become a pastor since she was a small child. A Trappist sister at Gedono Monastery in Salatiga, Indonesia felt called to become a Catholic sister as a teenager even though she was from a Protestant family. Growing up in the British Reformed churches, mission professor Kirsteen Kim felt the stirrings of the charismatic movement, kindling a lifelong interest in the Holy Spirit, an idea foreign to the preaching of the Reformed churches.[3]

Experiences did not need to occur only in childhood to be definitive. Convictions that developed slowly might be cemented by a particular occurrence. Sometimes an epiphany marked a new direction. Consistent

3. Kim, *Holy Spirit in the World*, v.

encouragement to move into mission or theological study by family or pastors could also become crucial in a woman's journey:

> As a teenager I felt an awareness of the power of the Holy Spirit.

> God started calling me my freshman year in college when the Urbana '84 ads started appearing. I was terrified that if I went God would make me be a missionary—worst that I would be in Africa where I've been for the last twenty-five years.

> My interests in theology began after I finished my MA in literature. I planned to teach but my father wanted me to study theology where he was teaching theology. I visited, walking around campus. Then I stopped. It was suddenly clear. Almost like a voice saying "you should come here and study theology."

Calling

Many women use the language of call to mark the event that led them into mission. Some put the work of the Holy Spirit at the center of that idea of call. Others mark a conversion experience as initiating that call. Many had more than one call, first a general call to follow Christ and later a more specific call to mission, teaching or pastoral work. For some women, a particular mission vision was at the heart of their call. Others sensed a call to a religious order, or a call to mission in general. For some, the call was to a specific task, for others, the call focused on a particular geographic area, culture, or people group. Each became convinced that God was taking them into mission or Christian leadership:

> For me there was an epiphany. But there is always an external and internal aspect of call. The epiphany was there and the circumstances confirmed it—I got full tuition, I could live with my parents, my father encouraged me. Now I'm doing my dissertation on Leslie Newbigin.

> I felt a strong calling to become educated. I knew education was "the way out."

> As a schoolgirl I felt called to become a pastor in my village. That call was renewed while at Seminary with a focus on teaching ministry. I felt called to teaching that would empower a local congregation.

For many years I was a pastor's wife, then a missionary wife. That seemed normal. I didn't question it or think of any other way to do things. Then I realized I was called to be more than a missionary wife. I was called to be a Christian leader. So I did my PhD at age fifty-seven.

Calling and Place

Some women link their experiences of God and their sense of call to mission to a sense of place. Remembering a particular church where they first experienced a sense of awe, a meadow or grove of trees where God had seemed real to them, or perhaps a people they felt called to serve. Being "in the right place" became a metaphor for becoming the person they felt called to become.

In the film *A League of Their Own*, women, recruited from all over the United States and Canada, played baseball in the All-American League during World War II. They left their homes to join traveling baseball teams. Some of them had husbands fighting overseas. They experienced fear and homesickness. They often felt misunderstood because women in that era were not supposed to play baseball as a major part of their life. The film uses a song composed by Madonna to describe that sense of being in the right place. The song is nostalgic, expressing a longing for feeling whole and well, a return to a "childhood playground." Years later those women understood that they "felt right" when they were playing baseball.

Women in mission feel a similar sense of dislocation and longing. They want to feel that they are "in the right place." Some express that place as being "in the center of God's will." Others express it as a feeling of "being home." One narrator described the relief she felt when she finally went to the mission field after years of feeling called to Christian mission but with no clear location in mind.

Others sense God calling them to a particular place or vocation:

> After college, while teaching school in Appalachia and working with a mission agency there, I sensed god calling me to the poor who didn't know him outside of the U.S. I also felt called to the disabled so I did a Master's degree in special education.

> Somewhere in the midst of a short term missions trip to a
> Kenyan orphanage God gave me an insatiable passion for the
> children in this community.

Some women expressed a more general sense of calling not related
to a particular place or even vocation:

> I didn't feel called to a people, a nation, or a cause. I just felt
> called. Even though I've been here going on three years, I feel
> that God is still shaping my call over time.

Sometimes missionary families or immigrants are displaced without
their desiring that move. When families are dislocated, they sometimes
reconstruct themselves. Christian immigrants from the West Indies found
that as women moved into higher paying jobs, family roles reconfigured
themselves in a less traditional way. The creativity of women in those
situations led them to function in key roles in the family and church:

> We learned how to live out our Christianity in a new situation.

> God's call creates a space for you to live differently.

Contextual theologians continue to focus on place as they do theology. Where they are and what the issues are in that place becomes a
source of theological reflection for narrators doing academic theology:

> My contextual method needs both Western systematic theology
> and context.

> In working with pluralism and religious dialogue, my focus is
> not on ends, like Moltmann but on paths using Koyama's bridge
> concept.

> I saw images of the Holy Spirit in the Bible. Then I began to see
> how indigenous spiritualities could be used in liberation.

Mentors and Encouragers

Many narrators spoke of encouragement from family, pastors, or friends.
A good number of those mentors were pastors, priests, or fathers, or male
teachers. Those men saw the potential in the woman and sought to influence her to reach that God-given potential. Even leaders that did not

believe in women's leadership in the church mentored women, sometimes as daughters, sometimes as bright students, sometimes as exceptions to the rule. Their influence on the directions narrators took was enormous.

Parents were at the forefront in some of the women's stories:

> My parents' affirmation was important to me. Also the support of my professors at seminary, especially the one that later helped me develop my ministry.

> My parents supported my decision even though I was their only girl and they hated to see me go.

> My parents were supportive although not involved in any church.

> My mother was very progressive. After finishing her education she returned home and set up programs for women.

> My father died when I was very young but he influenced me through stories shared about him.

Others recalled Christian leaders, teachers, or pastors that encouraged them to become leaders in mission:

> Cliff Schimmels challenged me to use my teaching training overseas.

> One summer my pastor encouraged me to consider a seven-week mission trip to Cote d'Ivoire that opened up my heart and mind to the need and possibility of serving God overseas.

> A mentor takes on "spiritual sons." There's a space there to reconstruct gender.

Relationships

Relationships played an important role in women's direction in mission and theology. In a context of supportive family and friends, people in their congregations or institutions where they received their education, many women took hold of their call to mission and followed it vigorously:

> The most rewarding part of my work as Moderator of the WCC Conference on World Missions and Evangelism is relationships so I focus on that.

> I'm enjoying working on an article with a friend in Jakarta.

> Truly and literally my greatest encourager has been God.

> Some good friends overcame many difficulties to visit us the first Christmas we were missionaries in Kenya. That gift of relationship was priceless.

For those with close relations that disapproved or acted to prevent them from following a call to mission, leadership, or studying theology, their call was delayed or put aside altogether. The case study on women in mission training in Brazil in chapter 11 tells the stories of women who were unable to pursue their call to mission or, on the other hand, were pressed into mission by husbands that had a call.

At the International Association of Mission Studies meeting in Toronto in 2012, women spoke to the issue of relationships that may harm the cause of Christian mission. Sister Rose Uchem noted that "internalized oppression keeps women from supporting one another in Nigeria. Girls are socialized to refer and defer to men. We marginalize ourselves—how can we help ourselves?" Jennifer Aycock, a participant from the United states reflected on the margins and center question for women in mission in a different way. "Relationships with marginal people have opened the way for me. The margins can empower other margins."[4]

Identity

We hold complex identities in our globalized world. Identifying as a missioner, a missionary, a religious, or a pastor may be only one part of a woman's identity. A woman may also be an African American, a mother, a wife, a teacher, an artist, a lover of the outdoors, a poor villager, a wealthy wife of a businessman. The narrators each tell their own story of their journey into mission and reflection on mission. The complexity of their identities, their ages, their locations, and other multiple centers of identity influence their stories:

> I have a strong sense of self. I know I am in charge of my own life.

> My family talks about returning to Florida but we have been in Kentucky for eighteen years. I am no longer from Florida.

4. Women's Track Discussion, August 20, 2012.

> I can't sit by myself and wait for people to come to me. I have to reach out.

Each woman is made in the image of God, given certain natural capacities to develop, and placed in a particular setting. Every story is unique. Yet the trajectory of the stories show that women desire to serve God in mission and to reflect on the meaning of Christian mission in their context. It is that trajectory that ties the diverse journeys together and yields insights for the Church:

> In the West Indies, tradition defines identity—but in Brooklyn girls and boys are socialized differently. Space is made for you to find new ways of being a family.

> In Nigeria women can't go to family meetings. If a woman's husband dies the men decide what happens to her. If she has no brothers or male children, she may become poor and have to prostitute herself.

> Girls are taught that they are inferior to boys. They can't inherit. Jesus didn't prefer males. We should imitate him.

Sources of Authority

Women use experiences, calling, a sense of place, mentors, and other sources of authority along with the Bible and church traditions as they develop mission theologies.

Women in churches that disallowed their participation in mission or leadership activities used their calling as a source of authority that validated their decision and gave them power to act. Speaking of a leader in the immigrant community one commented, "Because she's called by God, she won't give ground to any man."

A strong sense of identity also plays a role as a source of authority. Septemmy, a theologian from Indonesia remarked, "I claim my own authority as a contextual theologian. I set up contextual reading sessions with PERWATI, women theologians in Indonesia. We began reading the Bible in context—with new eyes.[5]

---

5. Interview, IAMS Quadrennial Meeting, Malaysia, May 2004.

Overcoming Obstacles

Women speak of many obstacles in their journeys into mission. Some obstacles are circumstantial: disabilities in the family, a need to care for parents, financial difficulties or spouses that wanted to move in other directions. Gender sometimes plays a part in those obstacles or presents other roadblocks:

> I have always felt "other." As a wife at Southern Baptist Seminary during theological discussions I would present an idea that would be ignored.

> Women cannot always do the big things. Women's leadership in mission societies and mission fields is not encouraged in Korea. In Korea women don't feel comfortable with the business strategy, structural approach to mission.

> Single women often are not accepted as mission candidates. Only married couples can apply for cross-cultural work.

Rather than retreating, women develop creative strategies for overcoming obstacles:

> I overcome obstacles by seeing life as a gift from God. Love for life makes it possible to work without ceasing or seeking recognition.

> I was feeling ignored and discounted, yet I continued to struggle with becoming a theologian. Now I am in seminary.

> I was a top high school student but no one in my family had a vision for college. I went but left on probation after a semester. I was determined to go back. I got my BA three weeks before my son graduated from high school! Now doing an MA in pastoral counseling at a seminary.

> When defending my thesis I insisted on a woman committee member.

Practices

Sustaining their professional and spiritual lives in the midst of struggles presents ongoing challenges for women in mission. Their approaches include spiritual practices and engaging in leisure activities:

I prayed silently before eating in any situation.

To take care of myself so that those pressures don't overwhelm me I do gardening. This year I planted violets, cosmos, and sunflowers.

I love to read the Bible with new eyes—through my context and local situation.

Those practices also included intentionally cultivating habits of character:

Peace and justice became important to me as a teenager living in the war-torn Middle-East. I could never throw a stone—so I had to ask what I could do. Violence is never a way of dealing with a problem.

I knew my ideas were worthwhile. I just had to persevere.

I must never take the victim role.

Direction

Sometimes women took directions that allowed them to pursue their work without battling theological or institutional limits on women's roles. Many became educators. They could teach, theologize, and encourage others to follow Christ sometimes without encountering significant resistance.

Sometimes a direction evolved from a combination of early experiences, theological convictions, and issues arising in the context. In Viola Raheb's story, those issues demanded a response. She grew up in a Palestinian family that was very involved with the Lutheran church in Israel addressing theological questions about conflict. Her father and later her brother Mitri influenced her own theology. In 1985 when she was in tenth grade, two of her classmates were jailed for reading Palestinian literature. What should she do? Although forbidden to express political views, she decided to speak out to the press about it. That led her to take a pro-active role, becoming a teacher using drama, music and art to work with traumatized children from Iraq and Palestine. The combination of theological convictions gained in her family milieu and circumstances around her demanded a response.[6]

Others saw ordination as the path for them, either in overseas settings or in home churches. Those women struggled with denominations, theologies, and both men and women in the church that wished to prevent women from achieving positions of authority in the church.

Conversations at the IAMS meeting in August 2012 in Toronto addressed the issue of the future of women in Christian mission. Some of the conversations in the Women and Mission Track yielded insights. Dorothy Oluwagbimi spoke of a scarcity of laborers but a huge harvest for Christianity in Africa. She said, "Mission work empowers, so women's marginalization in missions hinders the Kingdom. Women are the majority in African churches but they are excluded from preaching and witness. We must change gender relations to empower missions." Evelyn Parkin, an aboriginal from Australia concurred but took a positive approach to the future, "The church has been like a bird with one wing. That is not right. But we cannot stop the power of God. Women will be empowered."[7]

As women's experiences, calling, sense of place, identity, relationships, mentors, and desire to serve God's mission in the world coalesce, women choose directions and develop practices that enable them to find the place that suits their longing for God. The next chapters will explore those topics in more depth.

---

6. Interview, World Council of Churches Conference on World Mission and Evangelism, Athens, May 14, 2005.

7. Women's Track Discussions, August 16–25, 2012.

2

Sources of Authority

For it is God working in you both to will and to do of God's good pleasure.

—PHILIPPIANS 2:13

AUTHORITY HAS ALWAYS BEEN a big issue in theology. When women set out to think theologically about Christian mission, they encounter questions about authority. What kind of authority does the Bible have? On what authority can one interpret the Bible? How is the Holy Spirit involved in making theology? What about the Church? Where does the wisdom of influential theologians of the past fit in? Do one's own personal or communal experiences count as authorities in theology? What about practices and habits, rituals and liturgies, both past and present? How does one use any of those authorities in a particular context, time and place in history? How does one use any of them personally? What happens when authorities in theology or the church run counter to a woman's thinking or action in mission?

The bottom line on authorities for theology has yet to be discovered. That is because the authorities listed above are intertwined and receive more or less credibility in different eras and sectors of the church as well as in different contexts. The study of hermeneutics, interpretation of Biblical and philosophical sources of authority, will continue long after the author and readers of this book are gone. In fact, every generation in every time and place must struggle with sources of authority as they construct theologies. Those claiming the authority of Scripture alone or the infallible authority of the Church still must reckon with everyday interpretations of those authorities—interpretations that are sourced in community, history, and experience.

Women doing mission theology in the current era grapple with those issues. There is no one theology of mission for women. Major differences appear in their theologies—differences that stem from their context and use of sources of authority. Where do women go for sources of the theologies of mission they develop?

This chapter will describe the sources of theology used by women, and the next chapter will show how do they use those sources of authority in constructing theologies of mission.

Scripture

For the Jews following Jesus while he was on the earth, Old Testament Scriptures were crucial in interpreting the meaning of Jesus' life for them. Jesus refers to those Scriptures as authoritative sources in Luke's account of his first public proclamation. After reading Isa 61:1–2, he said, "Today this Scripture is fulfilled in your hearing" (Luke 4:14–20). In other words, I am the one who will fulfill this prophecy. I have authority because our own holy book, the revelation from God, tells of my coming.

The Hebrew Scriptures continued to be a major source of authority for the early church. The Epistles frequently refer to the First Testament writings to support their injunctions. The story of salvation in Romans, the resurrection of the dead in 1 Cor 15, the relationship between husband and wife in Eph 5:31 all include interpretations of Old Testament Scriptures. Not all of those interpretations of the Hebrew Scriptures are upheld today. Some are understood to be helpful interpretations for the contexts of the day, e.g. the relationship between Adam and Eve as an argument for the cultural practice of head coverings for women in public worship (1 Cor 11:3–10).

Church Tradition

As the early church became established those very Epistles and the New Testament Gospels were established as Scripture by church authorities. Church authorities took on the task of deciding what written accounts of Jesus' life and what letters of early church leaders should be included in the canon and considered to be revelatory Scriptures. Exploring the ins and outs of social and political history that influenced those choices makes a fascinating study. But however they came to be included, and with some differences among Protestants, Roman, Orthodox and Eastern Catholics, the books of the canon were established by the fourth century. Those books hold a special place in Christian study, preaching, and church life all over the world.

Besides establishing the canon, the early church instituted rituals, rules, and leaders to guide the ever-expanding company of Christians. Early church fathers wrote treatises on issues of the day and established hierarchies of official leaders. Later monastic communities modeled a life of simplicity and worship. During the second to the fifth centuries traditions that lasted for centuries were established. The church gained stability and continuity with the early church.

Despite those gains, disadvantages for women in ministry grew as church structures became established. Earlier Greek and Roman ideas about women's weakness and inferiority seeped back into the church. Women were barred from the leadership positions and activities that they had performed in the early days of Christianity—work as apostles, deacons, and teachers. Those traditions still hamper women's work in ministry and mission in many churches around the world.

Experience

Some theologians consider the use of experience as revelation for theology as a secondary, if not dubious, source of authority. Others, like John Wesley understood experience to be an important part of the way God communicates truth to humankind. And experience has been used as revelation by women for centuries. Since women were excluded from the making of theology, they often sought to override the Church injunctions that silenced them by claiming a special revelation of the Holy Spirit. The visions of Catherine of Siena, Julian of Norwich, and Hildegaarde of Bingen are well known examples of the power of experience as revelation from God. But there were many others.

The tradition of women's claim to the revelation of the Holy Spirit dominated views of women in the United States during the two great awakenings. Women became evangelists and preachers, and claimed leadership as deacons and elders by the power of the Holy Spirit speaking through them. William Andrews in *Sisters of the Spirit* describes the journeys of three African American women of the nineteenth century that claimed just that. Jarena Lee, Zilpha Elaw, and Julia Foote, the first woman ordained as deacon of the African Methodist Episcopal Church, speak convincingly of the effect of the Holy Spirit on their lives and work.

One way those women claimed authority was to speak of their call. *God* had instructed them to take up preaching and evangelism. They claimed that by virtue of the indwelling of the Holy Spirit they recovered their true identity and power.[1] That claim trumped the church authorities' view that they were ill-equipped to carry out such work. With dedication and perseverance those three women along with hundreds of others during the late nineteenth century carried out the work of mission in the United States. Women worked with the poor and formed mission associations, saving pennies in jars for God's work overseas. And at home, women worked against slavery, for temperance, for equal rights at the ballot box, and for the salvation of souls as Christian messages were preached.

The call of those women lay at the heart of their energy and authority. Aimee Semple McPherson, Harriet Tubman, Elizabeth Cady Stanton, and the American Quaker women fighting against slavery are just a few examples of women that sourced their authority to preach and lead in the call of God on their lives.

Experience also helped women develop practices that sustained them in their work of Christian mission. They saw visions, they fasted and prayed, they wrote letters to sisters in Christ, they held vigils, they traveled to revivals to gain fresh insights from ministers and worship in community. Women used the arts to communicate and to comfort them in their efforts to spread the gospel. They composed hymns and wrote poetry, framing their thoughts of God and God's desire for love and justice in artistic forms.

New sources of authority for mission theology grew out of women's experiences during two waves of influence during the nineteenth and twentieth centuries: the worldwide missionary movement and the third wave women's movement focused on spirituality.

Mission Themes: Nineteenth–Twentieth-Century Missionary Movement

Women in the United States and Europe from all denominations participated vigorously in the missionary movement. By the late nineteenth

---

1. Andrews, *Sisters of the Spirit*, 15.

century, numbers of women missionaries to non-Western countries were expanding.[2] When the Edinburgh Conference was held in 1910, focusing on evangelization of the world, women across the United States and Canada held simultaneous conferences on the topic of Christian mission to the world. Major themes of subordination, concern for women and children, holism, ecumenical cooperation, and a spirituality of self-sacrifice characterized women's work in mission during that era.[3] Those themes reappear in this study of contemporary women in Christian mission.

Women's response to subordination was twofold. First, lack of concern for ecclesiology grew up among women missionaries. That contributed to their ability to work ecumenically. As they were neither creating or given authority over ecclesial theology, they sometimes put it aside in the interests of the greater need of the community. Second, women focused on collaborative efforts that furthered the work of God's Kingdom. Fundraising and work with the poor did not require women to hold positions of authority in the church or public realm.[4] Although prominent public Christian women did valuable work during that era, other missionaries fostered relationships with people not in power—neighbors, the poor, and those in need of health and education services.

They turned to *work with women and children* since both opportunities and needs abounded in those arenas. "No country can rise higher than its women" became a rationale for intensive work in healthcare and education with women in many countries. "As the child goes, so goes the culture" became another refrain that pushed women missionaries into work with families and children.

Furthermore, in many countries in the two-thirds world, women were not able to interact with men but could work easily with women. Rural women in Africa and Asia spent their days with other women and with children. Whereas the men associated with one another and performed public functions, the women and children spent time together in the marketplace, in the fields, and in the home. This is still true in many countries today.

2. Robert, *American Women in Mission*, xx. That trend continued into the twentieth century during which two thirds of missionaries were women according to Robert in *Gospel Bearers*, xi.

3. Robert, *American Women in Mission*, 409–17.

4. Robert notes that leading women founded the New York Female Missionary Society, assisting missionary outreach through fundraising, an idea that spread among Methodist women in the United States. Robert, "Innovation and Consolidation," 129.

Another theme of the last century mission work of women was *holism*. Women rejected any mission theory that separated the spiritual from the physical realm. Healing the body was as important as healing the spirit. Health clinics sprang up for routine inoculations and childhood diseases. Physical education also found a place along with intellectual education. Schools for girls in South Korea brought physical education into play in a way that had never been done before. The YWCA began programs of yoga and exercise for girls and women. Whereas some missionary activity focused on proclaiming the Word and evangelization, women's work for women had a holistic emphasis, caring for both mind and body, intertwining the physical and the spiritual in mission theologies and practices.

Ecumenical cooperation was another theme of the women's missionary movement. Christian women founded some of the first ecumenical mission organizations. Some Methodists went outside of their denomination to fulfill their missionary callings.[5] Protestant and Catholic women worked together in healthcare. Conservative and mainline Protestant joined hands in efforts to care for the poor. Mission organizations that defied ecclesiastical divisions were created and sustained by the efforts of missionary women and their home churches.

Finally, a *spirituality of self-sacrifice* was fostered in the mission work that women did. Catholic women's model of the cross led many missionaries to dangerous regions of the world, to do work that required extreme deprivation and danger. Maryknoll sisters established missions in Central and South America. Baptist missionary Lottie Moon traveled to remote areas of China, training local women to take the gospel to Chinese people. Ann Wilkins founded the first Methodist girls' school abroad.[6]

The results of those efforts led to a vision of church less as an institution and more as a way of life. The mission theologies of women in that era remained hidden behind the practices that exhibited them. Due to the success of those practices in teaching, health care, work with children, and physical education, those theologies became incorporated into the churches as the twentieth century moved ahead. By the 1930s the mainstream missionary theologies included the innovations developed by women during the heyday of the worldwide missionary movement.

5. Ibid., 130.
6. Ibid., 129.

The Impact of Nineteenth–Twentieth-Century Themes on Contemporary Women's Mission Theologies

Theologies of Working in Community

Women in the missionary movement excelled in working in community. Rather than staying in their denominational enclaves, women missionaries often reached out to work with broader communities. The liberationist model of Catholic sisters in Latin America after World War II shows missionaries assisting the poor toward self-sufficiency.[7] A theology of working in community by women today influences women in mission. Narrators in this study spoke of many ways of working in community.

Adele Pucci who works with the Eagles, an international educational ministry centered in Singapore, spoke of the importance of community in her work. The Eagles are a close-knit community, participating in reciprocal giving, doing ministry together, caring for each other's kids, working together as staff and volunteers. The support staff and administrators live in a house together. They meet every Saturday for Bible study, going through books and worshiping together. Small groups are the heart of organizing this ministry. Adele spoke of the joys of shared ownership of work. Besides the teaching ministry, the Eagles put on outreach dinners, invite non-believers to jazz evenings, and take risks with creative formatting of conferences.[8]

In her interview, Lois McKinney-Douglas, a theological educator and missionary active in the Christian student movement in Brazil for many years, spoke of amazing work with the poor that students are doing. She talked about her large house full of students and the ways in which relationships among them and their work together strengthened their witness. Working together in community and as part of an international movement gave them both direction and encouragement.[9]

Both of those examples of working together in community have similarities and differences from work in communities in the last century. Contexts differ, modes of communication differ, but ministry centered in communities are central to the mission in both eras.

---

7. Robert, *Gospel Bearers,* 23.
8. Interview, Chiang Mai, Thailand, September 2009.
9. Interview, Techny, Illinois, June 18, 2012.

Non-priority of Doctrine

Women often worked across denominational lines in their missionary efforts, a pattern that deviated from the norm of mission activities during the missionary movement. Catholic women working with the poor in Latin America, women's work for women in the U.S. and kingdom-based theologies of mission all demonstrated the importance of collaboration across denominational lines. In the twentieth century, doctrinal differences defined not only denominations but also mission efforts. Presbyterians had a mission in the Congo, Lutherans in India, Anglicans in Rwanda.

Why then did the lives of so many missionary women demonstrate a non-priority of doctrine? One could argue that the women missionaries were untrained in theology and therefore, did not realize the importance of doctrinal divisions that separated denominations and influenced gender theologies. When Lutherans and Presbyterians worked together for women's causes perhaps they favored ecumenism because they didn't know any better.

As women missionary stories come to light, however, that argument proves to be a very weak one. In many cases, determining a higher good, i.e., **something more urgent or important that doctrinal differences**, surfaces. The grave needs of women in the cities of the United States motivated women in the women's work for women movement to put aside denominational differences in order to work together. Getting the job done was more important than correct thinking about Christian doctrines. Disregarding denominational differences, they worked together to alleviate human need. Working with the very poor became more important to Catholic women in Latin America than adhering to class, religious, or political differences.

Another interpretation might be that a praxis model motivated women. Doing the work itself became a priority. Integrating one's theology with that work happened simultaneously, or in other cases, a mission theology developed out of doing the work itself.

In other cases, the unction of the Holy Spirit trumped doctrine. In the African Methodist Episcopal Church founded by Richard Allen, Jarena Lee heard God calling her to preach. She approached the leader for confirmation of that call. She didn't receive that confirmation so she put aside her desire for many years. Eventually the voice of the Holy Spirit became more urgent than the doctrine of silence for women. One day during the worship service she stood up and spontaneously began to preach.[10] Fortunately, Richard Allen recognized her God-given gift and endorsed her preaching ministry. Although it was many years before women could be ordained as ministers in the African Methodist Episcopal Church, some male leaders and female preachers put the call over the doctrine that barred women from preaching. Named as deacons or traveling evangelists, African American women Christians traveled and preached in the late nineteenth century. That story has been repeated countless times in the lives of women called to ministry.

Another reason for the non-priority of doctrine in the lives of women missionaries was the call to unity. Aimee Semple McPherson's first national campaign held in Pennsylvania was a gathering for Pentecostals. Fraught with divisive conflict, Sister Aimee, in her advertising and presentations, stressed unity over doctrine. She wanted everyone to come to the conference. She not only resisted denominational differences, but in-house differences among Pentecostals—differences that were fragmenting the movement at that time.[11]

Ecumenism developed both as a theology and as a movement between 1910 and 1948 with the establishment of the World Council of Churches. Women missionaries supported the doctrine of ecumenical cooperation, not by writing about the theology of ecumenism, but by practicing ecumenism. Efforts to work together, to build relationships, to nurture and encourage one another were paramount for many women missionaries. Isolated as they were from the locus of power in their denominations, women missionaries banded together.

Ecumenism as a theological idea grew from the practices of the women. They worked together in mission efforts—efforts to spread the gospel, efforts to meet the human needs of poor women and children, efforts to educate, care for the sick, and bring healing to families. As women focused on the call of God in their lives, the sanctifying work of the Holy Spirit, the vision of unity in and among churches, and the efforts to build relationships for mutual support in furthering the work of God in the world, a theology of ecumenism grew. That theology grew up in and around the lives of women missionaries—its roots were in practices, the paths their feet followed became articulated in ecumenical theologies.

10. Andrews, *Sisters of the Spirit*, 29.

11. Barfoot, *Aimee Semple McPherson*, 73–75.

Subordination

Women in mission, particularly from conservative Protestant and Catholic denominations still experience subordination by their institutions and the theologies connected with their churches. Catholic women are denied full ordination and are sometimes corrected by the Church when their theologies "stray" from Vatican orthodoxy. A recent example is Pope Francis' restatement of concern that women religious in the United States are overly influenced by "radical feminism."[12] In Protestant circles, the Christian and Missionary Alliance decided in 2000 to deny women the opportunity to become elders.[13] Censorship by church authorities of certain theologies developed by women, e.g. Margaret Farley's sexual ethics and Sallie McFague's earth ethics also limit women's influence. Correspondingly, in conservative Baptist and some independent Protestant churches, a theology of women as subordinate to men goes unchallenged. During the 1970s the Southern Baptist Church in the United States began a systematic program of removing women from teaching positions in their colleges and seminaries. Both Catholic and Protestant women in mission experience discrimination in their work as well as a lack of authority to lead in their mission settings.

The women in the Brazil case study each experienced resistance from their husbands as they attempted to follow their callings, be it to mission or not to mission work. Their choice was to go along with their husband's calling or separate from their husband in order to follow their own God-given call.

Women in mainline Protestant churches in Asian contexts experience discrimination, especially in contexts where American women missionaries may be accepted but native women struggle for recognition. In parts of Indonesia, it is still difficult for a woman to become a pastor. She must either follow her husband's call as wife and helper in the work or remain unmarried.[14] In the U.S., more desirable pastorates still go to male candidates in the Presbyterian Church (USA) and other mainline denominations. Most bishops in the United Methodist Church are men. Although a theology of equality is in place in many denominations, in practice, women still lag behind both in opportunities and in financial remuneration for church leadership. Both Catholic and Protestant women

---

12. BBC News, April 15, 2013.

13. See Robert, *Gospel Bearers*, 4, for Missionary Alliance regulations.

14. Adeney, *Christian Women in Indonesia*, 88.

in mission experience discrimination in their work as well as a lack of authority to lead in their mission settings.

Concern for Women and Children

Concern for women and children still dominates much of women's mission theologies and practices of mission. A Brazilian missionary told me of a time when the mother of twin infants died. The missionary, breast-feeding her own baby, was called upon to breastfeed those twins. A strong bond developed through that sacrificial service.

Marilyn Headstand described her daughter's missionary work to members of the Hurley Christian Community Church in September 2012. Marilyn's daughter Amy has worked with an orphanage and school in Bogotá for eleven and a half years with Christian Vision, an independent Christian mission organization created for the purpose of establishing and running the orphanage and school.

The orphanage houses one hundred children. Most of them come before they are three years old. Often they have parents who cannot take care of them—drug addicts, persons with mental illness, prostitutes, children from abusive families, or women living on the streets of Bogotá. Few are adopted out. Parents come on visiting day to see their children and many have a close relationship with them.

The children are educated, learn English, and are helped to find work when they finish eleven years of school (equivalent to junior year of high school in the U.S.). Fifty additional children come for school every day. They are given three meals and receive uniforms through donations of sponsors or churches. They apply for work outside of school in an organized fashion even if there is no pay involved. That process prepares them for job seeking when they leave school. The older children perceive that they have opportunities to transcend the poverty of their parents if they learn English and stay with the program.

Amy lives in a *favela*, a poor neighborhood rated number two on a scale of eight in terms of poverty and crime. She lives with a ten-year-old girl whom she has been trying to adopt for a number of years. Amy's mother and dad go to Bogotá once a year to visit for two weeks. Her grandparents sponsor a child and communicate with the schoolchildren via Skype. Those conversations help the children learn English and use media technology. Amy returns to the States occasionally to visit for two to three weeks. Funds are raised through donations from churches and interested individuals.

The theology of the mission organization is conservative Protestant. They teach creation science and Marilyn's language displayed a conversion theology consistent with conservative Baptists views. According to Marilyn, Amy is committed to this work for the long haul, planning to live permanently in Bogotá.

Relationships are at the heart of Amy's work. She knows each child and mentors them through their childhood years. She and the other teachers care for the spiritual well-being of the children, even doing extra Bible studies during recess at the children's request. Amy feels that her long-term presence in the community not only helps her with cross-cultural issues but shows a commitment that receives respect from the local people. She is, however, concerned about her physical safety, a concern her mother mentioned repeatedly in her presentation.

In our conversation after the presentation, Marilyn again mentioned relationships—how Amy cared for all of the children and especially for Tayly who she was trying to adopt. Amy realizes that this is a long process. In Bogotá, children with darker skin are discriminated against. As a young blond Caucasion woman from the U.S., Amy is the target of discrimination as she enters society with a dark-skinned child. Roadblocks to adopting Tayly may also be related to racial discrimination. But Amy believes that God has put her in this place and given her this task to do. Marilyn and her husband already consider Tayly their granddaughter.[15]

Much has changed in the world and in the ways Christian mission operates since the movement of the nineteenth and early twentieth centuries. But many of the themes present in that movement still continue with vigor into the present day, becoming new sources of authority for women in mission today. Concern for women and children, working in community, ecumenical cooperation, and issues of subordination become not only issues but sources for theological reflection for today's women in mission.

15. In July 2013, the adoption process was completed and Tayly is now Amy's daughter.

Third Wave of Global Women's Movement: Spirituality

A second major historical and contextual influence upon women in this study is the third wave of the global women's movement that focused on spirituality.

The dominance of rationalistic scientific thinking in industrializing nations led to a loss of understanding of the relevance of the spiritual domain in human life. The search for universal laws of nature and the rejection of religious authorities during the 17th and 18th c in Europe led to great gains in human knowledge. But those gains have been in unlocking the secrets of the material world. Scientific and technological advances have affected every area of human life, bringing better health care, improved communication systems, more efficient industrial processes, and better education to a large part of the world's population. Those gains have been combined, however, with a lack of attention to spirituality and personal or communal knowledge of the non-material world. The desire to understand human significance and human relationship with that which is beyond the material was relegated to the "subjective" domain.

Gradually, however, scholars have come to understand the "situatedness" of all human knowledge. Human knowledge of any subject is always knowledge in context. Understanding arises in a particular community at a particular time for particular people. Furthermore, all knowledge includes a "subjective" dimension. Both experience and faith are active components of any kind of understanding. Knowledge of the material world, knowledge of human consciousness, knowledge of a transcendent dimension of life—each of these forms of knowledge is limited and connected to human experience and believing.[16] As that post-modern appreciation of the importance of location and experience grew, individuals and communities began to break away from socially accepted definitions of what is important in the search for knowledge. That "knowledge revolution" has resulted in a more open exploration of non-material concerns in intellectual and academic settings. Issues of spirituality, transcendence, and ultimate meaning are explored in the university alongside of scientific questions.

Since the conditions for understanding are no longer bound by traditional "scientific" definitions of what is important, authorities of custom, religion, and socialization are being questioned. Women scholars

16. See the work of Polanyi, *Personal Knowledge*, and McCoy, *When Gods Change* for accounts of this theory of knowledge and its implications for Christian theology.

are redefining their search for spiritual understanding in terms that are women-friendly. Socially accepted definitions of the realm of spirituality and the content of theologies are being laid aside. Women are exploring their own consciousness, drawing from their own experiences, and trusting their own intuitions in the search for spiritual understanding.

An example may suffice. In 1983 Hunter College produced a textbook of women's studies. Although attuned to the times, spirituality does not appear in the table of contents or in the index. It was during the 1980s that numerous books were published specifically about women's spirituality. Feminist critiques of history and social structures aided the critical process of reclaiming the biological and relational dimensions of women's experience as sacred, without succumbing to an erroneous view of women as more "natural" and less "intellectual" than men.

The early 1990s saw a proliferation of articles and books about women's spirituality as well as reproductions of collections of historical writings: spiritual writings, prose, and poetry. In its Classics of Western Spirituality series Paulist Press published editions of the writings of Julian of Norwich and Catherine of Genoa. Marilyn Sewell's collection of women's poetry *Cries of the Spirit: A Celebration of Women's Spirituality* came out in 1991 and includes classic as well as modern women poets on spirituality. *Women's Spirituality*, edited by Jann Wolsky Conn, and *Gaia and God*, by Rosemary Radford Ruether, also illustrate women's reflections on Christian spirituality from this era.

Contemporary Concerns of Women's Spirituality

Since the 1980s, women have more and more come to realize that women's work patterns, goals, and spiritual dimensions of life cannot simply be styled on male role models. The resulting movement of spirituality among women led to a number of distinctive concerns that define contemporary women's spirituality. Those concerns have influenced women doing mission and studying Christian theologies of mission

Embodiment is one of the primary concerns of women's spirituality today.

A body is not something a woman has—a container for her mind. Rather a woman *is* her body. She is a totality of body and mind, woven inseparably together.[17] Bodily experiences are part of a woman and thus

17. See Adeney, "Insights."

part of a woman's spirituality. Women in this movement do not say with Decartes, "I think, therefore I am." Nor do they agree with the Greek notion that bodily sensations are less valuable than mental sensations. The idea that the goal of spirituality is to rid oneself of bodily desire is also rejected. On the contrary, women celebrate their sexuality, their groaning in childbirth, their aging and their integration with all that is earthy. This too is part of women's spirituality.

Beverly Harrison's book *Making the Connections: Essays in Feminist Social Ethics* influenced the women's spirituality movement by positing embodiment as a central tenet of feminist ethics.[18] Making ethical decisions as embodied persons enables women to function holistically. Women can listen to what their bodies tell them about the good and the beautiful, the just and the holy. It is not only through thinking processes that women know—women's bodies also teach them.

Dorothy Day, founder of the Catholic Worker Movement in the U.S., found her spirituality awakened by her relationship with her lover, her exploration of the world of nature with him, and her months of pregnancy. Upon the birth of her child, she found the miracle of giving birth demanded a response from her. That response was to become part of the Catholic Church, an action that she knew would cause a painful separation from her beloved. The bodily appreciation of nature, the deep relationship with a loved partner, and the physical process of giving new life convinced her that God existed and must be worshipped.[19] Day is highlighted as an examplar of modern Christian mission in chapter 6.

That powerful appreciation of embodiment has led to many creative emphases in women's conversations and writings about spirituality. No longer are women's biological processes rejected as "unclean" but are appreciated as part of women's preciousness and destiny. No longer is childbirth seen as an intrusion upon adult life but it is celebrated as a gift—the ability to bring life into the world. No longer is the aging process viewed solely as loss, but as a process that is a natural part of life, bringing its own rewards along with its difficulties. No longer is women's focus on the importance of relationships lamented as feminine weakness, but it is appreciated as a talent that brings harmony to community life.

Those views have not gone unchallenged, however. Some of the pressures arising for women from an emphasis on the theme of relationships

---

18. Harrison, *Making the Connections*, 12–14.

19. Day, *Long Loneliness*, 132–35.

are brought out by contemporary theologian Mary Stewart Van Leeuwen. She offers an insightful analysis of the dangers of emeshment in relationships as well as the importance of relationships for women.[20]

Those changed attitudes expand the domain of spirituality. Not transcending the body but fully dwelling in and through the body becomes a goal of the spiritual life. Being present in one's experiences, bodily as well as mentally, broadens a woman's perception of spirituality. Much that was ignored becomes sacred. Women's part in bringing life, nurturing the young, offering the wisdom of life experience as one grows older—these areas somehow connect with a Christian apprehension of God and God's life in the world. It should be noted, however, that women who are appreciating this aspect of life no longer accept the traditional limitations imposed by male culture in this regard. Giving birth, nurturing life, and caring for relationships are not all that women can or should do. The talents and opportunities traditionally considered "for men only" are also areas of competence for women.

An example of this expanded notion of spirituality is seen in women's attention to the "earth-mother" concept. Romo Y. B. Mangun Wijaya of Indonesia, in his novel *Burung-burung Rantau (Wandering Shorebirds)* encourages modern independent women to also affirm their own role as bringers and sustainers of life in the world. Not a second-rate task, that nurturing mothering ability is essential to life on the earth. Seen in this way, the life-giving gifts of women take on a sacred dimension.

From this emphasis on embodiment grows an affirmation of the *sacredness of everyday life*. As women find their voices and begin to name the sacred, they speak of their circle of friends, of finding expression for the ache of existence, of the labors of childbirth and building a marriage, of creating a Sabbath space, and of finding a meditative aspect to doing housework and of sanctifying the space in women's homes and in women's emotions. Those topics were discussed by a circle of women at Harvard University when the wave of interest in women's spirituality was just beginning. The resulting book, *Sacred Dimensions of Women's Experience*, edited by Elizabeth Dodson Gray, celebrates women's everyday life. Those new sources for theology hark back to Martin Luther's revolutionary ideas about the holiness of family and ordinary life. Christian and non-Christian women alike are reviving and reforming the worshipful dimension of living life as part of God's good creation. The everyday

20. Van Leeuwen, *Gender and Grace*, 42–44.

practices of women in this study show the influence of those ideas on women's mission theologies.

Choosing presents another important theme in women's understandings of spirituality today. No longer seeing themselves as extensions of their fathers or their husbands, women are asserting themselves as agents. Freedom to choose, recognizing the ability to make decisions for oneself, and boldly taking action are crucial concepts of the women's spirituality movement.

In China, a professor at the University of Beijing who was also active in the women's movement emphasized the importance of women's choice in arranging child care and household tasks. "These decisions should not be made by the state. Socialization of household tasks is not the answer to the role conflicts women are experiencing," she said. "Rather, these decisions should be made in the family. Wives and husbands should discuss together how household duties can best be arranged for their family.[21]

In Indonesia during the same decade, more and more career women were choosing not to marry. That decision required great internal strength in a society that expects women to marry and focus their lives on children and husband. Women found spiritual resources for the task of independent life indispensable. The struggle to choose career over family and follow through on that decision directed them to their internal spiritual resources They began to understand their own ability to function independently, their talent in their work, and the spiritual resources in themselves and their communities that enabled them in that path. Christian women following a call to becoming pastors often chose this route.

In the U.S., during the 1980s and 1990s, women struggling with patriarchal practices in the church formed their own worshipping and political advocacy communities. "Women-Church" groups did not reject Christianity but separated themselves from the male-dominated patterns of leadership, claiming the tradition of the Exodus community for themselves. Choosing a feminist alternative allowed those women and women-identified men to develop spirituality by removing themselves from the anger-generating context of traditional churches.[22] Rosemary Radford Ruether put it this way: "Women can no longer nurture

21. Bohong, "Women's Double Burden."Lecture given at International Women's Conference, Hangzhou China, August, 1993.

22. Russell, *Church in the Round*, 105 and n. 72. Russell refers to Rosemary Radford Ruether's *Women-Church*, 238 and 57.

their souls in alienating words that ignore or systematically deny their existence. They are starved for the words of life, for symbolic forms that fully and wholeheartedly affirm their personhood"[23]

Self-trust developed as women depended on their own resources for their lives. Some felt freed from slavishly following male models of work or spirituality. As they developed their own styles and goals, women learned to depend on their unique perceptions of truth, their own apprehensions of the good, and their particular appreciation of beauty. Contemporary South Korean theologian Chae Ok Chun explains this point of view: "To develop my spirituality and relationship with God I spend time appreciating the beauty of flowers. I worship God through nature."[24] That development allowed women to critique views that were destructive to the interests of women. Professor Carol Robb outlined what a "women-friendly" economy might look like.[25] Trusting a woman's perspective on what is good leads to a critique of what was formerly hidden—structures and practices that appear normal but that actually hurt women. Virginia Woolf speaks about men writing books about women and how normal that seemed early in the twentieth century. She dubbed those practices "gentle violence."[26]

In the same vein, women's spirituality departed from male-oriented views of religion. Goddess worship began to be revived and made relevant to modern women in the U.S. At a Wicca Conference in Sacramento, California, in 1983, this author was impressed by the seriousness of women participants and leaders like Starhawk in seeking to devise women-centered rituals and celebrations. Since then Starhawk has published some of her ideas on women's spirituality. Eco-feminism grew as a movement, celebrating human connection with the earth and emphasizing the importance of protecting it. Christian women revived the reading of mystics such as Julian of Norwich and Teresa of Avila. Women began to define as "spiritual" what is important to them as women, and what moves them to worship. Revising religious traditions and reclaiming facets of religions that have been lost became more common as women trusted themselves to revise their notions of spirituality.

---

23. Quoted in Pope-Levison and Levison, *Jesus in Global Contexts,* 136.

24. Interview, Port Dixon, Malaysia, August 4, 2004.

25. Paper presented at the Graduate Theological Union Faculty Women's Retreat, Berkeley, California, April 15, 1990.

26. Woolf, *Room of One's Own,* 26–27.

For example, theologian Paula M. Cooey insisted that the Christian notion of redemption must primarily include redemption of the body, reworking a classic Christian doctrine from a contemporary feminist perspective. "A post-patriarchal understanding of incarnation must be committed to a redemption of the body," she declared. "In so doing, it must recognize that the transfiguration of pain begins with giving voice or bearing witness to injustice with a view to healing and nurture."[27]

That view clearly articulates the perspective of oppressed women— women who have, in silence, experienced both the pain of giving life and the pain of injustice towards themselves and those they love. Catholic theologian Sandra Schneiders asserts that such theology is sorely needed in a church that has, in the North and West, become powerful and complacent. If Christianity is to remain relevant in a postmodern age, the Church as a whole must take seriously the task of developing theologies that can liberate the oppressed, including women.[28]

Empowerment results from choosing and trusting one's perceptions. Women have found empowerment not to be an individualistic process only, but a group process. That empowerment results from sharing ideas, working together, and supporting one another's projects. Much- needed women-centered theologies are often created in dialogue. Christian women in Nicaragua during the Sandanista/Contra war in the 1980s showed this kind of solidarity in action. As part of a National Delegation of Women to visit war zones during that time, I saw women's theologies of solidarity in action in communities along the border with Costa Rica. It is such action and concern that enables academic and religious women to carve out new space for work in the world and to enjoy a new space of spiritual solidarity.[29]

Such empowerment occurred as *relationality* was affirmed, both as a spur to creativity and as a way of life during that third wave of the women's movement. Women realized that many of their "monuments" to history were acts that sustained and nurtured others. Being in interdependent relation to others was applauded as a life goal, not merely as a spare-time activity. "Giving birth to connection in the midst of separation, or giving birth to our own empowered selves, or daring to ponder our own spiritual journeys in a culture that devalues women's lives—this serious task

27. Cooey, "Redemption," 109.

28. Schneiders, "Does the Bible," 71.

29. An early example of this kind of working together is found in Moraga and Anzaldúa, *This Bridge Called My Back*.

of creating 'worth' is a task all women share in today. To bring into being that which is only potential is an art form of living which binds women together," declared Elizabeth Dodson Gray, a leader of this movement.[30]

The solidarity that occurred as women banded together to work for common concerns and explore spiritual connections could not be sustained without an emphasis on *celebrating difference*. The idea that women have *a* perspective, that there is *a* feminist viewpoint, is challenged each time a group of women gather together. Listening to other women and celebrating difference engendered both mutual respect and deeper creativity during the last decades of the twentieth century and it still does today as women of various racial backgrounds and religious orientations meet together to find new meanings in their diversity.

The Mudflower Collective exemplifies this trend. A group of diverse women theologians met in the U.S. to discuss theological education during the 1980s. The interaction that occurred, however, went much deeper than developing curriculum. Discussions about God, about doubt, about racial oppression, about power arose. Heated letters were exchanged. Conflicts were worked through and the resulting book, *God's Fierce Whimsy*, has been an asset to innumerable women educators.

Reasserting women's embodiment, learning to make and trust their choices, finding the sacred in the everyday, discovering empowerment in relationships, and celebrating differences characterized the global women's spirituality movement of the late twentieth century. Those trends have led in the U.S. to an emphasis on spiritual dimensions of life that seemed previously hidden.

Women doing Christian mission have not taken on all of the characteristics of the third wave of the women's movement in spirituality. However, many of the themes stressed by that movement have become part of Christian understandings, especially by women. Those trends provide new sources of authority that women in mission and theological education have incorporated into their thinking and experience.

Two waves of Christian activity and social energy in the last century have given Christian women in mission new sources of authority for doing mission theology. Themes from women's work during the missionary movement and themes from the third wave women's movement combine to offer rich resources for contemporary women constructing theologies of mission. How they go about doing that is the subject of the next chapter.

---

30. Gray, *Sacred Dimensions*, 3.

3

A Common Approach to Doing Mission Theology

Breathe on me, breath of God, fill me with life anew,
That I may love what Thou dost love, and do what thou wouldst do.
—EDWIN HATCH, *HYMNAL 1982*, 508

As WE SAW IN the last chapter, women use many sources of authority as they carve out a place for themselves in Christian mission. The Scriptures, early church practices, church tradition and experience combine under the wings of the Holy Spirit and in Christian communities to aid women in knowing and doing theology. Newer sources of authority from the missionary movement intertwine and make application of older sources pertinent to the times. The concern for women and children, a holistic approach, ecumenical cooperation, and self-sacrifice now become sources for theology in the contemporary era. Issues of subordination still operating in the church must also be addressed. In addition, a third wave of feminism focusing on spirituality provides resources for women doing mission theology. A focus on embodiment, the sacredness of everyday life, choosing and self trust combine to form a strong nexus for women's spirituality. That leads to new theologies of God, a sense of empowerment and a focus on relationality. Finally, dialoging and celebrating difference become important for women's lives. Those themes now become sources for theological reflection for Christian women doing mission.

That plethora of sources of authority does not influence all women in the same way or to the same degree. In fact, a diversity of theologies

35

mark the work of women theologians and practitioners. Contexts, cultural influences, church and family allegiances, and personal appropriation of sources of authority vary widely. One might ask what women have in common as they do mission theology across the diversity of the sources they use?

This chapter explores the theological methods that women use to construct theologies of mission. We discover a common approach that women use in utilizing sources of authority and applying theological methods to their work. As women practice Christian mission, they draw from those numerous sources. Experience becomes a major source of wisdom, especially experiences of God. The voice of the Holy Spirit becomes a source of direction as women strive to live out their calling within their context with chosen sources of authority. Their relationships and community inform their thinking. The Bible and church traditions influence their interpretations. Their character is shaped as they experience God in action and reflection. That common approach becomes a pathway women use in working with sources of authority and theological methods. Yet the results of using that approach do not reflect a single mission theology. We will explore those varied results in ensuing chapters.

Theology-Makers

During most of the history of Christianity, theology has been the domain of men. While women were leaders in the early church, as the church grew, women were relegated to positions of learner and follower. Men became the educated Christian teachers, the ones that studied the word and interpreted the Bible to others.

In its early stages, the radical good news of the gospel, that Jesus Christ died for all, and that, "in Christ there is neither Jew nor Greek, bond nor free, male nor female" (Gal 3:28) overturned the patterns of male rule in Greco/Roman society for Jesus' followers. Women traveled with Jesus, formed churches in their households, instructed Christian leaders, and even became apostles.[1] These missionary activities developed out of and supported a women's mission theology of action, leadership,

---

1. During Jesus' life, women traveled with him and helped support his ministry. After Jesus' resurrection, Priscilla and Aquila taught younger disciples, Lydia had a church in her house, and Phoebe is mentioned in Romans 16 as an early apostle.

and dedication to the gospel.[2] Women participated in church leadership even after the middle of the second century. Tertullian declared that women dared "to teach, to debate, to exorcise, to promise cures, probably even to baptize."[3]

As the institution of the church grew, however, it began to reflect the values of the surrounding society—values that not only held up male leadership, but rendered women and their work invisible.[4]

Throughout Christian history, however, there have been women that have defied this pattern. Monastics Julian of Norwich, St. Theresa of Avila, Hildegard of Bingen and others not only felt called by God to understand God's word and ways, but left written records of their theology and treatment of God and the world. Reformation women Anne Askew and Catherine Willoughby pioneered Protestant theology in England and joined other women to criticize the mass. Some were executed for articulating these theologies.[5] More recently, during the missionary movement beginning in the first great awakening in this country and moving on to the present, many women were called to be missionaries. Although they worked diligently alongside of men and often found themselves leading or instructing men, generally they did not hold positions of power, nor were they welcomed into the institutions of higher learning that have prepared theologians in Western societies. Even today, many theologians from Eastern and Southern nations are trained in Europe or the United States and experience the same constraints.

---

2. Jesus supported Mary, Lazarus' sister, in her desire to learn from Jesus teachings rather than help her sister Martha with food preparation and hospitality, declaring that Mary had chosen the better part (Luke 10:42). Biblical quotes taken from the New International Version.

3. Schüssler Fiorenza, "Word, Spirit and Power," 51.

4. Max Weber traces the growth of new religions through a prophetic stage, during which a prophet calls a religion back to its "original" message and values. The charismatic authority that leads this movement is inherently unstable and is followed by an institutionalization period during which stability of the new religion is gained through written texts, ritualized forms of worship, institutionalized structures of authority, and patterns of interaction among members. This period is one of legitimation and is inherently conservative, as the new religion attempts to become acceptable to the larger society. Charismatic power recedes as domination hardens into lasting institutions. See Weber, "Sociology of Charismatic Authority," 248, and "Meaning of Discipline," 262. During the first two centuries of Christianity, common views that women were not able to reason ethically and should not pursue public leadership roles reasserted themselves in the church.

5. See Zahl, *Five Women of the English Reformation*.

Nonetheless, women have been doing mission theology during these centuries, making their mark on Christian mission. Many records of women's mission work and what they thought about it have been lost, but much is being regained through historical work like that of Dana Robert, Dianne Reistroffer, and Bonnie Sue Lewis. Through those records, contemporary women are analyzing women's mission theologies and creating new and relevant works of theology that can aid the church in carrying out the mandate to go into all the world and make disciples.

Theology in Two Moods

The Imperial Mood

Besides recapturing and understanding women's mission theology and making it a base for future theological work, these records of women's mission theology suggest something about theological method. I would like to propose that women do theology in ways that are quite different from a traditional Western European method of theology-a method that I call the Imperial Mood of theology.[6] Theological work done in the Imperial Mood starts from the top down. In the thirteenth century the theologian Thomas Aquinas recovered some of Aristotle's wisdom and restructured knowledge in a hierarchical fashion. In that view, the most complete and correct knowledge is God's knowledge embodied in the eternal law. Humans do not have access to the mind of God but people in the church, men—literally—in the church, were believed to be closer to God than women and therefore able to articulate God's law and embody it in church law. Below that was the realm of human reason which Aquinas called natural law and finally human law which came in last and at the bottom.[7]

So, theology was done with God's eternal law as the highest thought. Theologians began with whatever they believed they knew about God's law. Theology began, for instance, with the attributes of God—God is omniscient, omnipresent, eternal, etc. Theology starts with God and works down from there. Using this Imperial Mood, theologians believe that their view is, in fact, synonymous with God's view. Their understandings

6. I first heard this nomenclature used by Prof. Charles McCoy in an independent study on Plato's thought at the Graduate Theological Union during my doctoral studies in 1986.

7. Aquinas, *Summa Theologia*, 217.

were backed up by church tradition, informed by mores of the society in which they lived, and influenced by the wealthy and powerful who ruled society. But these men believed that they were doing God's work, understanding God in an absolutely correct way.

Something of the same type of theology is done today when leaders claim that we must begin solely with the Bible.[8] The Imperial Mood begins at the top and works down. Issues of the influence of culture on biblical interpretation, social structures affecting human understanding of scripture—indeed the social construction of knowledge—are ignored in this view. Theology done in the Imperial Mood assumes that those sanctioned by society to develop theology know the Truth about God and show others how to interpret Christianity based on that absolute Truth.

The Contextual Mood

I would like to suggest that women do theology in a different way—from the bottom up. They begin with their experience much in the manner that St. Paul began *his* Christian theology. He was accosted on the Damascus Road—met by God—who turned him around and set his life in a different direction. Paul recounts that vision as the beginning of his true knowledge of God.[9] After that amazing experience, Paul went into the desert and studied for years, being instructed by the Holy Spirit. Paul's experience on the Damascus road can become a model for women who are accosted by God and called to a path of preaching, to a path of mission service, to a path of Christian ministry that may seem different from the path other women are taking—women around them.

This is theology done in the Contextual Mood. It begins with experience—often a life-changing experience that centers on a call—and results in taking a totally different direction in life. The Apostle Paul

8. This was not the view of R. A. Torrey, one of the editors of *The Fundamentals*, who wrote, "For without faith no one can explain the Holy Scriptures, and without scholarship no one can investigate historic origins." Torrey et al., *Fundamentals*, 1:10. Carl F. H. Henry, in speaking of the Word, stated that "the living God of the Bible inescapably and invincibly shows up and speaks out." Henry, *God Revelation, and Authority*, 1:17. Unfortunately, those views have been oversimplified by many who insist that the Bible stands alone in revealing truth to humankind. John Stott calls this mistake "total rigidity." One believes that in the Bible God has given a series of "precise formulas that we have to repeat more or less word for word, and certain images that we must invariably employ." Stott, "Bible in World Evangelization," A5.

9. Acts 9:3–9.

already had a calling. He was intent on stamping out the heretical teachings of a group of Jews who claimed that the Messiah had come—the new Christians.[10] After the experience on the Damascus Road, Paul's life took a new direction. He learned in a new way. He began doing theology in the Contextual Mood.[11]

Step 1: Encountering God

ACCOSTED BY GOD

For many women, an intense encounter with God—an experience of calling not unlike St. Paul's—becomes the first step in doing theology from the bottom up. These experiences occur in women's life situation, happening in their particular context and influencing their personal life choices.[12] Many women are called to preach, are called to leadership in a congregation, or they are called to mission service.

This experience of encounter and calling creates, for many women, a huge tension in their personal lives. A call from God demands a response—a response that involves a theological understanding of leadership roles and a supportive community. Many women called to mission have neither. They have been theology-followers, not theology-makers. And the theology they accepted usually excluded women from leadership. These women are thrown into conflict between the theology they had received—theology made by men as rulers of society and the church—and the inner unction of the Holy Spirit. For many this inner call is, as it was for Jeremiah, like a fire burning in their bellies.[13] Until they speak of this call, until they follow it, they cannot rest.

CALLED BY GOD

Jarena Lee, born a free black woman whose parents were hard pressed financially, experienced a call to preach around 1811. She was convinced

10. Acts 9:1–2.

11. Beginning with this experience, Paul grows into a theology of redemption, declaring "God was reconciling the world to himself in Christ." (2 Cor 5:19a)

12. For example, I developed an "inside-out" mission theology as I lived in Indonesia, experienced the culture, analyzed the context, and developed an understanding of listening and response through interaction with Indonesian Christian women. See "From the Inside Out" in Robert, *Gospel Bearers,* 172 and 182–84.

13. Jeremiah 20:8–9.

that God had called her to be an evangelist, preaching at the camp meetings and evangelistic services so popular in the late nineteenth century. Being a Methodist, she approached Rev. Richard Allen, told him her story and requested permission to preach. Permission was denied. Allen explained that women were not called to public ministry and the rules of Methodism, "did not call for women preachers."[14]

Jarena Lee accepted the Bishop's pronouncement. That judgment was based on a tradition of theology done in the Imperial Mood. It was not to be challenged. But Lee's spirit could not rest. She tried for eight years to suppress her calling from God. At length, in agony of soul, she returned to Bishop Allen's church to plead again her cause. Again she was refused. But the next Sunday, Jarena Lee stood up in the congregation and began to preach. So powerful was her preaching that Allen, by then the first Bishop of the African Methodist Episcopal Church relented, becoming one of her greatest supporters in what became a wide-ranging evangelistic work for Jarena Lee.[15] Bishop Allen even cared for Lee's children when she was away on preaching trips and, not surprisingly, in 1894, the African-American Methodist Episcopal Church became the first Protestant Church to ordain women as deacons, giving them a public leadership role in congregations.

Step 2: Grappling With Scripture

CONFIRMING THE CALL

Women who experience a call to a leadership role in the church are not at liberty to do theology in the Imperial Mood. Often the theology done in this way excludes them from making theology and bars them from following their calling. If they continue as followers of that theology they must give up their calling.

Jarena Lee attempted to do this. But like Jeremiah, she found that resisting the call did not quiet the voice of the Spirit. At last, feeling like Jonah, who ran away from God's call, she returned to her church, pleading again for community affirmation and permission from church authorities. When she did not receive permission the second time, her calling broke through in preaching and, at last, was recognized.[16]

14. Cited in Andrews, *Sisters,* 5.

15. Ibid., 45.

16. Ibid., 44–45.

Women that struggle with this tension are forced to examine their experience. Was it really a call from God? The next question quickly follows: If God has called me, Scripture must confirm that call. So women take their experience, which won't go away, to the sacred texts. And here they begin the process of searching the Scriptures for themselves—a search to confirm their calling, or set them straight. They leave off following theology and begin making theology. They begin with their experience because they must—since the church denies its validity.

REWORKING DOMINANT THEOLOGIES

So women begin to do theology to show how Christianity itself affirms their calling—how the Bible affirms the calling that they have experienced through the Holy Spirit. Some women begin this theologizing with the creation narratives and particularly the story of creation in Genesis 1 that pictures God placing men *and* women in the garden, giving them responsibility for all creation. Using this narrative, women can be seen as partners in the work of God in the world—equal partners since women and men were both created in God's image.

One of my students in Indonesia, Magdelena Tangkudung, did her master's thesis on this theme. It was very radical in Indonesia in the mid-nineties for women to do a higher degree in theology. It was even more radical, even considered subversive, for her to do a thesis that developed a theology of gender equality, using the Bible itself to resist the constrictions that women have operated under in both church and society in Indonesia.[17]

Some women look to the New Testament at what I call the problem passages—verses in Paul's epistle—which seem to require that women remain silent, that women not take leadership, that women remain in a position of following, not assuming leadership roles. For instance, the mutuality of Paul's admonition for wives and husbands to submit to one another has changed in some Christian circles to an emphasis on obedience of wives to husbands. For some, that obedience has been generalized to include obedience to other men. Subsequently, women are excluded from wielding authority in the church. This passage in Ephesians 5 and other problem passages can be worked with both by studying the Greek and also by studying the context in which many of the letters of Paul were

17. Tangkudung, "Mitos dan Kodrat."

written. By gaining an understanding of the original language and the context and style of Paul's letters, it becomes clear that they were written to women in a particular situation which may not be applicable to women in the church today.[18]

I can tell a story from own life when I was a teenager in the Plymouth Brethren that illustrates the confusion that some interpretations which limit women's leadership can create. Women were required to wear hats in church meetings following Paul's order of creation argument in I Corinthians. Here he was making an argument from nature that would insure the modesty that cultural standards of the day demanded for women in public settings. That didn't particularly bother me as a young person. But it did bother me that in I Corinthians 11 women are instructed to cover their heads when they are praying or prophesying in the church. My question to the elders was, "Why aren't women praying and prophesying in the church meeting?" This, after all, was clearly the setting in which a head covering was required. It was the public speaking role of women that called for the requirement that women dress modestly and in accordance with custom. But the Plymouth Brethren chose to emphasize only the head covering, requiring silence of women in all public meetings. As a teenager, I looked to Scripture to sort out such contradictions. I still do.

Step 3: Religion-Identified Resistance

Many such contradictions must be worked out so that women may find congruence between their call from God and their manner of following that call. Jarena Lee's story illustrates how very frustrating it is to believe that one is called by God to preach and then be barred from preaching. When Lee returned to plead with Bishop Allen after years of this frustration, she spontaneously stood up in the congregation and declared that she had been called to preach but like other fallen sons and daughters of Adam's race had lingered and delayed to go at the bidding of the Lord.[19] In the end, it was in the demonstration of her preaching, an act of resistance against the authority of the Bishop, that her call was confirmed. Even then, the bishop of the African Methodist Episcopal Church did not ordain Jarena Lee. It was quite a few years later that women were ordained as deacons in that church and not until 1948 that they were or-

18. See Gundry, *Woman, Be Free*, and Scanzoni *All We're Meant to Be*.
19. Andrews, *Sisters of the Spirit*, 44.

dained as pastors and able to lead congregations and preach—still years earlier than many other denominations in the U.S.

Women in this situation (called but not affirmed by the church) and the tension it produces (called but not able to follow God's calling) propel women into a more formal study of theology. They need personal confirmation that their encounter with God produces a valid call to service. And they need sacred texts to show that a theology of women's mission and leadership can become acceptable in the church. They use Scriptural teachings to *claim inclusion* in church leadership and in the circle of those that make theology—an inclusion necessary for them to pursue their God-given calling. In the late twentieth century when women began entering doctoral work in theology, many chose biblical studies as their focus. A similar process has occurred in other world religions: Islam, Buddhism, Hinduism, and Judaism.[20]

Women begin their mission theology with experience because they must. It is their experience of God's call that has been denied by the church. Women's experience pushes them to study the Bible to confirm their calling. They then resist the theologies that prevent them from following their calling, using Scripture itself to argue against the dominant theology in their setting. This religion-identified resistance speaks powerfully to the church and engenders change.[21] Women doing mission theology in the contextual mood have broken through barriers that prevent them from doing the work of God in the church and in the world.

Step 4: Shaping Practices

Opening a path for women called to do the work of the church sets women on a creative course. Many women have gone before, but few records of their actions, thoughts, or behaviors, have been preserved. Records of the practices they developed and their theological reflections that their experiences and study of Scripture produced are being recovered in our generation. But much has been lost.

Based on a small pilot study of Christian women leaders in Indonesia, I suggest that the practices developed by women doing mission

20. See Gross, *Feminism and Religion*. "Buddhist teachings directly prescribe gender equity and equality, and the religion lacks any patriarchal symbolism for ultimate reality" (ibid., 140).

21. See the summary of my research findings in Adeney, *Christian Women in Indonesia*, 13–15.

theology are of two types: practices to gain competence in fulfilling their calling and practices to sustain them in their life of difference.[22] Their life is one of intentionally choosing otherness. They are not like the men with whom they lead because they are women. And they are not like the women of their class or generation because they have a special calling, and special tasks to fulfill—tasks that have traditionally been the domain of men.

COMPETENCES

Women leaders, therefore, must develop practices that suit them as women but still enable them to fulfill their calling. Pursuing theological education, studying the Bible, writing sermons, traveling to places and engaging people in this public role are all actions that the women took and things that they learned to do as practices that shaped and formed their lives. Yet, each woman leader developed a unique style of leadership and her own understandings of issues facing the church. The competences they developed were crucial to their work and by developing those practices, women also learned about the nature of God and nature of the world around them and the nature of sin. As those practices developed, reflecting on them yielded new theological insights.

Not only did those understandings differ from the male-oriented theologies that women inherited in the church, they also differed from the understandings and practices of women around them. Sometimes those differences separated women leaders from other women.

NURTURANCE

In order to maintain the important social ties that women depended on in Indonesian society, women leaders developed another set of practices—practices that nurtured and sustained them as they lived their lives. In Indonesia I identified three practices that nurtured women leaders—no doubt there are more. The first was *honoring relationships*. None of the women that were called to leadership believed that they should be resisting men that were in positions of power, or that they should be overthrowing systems instituted by the church. Instead they honored the

22. Ibid., 104–6.

relationships and they gave the respect that was culturally expected to the men that were the leaders of the church.[23]

A second practice that they developed was the practice of *hospitality*. This traditionally has been the domain of women, women practicing hospitality in the home, serving meals, giving shelter. The women called to leadership adopted this practice of hospitality in many generous ways.[24]

One of the effects of developing this practice alongside of their practices of preaching and teaching and doing theology was that it bonded the women to other women in the society. The women called to leadership, called to be evangelists, did not seem quite as strange to other women because they participated in similar activities of cooking, marketing, and bringing gifts to neighbors and practicing hospitality. This sustained the women in their life and work.

A third practice that characterized the women leaders in Indonesia was the practice of *creating beauty*. They created beauty in worship services where rituals were augmented and changed to reflect women's ideas of what is appropriate and what is beautiful. I remember one service prepared by a woman, a worship service that included communion servers dressing in traditional Indonesia dress. The service was held outdoors and the elements of bread and wine were transformed into yellow rice and special Indonesian wine. The service was an international and ecumenical service that became a thing of beauty that brought praise to God in a very special way.[25] Women leaders also created beauty in their homes with plants or gardens, with portraits or photos, with cloth and textiles. This practice of creating beauty around them sustained those women in the difficulties of charting the new course of women becoming leaders, called by God.

Step 5: Theological Reflection

INTENTIONALITY

Through developing practices that further their work and nurture their lives and communities, women sustain themselves and their communities

---

23. Ibid., 112–14.

24. Ibid., 107–10.

25. Ibid., 110–12.

in the new work to which God has called them. In so doing, they lay a groundwork for theological reflection—reflection that is unique since the experience of women becomes the basis for making theology.

Theological reflection is then, the next step in women developing mission theology. Of course reflection occurs through all of these steps: the encounter with God, the study of Scripture, the resistance that seeks inclusion, the development of competence and nurturing practices. Reflection is going on through all of these stages. But to develop mission theology, women need to *intentionally* take this next step , taking time out to reflect on their experience and to interpret Scripture in the light of the acts of God in their own lives and communities.

COMMUNITY

Women often do this in community. Through informal discussion with others, women identify the areas of life which touch on the deep meanings of Christian faith.[26] In Indonesia, ongoing dialogue about Imperial Theologies and Contextual Theologies growing out of women's experience forms a dialectic that is informing Christian theology.

Step 6: Articulating Women's Mission Theology

IMPLICIT TO EXPLICIT THEOLOGY-MAKING

New insights into the nature of God and the world, the nature of sin and the virtues of Christian love and faith are being discovered by women as they reflect on their lives as missionaries and Christian leaders. My theological understandings were broadened and deepened as I learned from women theologians and aspiring Christian leaders in Indonesia.[27] Subsequent chapters will highlight theological reflections of women in many countries, both academic theologians and mission workers.

The partnership theology developed by women theologians in Indonesia is a wonderful example of a way of doing theology in a new mode by women that are called to be leaders. They have developed a culturally

26. The Graduate Student's Women's Association at Satya Wacana Christian University is one example of this kind of discussion. See Adeney, *Christian Women in Indonesia*, 71.

27. See Adeney, "Feet First," 17.

appropriate theology of partnership in which women and men are seen as working in the world building God's kingdom together. This is a pattern of doing theology that grapples with reality as Christians experience it, as we engage one another in Spirit-led dialogues in our communities.

Theology needs to be done in every generation. Not that God changes or the basic eternal truths of Christianity change but that in order to understand these truths they need to be apprehended in new ways in particular contexts, new social locations, and changing historical situations. Theologies need to be articulated in ways that are consistent with the life experience and the questions of meaning of communities of Christians.

CONTRIBUTIONS OF MISSION WOMEN AS THEOLOGY-MAKERS

And these theologies need to include the experiences and insights of women. Asian theologians Chung Hyun Kyung and Marianne Katoppo have written theologies in the contextual mood—theologies that have greatly contributed to Christianity today.[28] The work of women missionaries and women leaders that is currently being recovered contains significant theologies developed by women. Because women have not been considered theology-makers, much of that theology is implicit in the writings and records of women. The historical work of Dana Robert and others is reclaiming and reinterpreting the theological significance of the impact and role of women missionaries, thereby influencing current understandings of women in mission and contemporary views of mission theology.[29]

Step 7: Changing Situations for Theology

Theology is not done by individuals. Nor is it done in a vacuum. Experience and context are crucial components of making theology. Both tradition and communities of interpretation are important in the ongoing process of making theology. Through different circumstances, new situations, varying cultures, unique experiences, and changing historical

28. The relationship between their theologies and religion-identified resistance is described in Adeney, *Christian Women in Indonesia*, 116.

29. See Robert, *Gospel Bearers*; *American Women in Mission*; *Christian Mission*; and *Converting Colonialism*.

locations, God works with Christians to make theology that is relevant and contemporary. For, in order to say the same thing—the thing that is truth—we must say it differently. We must say if from our perspective, to our generation, with our insights from Scripture freshly pressed into the service of helping us to solve contemporary problems and articulate Good News.[30]

Since contexts and circumstances differ widely in the global church today, the common approach to theological reflection outlined in this chapter results in diverse theologies of mission among Christian women today. The next chapter outlines some major theological differences among women in Christian mission and explores reasons for those diverging theologies.[31]

---

30. An example of this important work of collaboration and contemporary theological discourse is found in King, *Feminist Theology*.

31. This chapter was published as "Women Doing Mission Theology," in *Missiology: An International Review* 23 (2005) 277–86.

4

How Diverging Theologies of Mission Arise

> To this day I bring my life
> born of hope, born of sand
> Yearning joy where now there's strife
> all I have, all I am.
>
> MCDADE , "PRAYER TO FRIENDS"

How is it that women using a common approach to theological reflection end up holding very different mission theologies? Some Christian women understand mission as liberation, others as serving women's needs, others as accompaniment, others as bringing Christianity to individuals or cultures, others as empowerment of women, others as friendship and cultural understanding. Some of those theologies overlap but they also include marked differences—differences that exclude other mission theologies.

This chapter explores reasons for theological differences in women's mission theologies: historical reasons, differences in traditions and received theologies and the blending of various methodologies operating in different contexts. Post-modern influences and overlapping theoretical patterns result in a blending of Imperial and Contextual methods and the development of a common philosophical hermeneutic. This chapter explicates those methodological issues, sometimes illustrated with specific theologies. A fuller description of some of the contemporary theologies that result from those historical and methodological complexities will be the subject of chapter 6.

Historical/Denominational Differences

Differences between American Catholic and Protestant women's mission movements illustrate historical differences that go back many centuries.

Roman Catholic Women

Catholic women struggled from the seventeenth century onward with rationalistic theology handed down by the church. The recovery of Aristotle's thought by Aquinas in the twelfth century put reason at the forefront of Western Christian theology. Church authorities stressed natural law, reasoned analysis, using the imperial mood as their central theological method. Women struggled with the resulting doctrines in a number of ways.

As the missionary movement gained steam, women in Catholic religious orders struggled with the role of women vis a vis the cloister. The subjection of women in orders to central authorities of the Catholic Church restricted the freedom of women to minister in needy areas, individually or in a group. The formation of lay orders addressed this problem for some women. Others in consecrated orders, questioned the necessity of having a male priest or bishop overseeing matters of women religious. They sought pastoral roles for women in the Church. Women in South America used new liberation theologies as an avenue for expanding their work. Those theologies departed from natural law theology and Church tradition by developing contextual theologies beginning with the questions and issues of local people. The question related to the larger issue of how God/God's Spirit works through women—what callings, duties, roles, avenues of service were open to them and why?

Contemporary Roman Catholic women respond to those problems with theologies of mission. Some argue theologically for independence in following God's call communally or individually. Others seek changes in Church structures that would allow them more freedom to pursue their ways of knowing and doing theology into action. Some contemporary feminist theologies of mission dovetail with Catholic Church Imperial Mood theology and others diverge sharply from traditional understandings. Their experience moves some women to study theology. That approach is directly related to context. Yet their resources push them to use tools of the Imperial Mood in doing theology. Other women move from an imperial method to a contextual method wholeheartedly.

Susan E. Smith argues that the Holy Spirit, operating before Christ's advent in creation, gives a stronger basis for women's direct following of the Holy Sprit than traditional New Testament based theologies. Without departing from traditional methods of doing Catholic theology, she emphasizes a different way to interpret the Bible—a way that makes room for more independent thought for women. Understanding mission as liberation, as interreligious dialogue, and as inculturation, she sources those ideas in an incarnational theology that allows women missionaries to move into ordained ministry. She calls that a "reignocentric" view since it focuses on the coming reign of God rather than on saving souls or establishing the church. Smith stays within the parameters of respected Catholic theologies and official documents even as she points a way forward for women in ministry.[1]

Catherine Mowry LaCugna turns to Eph 1:3–14 and to theologies of the Trinity from the forth and fifth centuries to argue for a redemptive history that begins with "God turning toward the creature in love and ending with all things being reunited in God."[2] In so doing she bypasses the imperial method that developed between the twelfth and sixteenth century. For LaCugna, "The central theme of all Trinitarian theology is relationship: God's relationship with us, and our relationships with one another."[3] Rather than an abstract theological idea, LaCugna asserts that "the doctrine of the Trinity is, in fact, the most practical of all doctrines."[4] It tells us what the gospel demands, how personal conversion relates to social transformation, and much more. LaCugna moves out from under the umbrella of the Imperial Mood in theology, developing a view of the Trinity that is focused on relationships and grounded in practices of daily life, in liturgy, and in Christian community. Applying her view becomes an exercise in contextual theology.

Rosemary Radford Ruether distinguishes the modern Western focus on a limited rationality from natural law theology. It seems that she

1. Smith, *Women in Mission*, xix.

2. LaCugna, "Practical Trinity," 275.

3. Ibid.

4. Ibid.

would like to preserve the rationalistic method of doing theology in the fuller way that it was initially understood. "Modern Western rationality screens out much of reality as 'irrelevant' to science and reduces scientific knowledge to a narrow spectrum fitted to dominance and control. But the systems it sets up are ecologically dysfunctional because they fail to see the larger *relational patterns* within which particular 'facts' stand."[5] Ruether goes on to recommend a balance between linear thinking and right brain thinking that includes spatial and relational dimensions. Relationality thus becomes central to her theological method.

She uses that relational method to critique traditional theological views of women. Tracing the history of views of women as inferior from Augustine to Karl Barth, Ruether outlines three egalitarian anthropologies and then puts forward her own feminist anthropology that combines liberal and romantic views.[6]

In so doing she departs from traditional theological methods to include relational apprehensions of reality. She states, "We need to recover our capacity for *relationality*, for hearing, receiving, and being with and for others but in a way that is no longer a tool of manipulation or of self-abnegation. We need to develop our capacities for rationality, but in a way that makes reason no longer a tool of competitive relations with others."[7] Ruether uses contextual methods to do theology—methods modeled on women's experiences from many times and cultures.[8] Finally Ruether asks if the use of traditional Christology might be used as a tool for enforcing female subjugation in a patriarchal society. Women must seek an alternative useable Christology centered in the praxis of the historical Jesus.[9] Here she has left behind the methods of the Imperial Mood in theology. For Ruether, relationality and praxis become paramount as women do theology out of the experiences of women in history and contemporary societies.

Elisabeth Schüssler Fiorenza makes an even more radical move. She changes her critical standard on how to evaluate texts and doctrines of the Church. No longer is the Bible or Church doctrine the ultimate arbiter of truth. Rather, what is good for women becomes the basis for evaluating

5. Ruether, *Sexism and God-Talk,* 90. Italics mine.

6. Ibid., 109.

7. Ibid., 113–14.

8. Ibid., 114.

9. Ibid., 115.

the worth of a theology. After a session at the American Academy of Religion in the late 1980s, she said to me something to this effect: Most people think that the Bible forms the basis for my evaluation of theologies. It doesn't. I think that what is good and just is what is good and just for women. Women's welfare is my critical standard. Schüssler Fiorenza departs from traditional Imperial Mood theology, doing a contextual theology with women as both the context and the critical standard.

Protestant Women

In their nineteenth–twentieth-century mission movement, Protestant women did not consider themselves "theology makers." This freed them up to hold official church denominational theologies more lightly and implement creative strategies in mission. Methodist women who founded the Woman's Foreign Missionary Society in 1869 made a commitment to "Woman's Work for Woman."[10] Their focus was on practice and working together with other Christian women especially in education and piety. They became a strong force in mission in many countries by putting their efforts where the need was greatest.

As women worked with the needs of poverty, women's health, and education, they developed theologies of mission. With a few exceptions, they were not church leaders. Many worked well ecumenically because they were not responsible for theology in their denominations. Practices led the way: they did not write "formal" theology but put their theological convictions in letters, diaries, and actions in their lives.

Contextual theologies developed. Women based their actions on their context—what was required in their situation by Scripture and the heart of God known to us through the Holy Spirit. In the late nineteenth century, Catherine Booth led the way for wealthy women in London to do mission work with the poor. She focused on raising money from wealthy women, arguing that they were as much in need of the gospel as the poor. She also persuaded wealthy women to do actual work with the poor, getting them to experience the awful conditions that shackled poor women of London during that era.[11]

---

10. Robert, *American Women in Mission,* 141.

11. See ch. 11, "Variety," in Muck and Adeney, *Christianity Encountering World Religions,* 162–73.

That type of contextual theological development was common in the Protestant women's mission movement between 1850 and 1930s when independent women's mission societies were merged into general church budgets. The lack of leadership roles for women in the churches at that time resulted in their loss of voice and mission projects and funds were directed by male leadership. This marked the end of the powerful women's mission movement in the USA.[12]

Three Methods for Mission Theology

The post-modern turn leads to a diversification of methods as women do mission theology. The last chapter outlined two methods of theological reflection, imperial and contextual, arguing that women used contextual methods since their experience pushed them to do theology. In a post-modern framework, *all* theological methods are deemed contextual, originating and operating within boundaries of society and historical situatedness.

That insight changes two things: First the way that the Imperial Mood is apprehended and used. No longer seen as a pathway to universal truths, the imperial method can uncover insights for a particular context. And second, the recognition that theology can be done by non-Western, non-male theologians. Because theology itself no longer eminates strictly from "universal" rational discourse originating with European scholars and church authorities, women and two-thirds world theologians have as strong a basis for doing theology in their own context as Europeans have in their context.

Consequently, the imperial and contextual methods can be used dialectically or even together creating a third theological method, the Transitional Mood in theology. Traditionally theology-followers, the post-modern turn moves women from theology- followers to theology-makers. Self-consciously embracing that new role, women mission scholars are doing theology within three methodological frameworks.

Women theologians use those methods to do mission theology as they move through the six steps of theology-making presented in the last chapter. By using both frameworks together, differences in both in method and theologies of mission can be identified within the larger paradigm of women doing mission theology in the six-step model. For

12. Robert, *American Women in Mission*, 302–3.

although the six-step model is an experiential and contextual paradigm, Imperial Mood theologies and Transitional Mood theologies are also used as women journey into mission theology.

Let us amplify the descriptions of the imperial and contextual moods in theology, showing how a third transitional method arises.

Theology from Above: The "Imperial Mood" in Theology

This theological method begins with three sources of authority: philosophical/theological traditions, Scripture, and institutional authority. All-encompassing theological issues such as the attributes of God, questions regarding salvation, and the ordering of society under God's laws are the focus of study. The search for universals in theological discovery guide theology-making. History and social location become less important than finding transcendent perspectives. Philosophy defines both the method and style of theology in the Imperial Mood. A rationalistic and discursive style predominates. Binary categories of the Western intellectual heritage such as subject/object, existence/essence, freedom/necessity, noumenal/phenomenal, and theoretical/practical are used to further the development of theological ideas. Often the resulting theology is dependent upon a philosopher or school of thought such as Aristotle, Augustine, or Aquinas.

Theology in the Imperial Mood depends on ecclesiastical authority. The church decides what theologies are acceptable and what theologies constitute heresy. Decisions of the church councils and later the popes and bishops authenticated right theology for the church. Since Aquinas' integration of Aristotelian and Christian thought in the 12th century, the Imperial Mood in theology has predominated in the West.

The impact of the Reformation refocused this method for Protestants. An emphasis on the authority of the Bible supplanted the stress on the philosophical and theological sources in the Christian tradition. Institutional authorities in the protestant church appealed to the Bible as a theological authority rather than church councils or institutional authorities. Protestant theologians and church leaders still decided on the content of orthodox theology and so passed "biblical theology" on to congregations and lay people. Not until the post-modern turn was the impact of *context* upon biblical interpretation fully recognized.

Women Doing Theology in the Imperial Mood

Women doing mission theology in the Imperial Mood use Western European systematic ways of doing theology. Appealing to philosophical/ theological traditions and the authority of Scripture as interpreted by the church, utilizing European theological sources and methods, those women follow the traditional theological interpretations under the institutional authorities of their particular traditions.

What is new is that it is *women* who are theologizing. Women having the opportunity to become theology-makers, mold their theologies using the methods passed down by the tradition. Some differing interpretations of traditional theological positions may occur as women do theology in the Imperial Mood but, for the most part, interpretations follow traditional patterns and theologies.

The message lies in the method. Because the method itself minimizes the role of context, location, and personality, those factors are kept out of the process of theology-making as much as possible. Universal theologies that mirror traditional Roman Catholic, Protestant, Free Church, and Orthodox theologies result.

Women doing theology in the Imperial Mood do not emphasize their context or gender in doing theology. When asked about her methods, a Dutch theologian teaching theology in Hungary said that she did theology in "the normal way." Being a woman had nothing to do with how she approached theological issues, she said. She did theology "as an academic." In fact, she suggested that if I wanted to know about how *women* do theology, I should "ask the men."[13]

This theologian and many others are doing theology in predominately male academic settings. They are pioneers of women's mission theology, having broken the barrier between "real theology" done traditionally by men and "women's theology." That, in itself, is revolutionary. To go beyond traditional theologizing, either in content or in method, could threaten their positions and undo the gains they have made. Having been accepted in the academy, women doing theology in the Imperial Mood tend to conserve those gains, working with and through the traditions.

Those academic theologians are an asset to the academy and to the church. They act as role models for women aspiring to be theologians.

13. Conversation at IAMS Quadrennial Meeting, Port Dixon, Malaysia, August 1, 2004.

Their presence and practice announce the competence and importance of women doing mission theology. Yet they miss out on opportunities to use their experience as women to augment their theological insights, confining their theologies to traditional methods and outcomes.

Theology In-Between: The "Transitional Mood" in Theology

Doing theology in the Imperial Mood works well for some academic women doing mission theology in Western settings. As they work with a predominantly male faculty, they can pass on traditional views and support institutional authorities while modeling a new way of doing theology—women as theology-makers.

Difficulties arise, however, when, either because of the direction of the woman's calling, or because the context is shifting towards gender equality, the question of women's authority to do theology becomes too apparent to disregard. The "in-between" quality of such situations leads women theologians to become more intentional about the roles and abilities of women in the theological realm.[14] The "women question" cannot be avoided but must be addressed.

A **struggle ensures, often beginning in the mind of the woman** theologian, but also very much "in the air" in the context of the church or academic setting. The unspoken challenge to the authority of traditional interpretations of Scripture about women and leadership are voiced. Should women become theology-makers? If so, what should be done about certain "problem passages" in the Pauline epistles? Can women do theology and still remain submissive to male authority? How does this work in practice?

Woman theologians in such settings are forced to shift from the Imperial Mood to a more self-reflective methodology. Their context becomes a crucial as the tension between the views of women in leadership developed in the Imperial Mood and supported by church authorities collide with their own sense of calling and their theological insights. Their position in academic settings requires them to theologize and become leaders in direct contradiction to theologies developed in the Imperial Mood.

14. This crucial insight was made by Eunice Irwin, now retired professor of anthropology at Asbury Theological Seminary's J. Stanley Jones School of World Mission, in one of our women's study group meetings at IAMS, Port Dixon Malaysia, August 6, 2004.

The church in Sulawesi, Indonesia is one example. Established by Dutch Reformed Churches, the Sulawesi Protestant Church followed traditional theologies of the Dutch Calvinists in every theological area save one. After World War II, when the Indonesian church became independent from Dutch control, women became church leaders in the Sulawesi churches.[15] Women had held prominent roles in traditional religions in Sulawesi such as the Minahasa culture in the North and the Torajan society in central Sulawesi. When Christianized, women found their position as community leaders compromised in the Protestant church. Women's movements for political and social equality in Indonesia had also been strong during the twentieth century. When independence was declared in Indonesia in 1945, women gained equal rights as partners in the development of the new nation. Those factors influenced the Protestant churches in Sulawesi to recognize women's leadership in the churches despite an inherited theology that prevented women taking on leadership roles.[16]

Indonesian Christian women in other areas of Indonesia who aspired to leadership in the church and the academy found themselves called to positions that they were automatically disqualified from. In Sumatra a woman could not be a solo pastor but if she and her husband pastored a church, the husband became "the real pastor." In Java, if unmarried, a woman was required to follow her husband rather than accept a call. An emphasis on calling that gave their call more authority become crucial for those women.[17]

As women theologians work in changing settings, they need to address the issue of received theologies when those received theologies contradict the woman's calling from God. Some women argue for inclusion of women in leadership positions. Others see themselves as an exception to the rule. While most women are not called to church or academic leadership, *these women are called* to it. In such cases a traditional theology of women as theology-followers can be upheld while the woman theologian herself does indeed do theology.

Elizabeth Elliot exemplifies this position. As the widow of missionary to the Aucas, Jim Elliot, she has become a prominent mission speaker. Yet her public role as a Christian leader does not prevent her from espousing a theology for women that emphasizes women's role in the home

15. Adeney, "Factors," 32.

16. Ibid.

17. Adeney, *Christian Women in Indonesia,* 77–78.

and family. Somehow her role as church leader and public theologian has not been seen as contradictory to her theology of women as homemakers and supporters of male leadership.

Another response to the in-between context where gender equality is discussed and women are taking on leadership roles, but a traditional theology of male headship and authority is still in place, is to develop a theology of special circumstances in which women may take leadership roles. Missionary-sending institutions in the nineteenth century often took this view. If there were not enough men to do the work in other countries, women were then asked to do it. Biographers of Baptist women missionaries in Burma in the nineteenth century usually made a disclaimer that women were not really preaching when they did evangelistic work. Sometimes the work of Bible translation and church planting was viewed in a similar manner.[18]

A third response is to develop a theology of gender equality that emphasizes the complementarity of women and men and stresses a noncompetitive leadership role for women. That complementarity defies a simplistic view of gender roles. Mary Stewart Van Leeuwen's team of evangelical researchers on gender state that, "The concepts of reciprocal agency, negotiation, and dynamic change are central to an adequate understanding of gender."[19] Christians for Biblical Equality is an organization of women in the United States that works within this theological framework. Their methodology stresses the authority of the Bible and interprets the problem passages in ways that allow women to become leaders in the church. They use a transitional method in doing theology.

Indonesian women theologians in EATWOT took a similar stance when they hosted a national conference on the theme of women and men in partnership in 1995. Throughout the conference, men were honored and included in activities and theological reflection. Scripture passages emphasizing partnership were discussed and women leaders emphasized their desire to work with men in building God's church.[20] Here again, a Transitional Mood method was used as women drew both from their experience and from authorities of the Imperial Mood method in doing theology.

18. Robert, *American Women in Mission*, 56.

19. Van Leeuwen, *After Eden*, 43.

20. Adeney, *Christian Women in Indonesia*, 113–14.

The in-between situation for many women theologians is a difficult, yet promising one. The need for change and inclusion of women in leadership is recognized even though the paths to that leadership may remain narrow. Women leaders in protestant churches in the United States find remarkable ways to acquire inclusion in leadership on the way to acceptance of full gender equality in their settings.

Whether women in an in-between situation see themselves as an exception to the rule of male leadership, whether they develop a theology of special circumstances, or whether they stress inclusion on the basis of complementarity and partnership, the actions of those women theology-makers is pivotal to women doing mission theology. By coordinating their activities and theology with male leaders, those women theology-makers break new ground in mission theology without disrupting institutional structures. As reformers, not revolutionaries, those women pave the way for others to follow. They resist the constrictions of the church on their activities as leaders without rejecting the church and its traditions. Their religion-identified resistance has brought the recognition of Christian women's calling as leaders and theologians to the contemporary church in many countries.[21]

Theology from Below: The "Contextual Mood" in Theology

Many women doing mission theology today are working from a postmodern contextual methodology. This method begins with experience in context. Women start doing theology where they are: the historical and situated perspective predominates. Theology in the Contextual Mood is first of all connected to one's narrative. It is a theology connected to the past, yet related to one's present situation. Rather than beginning with sacred texts, texts are understood through experience. A narrative retelling of texts through the lens of women's experience characterizes theology done "from below."

Theology from below is at the same time a community-centered theology. Not only personal narratives but communal understandings and memories are important resources for doing theology in the contextual mood. As communal memories for women are often related to oppressive church and societal structures, theology from below becomes

21. See ch. 5, "Strategies of Resistance," in Adeney, *Christian Women in Indonesia*, 76–103.

a self-conscious liberation theology. Solidarity among women and net-
works relevant to theology became an important resource for theology-
making. Women of the International Association of Mission Studies
(IAMS) demonstrate this mood in theology as the women's group works
to understand theologies through conversations and shared experiences,
highlighting and valuing differences among them.

Experience defines the method and style of theology in the Contextual Mood. A narrative story-telling style is not an add-on but becomes
integral to theology-making. *Kitchen Table Talk: Sharing our Stories of
Faith*, edited by Jane McAvoy published in 2003 is one example of a theology that gives authority to personal narrative, using women's experience
as a source of theological reflection with the goal of mutual support.

Contemporary missiologist Kirsteen Kim outlines a theology of
the Holy Spirit using a contextual method. Studying at Fuller Seminary,
teaching missiology in India, and spending years in Korea led her to the
view that missiology is a global conversation among contextual theologies. Different theologies are compared across contexts. To do that, Western systematic theology must take its place alongside of other theologies.
Rather than the standard for theological inquiry, systematic theology
must be seen as one view among many. As that happens, comparisons of
theologies become easier.

In her interview for this study Professor Kim made these remarks:[22]

> We must see Western theology as contextual.
>   I began to see missiology as a global conversation of contex-
> tual theologies.
>   I'm interested in theologies plural.

Kim contrasts views of spirit across cultures. Views of spirit in different
cultures led her to focus less on specific views and more on spiritual experience as a common ground. She saw many spirits operating in Korea.
In India, people took one common overarching understanding of spirit.
When Chung Hyun Kyung gave her famous address at the World Council
of Churches meeting in Canberra in 1989, Kim saw in it the potential for
new theologies of the Holy Spirit.

As a feminist theologian, Kim is concerned with how different theologies affect women. In her own journey she began to see Holy Spirit
images in the Bible that emphasized the helping and nurturing aspects
of God's Spirit. Many indigenous theologies in Korea also emphasize the

---

22. Interview, Parliament of World Religions, Barcelona, Spain, July 10, 2004.

female aspects of Shamanistic spirits, in contrast to a male Confucian focus. Kim remarks, "Ignoring indigenous spiritualities can lead to ignoring women."

Kim's own life journey reflects something of that problem. Her early experiences in the Christian community did not provide female models. She says:

> I didn't consider ordination early in life. In my evangelical context, women were not ordained. They didn't become president of the Christian Union. So I was more interested in mission and para-church work.

Kim's growth into a fuller view of both indigenous spiritualities and Christian views of the feminine in contextual theologies informs both the content and method of her mission theology. Her Holy Spirit theology offers a way for Christians to enter inter-religious dialogue with a common ground of spiritual experience without departing from a Christology that emphasizes the historical Jesus.

In the Contextual Mood, faith moves from historical knowledge to a hope that connects the past to the future. Historical interpretations of women as partial or inferior males is replaced by the conviction that wholeness of the church is possible as women are recognized as full human persons—theology-makers. Wholeness in time, through community, wholeness of faith and knowledge, and an understanding of God *with* the world characterizes contextual theology.

Women theologians at the International Association of Mission Studies (IAMS) represent a world-wide movement of women doing theology from below. Women theologians in EATWOT and PERSETIA, an association of women theologians in Indonesia, are Asian examples of this global movement. In addition, the research of this study illustrates theology-making in the contextual mood. Many other women theologians are working in this way.[23]

The Problem of Diversity

As human persons, we cannot live in a post-modern matrix of incommensurable diversity. Paul Rabinow's insight into cultural anthropology showed that if one tries to equally value every culture's ethical standards

23. See for example Johnson, *She Who Is*; Van Wijk-Bos, *Reformed and Feminist*; and Njoroge, *Kiama Kia Ngo*.

and religious practices, we actually value none of them.[24] A peculiar anthropological nihilism results that undercuts that undercuts all particular
values.

Feminist methodologies respond by asserting the importance of the
good for women as a critical standard in doing theology. Many women
in mission argue for a universal value of gender equality. Positing a universal value allows theologians to use contextual methods without falling
into a radical relativism that isolates them from conversation with those
of differing theologies (see chapter 14).

Women doing mission theology do value the diversity of methods
described above. However, a problem arises as we see the divergence of
resulting theologies. What, if anything do women have in common as
mission theologians? Is the diversity incommensurable?

A Common Philosophical Hermeneutic

Looking for commonalities, we find that all three methods begin with
experience, a major deconstructive insight of post-modernity. Yet in
beginning with experience, women do theology differently as described
in the three methods above, ending up with diverging theologies. What
they do have in common is a women's *way* of doing mission theology.

The last chapter took the next constructive step—finding common
ground, yet valuing diversity. A common thread runs through the three
different methodologies. While beginning at different starting points, the
methods themselves go through the same set of steps. After applying the
localizing insight of post modernism, experience and location determine
the starting point of doing theology. The resulting method looks different
depending on where one starts—yet a common philosophical hermeneutic framework ties all three methods together.

Depending on the context where one stands while using one of the
three methods three different starting points become apparent: First, a
traditional matrix of modern theology. Second, a changing matrix in between modernity and post modernity, and third, a thoroughly post-modern context oriented toward local knowledge. The resulting theologies
when beginning with one of those starting points look different. Women
mission theologians may or may not value those differences.

---

24. Rabinow, "Humanism as Nihilism," 52.

The IAMS quadrennial global conferences give mission theologians the opportunity to interact with theology-makers from different settings and starting points. Their different conclusions about mission theology can be valued and perhaps better understood when viewed with the heuristic device of a post-modern theology of mission that places each theology on a context-dependent continuum. The contours of that continuum result in modern, and in-between, and post-modern theologies of mission. The steps remain the same. The starting points and therefore the results differ. Women at IAMS do theology from each of those vantage points, resulting in varying theologies of mission.

Overlapping Patterns

There are two theoretical patterns involved here that overlap. The more general one, applicable to all three types of theology illustrated by women at IAMS is a philosophical hermeneutical method that outlines six steps in women doing theology. Used as an overlay one can see that common method occurring in varying theologies of mission. To review, the six steps are:

1. Encountering God and experience of call.

2. Study of Scripture to confirm call.

3. Use of Scripture in religion-identified resistance that demands inclusion.

4. Shaping practices of competence and nurture.

5. Theological reflection on experience of calling, study of scripture, and interaction with community and church institutions.

6. Articulation of new theological insights

When these steps are applied to specific philosophical contexts, a diversity of results occur: Modern—traditional theologies from above result with the difference that women include themselves in the categories of leader and theology-makers. In-between—traditional starting point gives way to assertion of a more located stance in theological work—owning of calling and assertion of its centrality in doing theology and mission. Post-modern—local starting point affirmed—experience of calling in a particular context leads toward a liberative model as theology moves intentionally in a localized context.

The resulting theologies, of course, do differ. However, the six-step path to those insights in each of the three methods used by women, shows remarkable similarities. Reasons for those similarities were identified by women in the research group of this study:

1. Similar patriarchal structures exist across cultural lines, in east and west, north and south. Public roles, family patterns, and social expectations in many societies relegate women to secondary status and deprive women of power in economic, political, and social spheres.

2. Institutional Christian theologies have supported those patriarchal structures by outlining theologies that place women in subordination to men, reducing their authority and relegating their calling to privatized settings.

Consequently, development of women's theologies follow a similar pattern. The calling itself runs counter to the expectations of the women and their social institutions. As the calling is confirmed by study of scripture, resistance occurs. That resistance centers on the institutional configuration of the church. Women called to church leadership remain in the church but resist patriarchal theologies and structures in that setting. Reflection on those struggles results in articulation of new women-empowering theologies.

However, if the theological milieu of the woman is set against women-empowering theologies, the same pattern of theological development results in less confrontative theologies. Women called in such settings survive by collaboration with men in authority and articulation of theologies that go along with the dominant Imperial Mood theology paradigm. A woman, for example, may articulate a theology of women's submission even while becoming an outspoken Christian leader herself. Elizabeth Elliot demonstrates this by writing and speaking publicly, admonishing women to do the opposite of what she does, stressing the importance of women remaining in the home and not seeking a public role in the church.

This chapter illustrates that the diversities in women's mission theologies cannot be captured in a neat model. Women's agency, differences in cultures, backgrounds, status, and situation result in diverse approaches to Christianity and the mission task.

Those diversities can be better understood, however, by utilizing overlapping models of theological methodology. Particular theological methods—imperial, transitional, and contextual—provide insights into theological methods used in modern, in between, and post-modern settings. An overarching philosophical hermeneutic outlining steps taken by women to advance their leadership and ability to be heard in theological discourse illumines some commonalities in the more specific theological methodologies used by woman in doing mission theology. Juxtaposing those models reveals both differences and cross-cultural similarities in women's contexts, differences in approach, and varying results as women do mission theology.

Women in this study represent all of the above ways of doing mission theology, striving to clearly articulate their mission theologies and value the theologies of others. The next chapter explores specific theologies of contemporary Christian missiologists. Rather than focus on the methods used, that chapter will outline the content of the theologies of numerous contemporary women missiologists.

5

Contemporary Missiologists

If the disciples had watched with the same assiduousness, as Mary did at
the Sepulchre, they would have had the joyful tidings to preach.

—DOROTHY RIPLEY, *BANK OF FAITH*, 1

THIS CHAPTER PRESENTS SOME of the diverging theologies of mission
that arise from the use of differing methodologies in different contexts.
The idea for this chapter is not to emphasize their differences, although
there are many. Rather, the goal is to find common threads among them.
Do women's ways of knowing and doing theology result in commonalities among their different theologies? Theologies of contemporary missiologists from three groups are analyzed: World Evangelical Alliance,
Roman Catholic women, and theologians from the American Society of
Missiology. Historical theologies and methodologies of women in mission since World War II set their thinking in the global context of today.
We see how women's mission theologies from those sources both connect with traditions in mission theology and display divergences from
mainstream Western missiology. Questions are posed, many of which are
addressed by narrators in this study.

Changes in Women's Mission Theology since World War II

Let me begin with a story, told to me by Rev. Carol Chamberlain Rose
Ikler, one of the narrators of this study. Reverend Ikler was ninety-two
years old in 2012, the first woman to be ordained by the Presbytery of

Philadelphia in 1958. Her life illustrates the changes for women doing mission theology since World War II. She lived through those changes.

Born into a family of four generations of ministers, Carol's youth was marked by the hospitality of parents deeply involved with social issues of the day. Her father, a Congregational minister, did inner city ministry in the slums of New York City and her mother led the choir at Riverside Church. As a young person, the influences of Walter Rauschenbusch and Harry Emerson Fosdick shaped her theology of mission.

During her college years, Carol spent summers doing mission work. She cared for patients in a mental hospital in Europe, worked with Japanese children in internment camps in the United States, and gave children made homeless by the war opportunities to do outdoor camping in the mountains of Switzerland. Graduating in 1942 from Mt. Holyoke College, Carol went on to study at Union Theological Seminary in New York and Columbia University in a joint program. She then went to Hawaii where she spent eight years working with a Congregational Church as director of children's ministry.

On her return, a crisis of faith led her to Yale Divinity School where she studied with Reinhold and H. Richard Niebuhr and other prominent theologians. Her professors helped her to solidify her progressive theology and she went on to become one of the editors of the Faith and Life Curriculum for the Presbyterian Church. "H. Richard Niebuhr came nearer to being Jesus to us than any other professor," she said frankly.[1]

Carol Ikler's journey illustrates the changes in women doing mission theology since World War II. Both the ecumenical movement and the women's movement in the church were vibrant during the 1940s. Her time at Union and Columbia coincided with the birth of the World Council of Churches. Carol said it was a time of great excitement and expansion in the intellectual and practical worlds of theology. Those changes created opportunities for women. Women students were welcomed at Union Seminary. Ordination for women began to be considered as talents of women began to be recognized and utilized by the church. Women found opportunities to do mission work that was usually the work of men.

Studies at Yale continued to open paths for Carol Ikler and other women to do serious work in theology. In 2011, Yale celebrated "70 years of women at Yale." Carol was one of the pioneers of women doing mission theology. She looked back at the changes with humility, grateful for the

---

1. Interview April 26, 2012, Louisville Presbyterian Seminary.

opportunities she was able to pursue. She spoke of theology as a practice, something she did every day. Grappling with theological ideas, studying the works of others, and reformulating her own thoughts in light of Scripture formed an important part of Rev. Ikler's spirituality. She credited the Holy Spirit for direction in those endeavors and the church for nurturing them. "Young women today," she said, "seem surprised that there was ever a time when women were not ordained, were not leaders in the church, were not doing theology." For that we can be grateful to women like Carol Rose Ikler.[2]

Social changes in the United States and around the world since World War II make finding theologies of Christian mission by women much easier. World War II itself laid the groundwork for women in the United States to participate more fully in the workplace. A wave of feminism in the 1970s furthered that freedom. Academic positions began opening up for women and Protestant churches began to ordain women, recognizing their leadership capabilities. Women's independence on the mission field also increased as para-church organizations developed in the second half of the twentieth century. Immigration from Africa and Asia and the proliferation of world religions in the U.S. brought the mission field home, giving women more opportunities to work and reflect on mission and Christianity. Finally prominent Christian women like Frances Willard, Eleanor Roosevelt, Mary McCleod Bethune, Dorothy Day, and Mother Theresa provided role models for women called into mission service.

Evangelical Women's Mission Theologies

Evangelical women participating in the World Evangelical Alliance provide insights into the content and methods of evangelical women's mission theologies. In 1999 the Iguassu Missiological Consultation brought together 160 missiologists in Brazil. The publication of the papers from that consultations along with "The Iguassu Affirmation" outlined the mission theology of the World Evangelical Alliance (then known as the World Evangelical Fellowship) at that time. It also included thirty-five articles by men and five articles by women. One article was co-authored

2. Reverend Ikler died in 2013, a loss to the Presbyterian Church and the seminary where she had remained active until her death. She organized a monthly Presbyterian Book Review meeting, inviting faculty from the seminary to present books they had recently read or published.

by seven men and one woman. Additional articles by Samuel Escobar and Christopher Wright were added before publication.

The Iguassu Affirmation provides a base line of evangelical mission theology. It was crafted by World Evangelical Fellowship Missions Commission leadership David Tai-Woong Lee and Jim Stamoolis, revised by a team of seven theologians from various continents, and discussed in groups at the meeting itself.[3] The Affirmation includes fourteen declarations of evangelical mission theology that stress the foundations in the authority of Scripture, the saving work of Jesus Christ, the Trinitarian basis for mission, and the importance of the church in fulfilling God's plan for the world.[4]

The articles by women reveal a number of theological themes and emphases that differ from the text of the Affirmation developed by their male colleagues. It is those views that we wish to explore here.

Antonia Leonora van der Meer's article stresses the missionary's ongoing relationship with God and the calling from God that drives the work of mission. She uses the Scriptures to emphasize the unity of the human race, and the love of Jesus for all nations—a love that broke through the disciples' prejudices, preparing them for a worldwide ministry.[5] She relies on the mission theology of David Bosch, drawing out the thread of God's relationship of love as a basis for mission.[6] Mission, according to van der Meer, is "the fruit of the love of God."[7] It is "caring for whole human beings with the compassionate love of God."[8] Van der Meer brings her emotions into her theology. "When Christians and even missiologists call Africa 'the cursed continent,' call African culture 'demonic,' and look down upon our African brothers and sisters, I become very angry."[9] She shows empathy for the suffering of extreme poverty many faced in Angola and declares that "in response to my caring, many believed."[10] She stresses enabling the local people to do the work of mission, not rejecting some groups as heretics but treating all as those who have the right to

---

3. Taylor, *Global Missiology*, 2.

4. Ibid., 17–21.

5. Van der Meer, "Scriptures, the Church, and Humanity," 151.

6. Ibid., 153.

7. Ibid.

8. Ibid., 154.

9. Ibid.

10. Ibid., 155.

learn and understand what Jesus commanded us in Matt 28:20.[11] In those and other ways, Van deer Meer changes the tone of evangelical mission theology from one of authority and effectiveness to one of respect, compassion and whole engagement of the mind and the emotions in the work of mission.

Miriam Adeney's essay centers on the theme of unity-in-diversity, couching respect for American subcultures in the language of Eph 1:9— the mysterious plan of God to bring all things together in Christ. She advocates seeing the subcultures of the United States as unique and precious particularities to be explored and embraced. "This means teaching unity at every opportunity," she declares.[12] It is in Adeney's essay that we hear the condemnation of racism and classism, ideas that seem distant from the formal Affirmations of the consultation. Adeney connects her anthropological insights and social analysis about American compartmentalization with her convictions about the respect and unity that American Christians must foster in order to tell the story of how God in Christ brings together all things.

Rose Dowsett's essay gives an overview of problems in the West, an analysis possibly sourced in Os Guinness' work. The creative part of her theology appears somewhere in the middle of her discourse when she introduces the topic of listening. She calls upon Christians to listen, not only to the Word, but also to non-Western churches. She describes the preferred attitude of that listening as humility.[13] Dowsett argues that critical contextualization begins with humility and continues as a practice. Rather than a thought process, she describes contextualization as something the missionary *does*—"a living out of biblical truth in the here-and-now."[14] Here, as in Van der Meer's essay, Dowsett brings emotions into her theology. She says, "The Western church must listen with tears and pain and penitence."[15]

Paula Harris' article on the Nestorian church brings up the question of women's influence in earlier times. She wonders what influence clergy wives had on the church through their husbands. She speculates that queens and mothers of queens could have affected the course of

11. Ibid., 157.

12. Adeney, "Telling Stories," 385.

13. Dowsett, "Dry Bones," 454.

14. Ibid., 455.

15. Ibid., 456.

Christian history in that part of the world. These wonderings show a keen interest in women's mission theologies and the desire to recover women's voices. Although she does express unity as a theological concept, Harris admires the Nestorian communities for their ability to display unity in the face of diversity.[16]

Cathy Ross' reflections on the Iguassu Affirmation laments the lack of women's voices at the consultation. Here again, emotions are not ruled out as part of theological reflection as Ross says she is "shocked and disappointed" that women's perspectives are not heard.[17] She brings out that although women represent two-thirds of missionaries worldwide, only nineteen out of one hundred sixty delegates were women. She speaks of the need for evangelicals to address women's issue as a response to the injustices that women suffer.[18] Finally she stresses the importance of developing partnerships of equals in mission and advocates for humility in the process of interacting with Christians from other cultures and contexts.[19]

The common themes in these articles by women are not difficult to find. Unity in diversity, the need for women's voices to be heard, careful listening, critical practices of contextualization and compassion, emotional expression, and humility are stressed in these articles. The Iguassu Affirmation might read differently if those themes were added to the evangelical mission theology presented in the document. Its tone would change—perhaps to a warmer, more friendly theology of mission for the twenty-first century.

Catholic Women's Mission Theologies

Women's Catholic mission theology has gone through major changes since World War II. In her book *The Missionary Movement in American Catholic History*, missiologist Angelyn Dries, OSF describes World War II itself as an important marker for Catholic mission theology. Between 1946 and 1959, Maryknoll founder John Considine developed a broad vision to frame human societies into a Christian social order. Women in mission took on the fourfold goals of "world Christianity": regard, love for, and knowledge of all cultures; promotion of the welfare of all; justice

16. Harris, "Nestorian Community," 497.
17. Ross et al., "Iguassu Affirmation," 521.
18. Ibid., 530.
19. Ibid., 536.

according to Christian ideals, and the transmission of Christ's teaching to non-Catholics, and non-Christians.[20] The women who developed the U.S. Catholic school curriculum of this era focused on those goals, thus having a profound impact on future leaders of the Church. The curriculum emphasized the evils of racism and attitudes of superiority toward others, themes not dissimilar from some of the voices we heard by women in the World Evangelical Alliance.[21]

By the 1960s mission to Latin America involved women in both pastoral ministry and education for women's leadership. The Sisters of St. Joseph brought a theology of the Mystical Body to Peru in 1965. They stressed the importance of living with the same privations as the people they were serving, becoming willing to receive gifts of religion and social warmth from the people.[22] Mary McCormick, a widow and lay volunteer, demonstrated that theology spending twenty-seven years in Colombia. She organized a nutrition and milk program for young mothers, started a daycare center, and managed a loan program focused on housing. In addition she organized a four-week "conscientization" program for North Americans so they could live with local families in Bogotá and assist her in her work in the barrio.[23]

Two-thirds of the Papal Volunteers for Latin America (PAVLA) during that time were single women.[24] Those women had the opportunity to practice the Latin American liberation theology that was being developed by Gustavo Gutiérrez and others. Many women missionaries focused on education with a two level approach. Educating the elite was crucial for the growth of the church but women missionaries also emphasized educating the poor, grooming them for a way out of poverty, and demonstrating the love of Christ at the same time.[25]

In the area of pastoral formation, Gretchen Berg, a Franciscan from Rochester, Minnesota started Regina Mundi, a two-year program that prepared Peruvian women to enter university. Through weekly seminars on liturgy, ecclesiology, Scripture, and the church in the modern world, the Sisters learned and discussed the latest theology. Conferences were

20. Dries, *Missionary Movement*, 168.

21. Ibid., 269.

22. Ibid., 185.

23. Ibid., 195.

24. Ibid., 196.

25. Ibid., 225.

sponsored that brought rich and poor congregations together for the first time.[26] Although conflict between rich and poor communities ended this effort in 1967, the women educators were at the forefront of practicing a theology that would significantly influence the Catholic mission theology in the coming decades.[27]

An important aspect of that theological vision for mission had to do with method. Mary Xavier O'Donnell, MM stressed a new approach to evangelization of Hispanic groups in Chicago. In teaching the catechism of the Family of God, she affirmed the traditional family values that the people embraced, using what they already knew as a basis for understanding God in their lives. The emphasis was on hearing the Word of God in experience and community which then led to action.[28] That liberation theology praxis model was used in women's groups: observe, act, judge.[29]

During this time, many women religious moved from educational institutions into more pastoral work.[30] The formation of communities of the Word, an emphasis on team ministry and the development of lay leadership provided important trajectories for the new ecclesiology that the Church was embracing at the time of Vatican II. Women were at the forefront of implementing an ecclesial model that challenged the passivity and dependence that had marred the experience of many people in Latin America. Dries describes that ecclesial model as one that "emphasized the sacramentality of human beings, promoted cohesiveness and collective experiential knowledge, and brought the Word of God to bear on daily life.[31] As missionaries listened to people telling the stories of their own experiences, a spirit of humility developed among pastoral ministers.[32]

Another important theme of women's Catholic mission theology since World War II has been the theme of self-sacrifice. Living with the poor, seeing God's face in their visage, and being willing to do whatever it takes to follow the mission call cost a number of Latin American missionaries their lives. Maura Clarke, MM and Maureen Courtney, CSA are

26. Ibid., 207.
27. Ibid., 213.
28. Ibid., 218f.
29. Ibid., 225.
30. Ibid., 243.
31. Ibid., 244.
32. Ibid.

only two of the women that gave their lives working among the poor in Latin America. Their contributions left us an unforgettable legacy.

Although the number of Catholic missionaries has decreased since the 1970s, the gains made through use of new educational and pastoral care methods are still with us. Women's influence on educational programs that included anti-racism and equality dimensions, their pastoral work in empowering local communities, and their dedication to the mission task provide cogent tools for mission theology today.

Although gender roles were at issue in many communities and women's ideas were sometimes not celebrated by the establishment, women's mission theologies moved ahead in educational and pastoral formation forums. Before 1960, a theology of the Mystical Body was emphasized, along with an emphasis on world Christianity as it was then defined. Developing curricula that emphasized equality of all peoples had great influence on future Catholic leaders. During the 1960s a horizontal ecclesiology and an option for the poor were at the forefront of women's educational efforts and mission practices. Those contributions by Catholic women to mission theology and methodology stand out as salient as we reflect on mission theology since the middle of the twentieth century.

Comparing those contributions to the evangelical women missiologists we see similar themes emerging. Parallels between Christian unity and a theology of the Mystical Body are clear. An emphasis on anti-racism and equality among all peoples can also be traced as similarities, as can promotion of an attitude of humility and a goal of shared leadership. An emphasis on contextualization also runs through both evangelical and Catholic women's mission theologies.

A major difference can be seen in the beginning points of their methods. Catholic women theologians use a liberation theology methodology. They begin with experience as a field for hearing God's word in community. Evangelical missiologists tend to emphasize the Word first and then the hearing of the Word in community rather than starting with experience and seeing God's word primarily through that lens. They begin with the Imperial Mood method of doing theology.

American Society of Missiologist Women Missiologists

American Socity of Missiologists women are recovering the history of women in mission in both Protestant and Catholic traditions, analyzing theological streams and critiquing mission methods, making theological contributions to the academy and the church, and utilizing insights from social science for mission. Their focus on context and the needs of local settings are contributions to mission theology made by ASM women.

Beginning historically, significant mission history has been done by Sister Angelyn Dries, OSF and Dana Robert. Much of that work reclaims the history of women in mission in both Catholic and Protestant realms. The last section of this chapter explored some of the theological themes that Angelyn Dries recounts of Catholic women's mission theology and methods.

On the Protestant side, significant historical recovery of women's theologies of mission has been captured in Dana Robert's *American Women in Mission: A Social History of Their Thought and Practice* (1997). She documents the rise and fall of the women's missionary movement, highlighting theologies that emphasized the personal and ethical dimensions of mission work, ecumenical cooperation, women's missionary work with women and children, and issues of women's leadership.[33] Unfortunately, in mainline denominations, that movement was quelled after World War II, which Robert notes marked "a prelude to foreign missions becoming a lower priority for the (mainline) churches.[34] Looking more broadly at mission history, Robert outlines the major themes of women in mission as service, healing, teaching, and hospitality.[35] She notes that because they were barred from ministerial roles, women missionaries became educators, establishing schools and training girls and women as well as boys and young men that would later become denominational leaders. In so doing, women have left a legacy of educated women and efforts to claim human rights for women all over the world. She describes women's mission method as one of building relationships, a method that not only allowed women access to women of other cultures but kept them from charges of cultural imperialism as they partnered with local and national leaders to establish hospitals, work for human rights, and educate women for leadership.

With such a legacy, Robert asserts, "The history of mission must focus on women for the majority of the Christians in the world are

33. Robert, *American Women in Mission*, 409–12.

34. Ibid., 306–7.

35. Robert, *Christian Mission*, 141.

women."[36] Looking at recent decades, we find that the decline of mission efforts in the mainline Protestant churches of the United States after World War II is not reflected in the Catholic, Pentecostal, and conservative Protestant traditions. During this time Catholic women in Latin America implemented new forms of mission theology. Conservative Protestant women developed specialized forms of mission, producing Bible translations, Gospel recordings, and the training indigenous pastors.[37] Pentecostalism grew exponentially after the 1960s spawning interest of women in mission in Central and South America. Protestant models of family life brought many into the churches in Latin America and in Africa, views of the missionary as mother played a central role in the spread of the gospel.[38]

Another scholar that has reclaimed part of women's theological work in mission is Bonnie Sue Lewis. In *Creating Christian Indians: Native Clergy in the Presbyterian Church*, Lewis highlights the productive relationships women missionaries developed with Native American pastors. Despite frequent conflict, women missionaries educated and empowered the elders of Native American congregations to take leadership. Missionary Kate McBeth saw the wisdom of the Nez Perces' desire to establish their own churches with Native leadership.[39] Part of the appeal of the Christian gospel for Native Americans was its call to the weak and impoverished. Women missionaries reached out to the poor and lowly, practicing hospitality and honoring Native American leaders who had to depend on persuasion to get support for their decisions. Between 1874 and 1932, eighteen men became ordained Presbyterian ministers under the training of women missionaries.[40]

Besides reclaiming histories of women in mission, missiologists are reorienting mission theology to benefit from women's experiences and theologies. Robert notes that the majority of Christian missionaries have been women and the majority of Christians in the world today are women.[41] Mission theology by women provides a tremendous resource developing a fitting response to those facts.

---

36. Ibid.

37. Robert, *American Women in Mission*, xxii.

38. Robert, *Christian Mission*, 130–31.

39. Lewis, *Creating Christian Indians*, 119.

40. Ibid., 121.

41. Robert, *Christian Mission*, 141.

Sherron George's theology of mission provides one resource for that reorientation. Postcolonial critiques have shown the necessity of working in partnerships with the people whom North American missionaries serve. George's *Called as Partners in Christ's Service: The Practice of God's Mission* describes how to develop those partnerships with the 70 percent of Christians in the two-thirds world.

George focuses her theology on the mission of God, a Trinitarian mission that is part of redemption. She first describes God's mission of love and light to the world as portrayed in the Gospel of John. Turning to contemporary missionaries, George stresses attitudes and practices that give Christianity the appeal that inheres in it—compassion, respect for others, humility, and the ability to receive as well as give.[42]

As she tells her own story, Sherron George traces a movement that reflects important changes in her mission theology.[43] Mutuality was her paradigm for mission in the 1970s. She immersed herself in the life and culture of rural congregations in southwest Brazil.[44] During the 1980s she gained a new perspective from her doctoral project—an understanding of solidarity as a missional stance.[45] In the 1990s, George was called to teach at the IPB Seminary of the South in Campinas. As the first ordained woman to teach at this oldest and largest Presbyterian seminary in Brazil, George felt herself moving into marginality as a new identity.[46] George was transformed by "mission in reverse" during her twenty three years in Brazil. From there she could move to a new attitude, a "bold humility." In that attitude she crafted a new definition of mission: "Mission is everything the local-global church is sent into the world to be and do as a participant in God's mission and every person and gift the local-global church receives in Christ's name and way."[47]

The work of Marsha Snulligan Haney provides insights into evangelism and Africentric approaches to Christian ministry. Standing in the prophetic tradition of the Black Church, Haney sees God as a liberating relational God interested in all peoples. Firmly rooted in Biblical texts, Haney stresses the importance of addressing contextual challenges in

42. George, *Called as Partners,* 60.

43. George, "From Missionary to Missiologist," 40.

44. Ibid., 43.

45. Ibid., 45.

46. Ibid., 51.

47. Ibid., 52.

diverse urban settings. That concern has taken her into studies of Prot-
estant/Islamic relations and African American Presbyterians who work
in a pluralistic denomination. From the Afrocentric perspective, Haney
says "there is no validity to our spirituality if it does not result in social
action."[48]

Unpacking Haney's substantive mission theology takes us into the
middle of urban, pluralistic, and post-colonial contemporary contexts. In
telling her own story, Haney speaks of listening, seeking peace, and staying connected to a missionary liberating God.[49] Using a pilgrim metaphor for missional identity allows Haney to focus both on the meaning
of faith for the individual as well as the structures and systems that need
the transforming power of the gospel.[50] Unwilling to leave her theology
at the level of generalizations, Haney goes on to describe six steps for
changing the "traditional, convenient, and familiar patterns of mission
defined by paternalism, exclusion, and elitism" into a new paradigm that
responds to the "*missio Dei* from the ecclesia of every nation, language,
and people group."[51] Those include understanding the relative nature of
truth, centering on ways of being in the context of relationsips and af-
firming diversity in a way that appreciates the gifts of others.[52] Haney's
thinking and her process in developing a new mission identity offer crucial guideposts to women missiologists as we formulate our theologies in
a fast-paced world of diversity.

Miriam Adeney, whose work was cited earlier in this chapter, brings
anthropological insights into play in her theology of mission. Her work
is both global and focused on issues in North American contexts. According to Adeney, reaching across cultural boundaries happens everywhere and has always been the Christian's call.[53] Adeney puts action
behind her words by modeling a cross-cultural mission in her practice
of teaching writing skills to Christians all over the world. Her stress on
unity-in-diversity colors her work with both ecclesiological and egalitarian overtones, which she displays in her work on Muslim women. "Can a

48. Haney, "Africentricity," 162.

49. Haney "Development," 79f.

50. Ibid., 89.

51. Ibid., 91.

52. Ibid.

53. Adeney, *Kingdom Without Borders*, 33.

single woman who follows Jesus thrive in the Muslim world?" she asks.[54] Adeney also contributes to the conversations among missiologists with her cogent critique of the compartmentalization in the academic field of missiology as well as in American life.[55]

ASM missiologists have made significant contributions to reclaiming the history of women in mission as well as helping us to reorient our current understandings of mission theologies and methods.

Salient Themes and Questions

This whirlwind tour of women's mission theologies barely scratches the surface of the work that women have done and continue to do in mission theology, education, and practice. Identifying a few salient themes provides us with questions and directions for further mission theologies.

First, the theme of God's relationality and the claim that places on Christian mission to work in love with others stands out across all of the theologies observed in this chapter. It was also a strong theme in my own study of Christian women in Indonesia. Women there sought to sustain relationships with women and honor leaders even as they pursued theological education and leadership in the church.[56] This is not a theme unique to women missiologists, however. But it does demand more study of women's interpretations of relationships with God and others. How are those views unique, and how are they influenced by gender considerations—sociological, ecclesiological, and biological?

Second, the themes of unity, of God's love for all humanity, and of the importance of treating others with respect comes through strongly in much of the women's work in theology we have looked at. Whether couched in terms of compassion, justice, or unity, the focus is on the mission of God in the world as a mission for all peoples, to be carried out through work that shows honor and love to all. As Christian communities reach out to those of other religions, respect becomes a baseline practice for interacting with others in our pluralistic world.[57] How can missiologists tie together unity-in-diversity, liberating justice for marginalized people, and ecclesial practices of worship and welcome together?

---

54. Adeney, *Daughters of Islam,* 110.

55. Adeney, "Telling Stories," 384–85.

56. Adeney, *Christian Women in Indonesia,* 113–14.

57. Muck and Adeney, *Christianity Encountering World Religions,* 174.

Women's concern for those themes puts women missiologists at the fore-front of that endeavor.

Third, the emphasis on Christian values, particularly attitudes of humility and willingness to receive from others as an incarnational witness run through many of the studies. A further emphasis on family values was stressed in some of the work. The questions arising from this focus include parameters of family values as societies change, how humility presents itself in different cultures, and how to become receptive to the gifts that others have to offer. Some of those questions are tackled by George and Haney. I also deal with them in my work on giftive mission and graceful evangelism.[58] But there is much more to be done.

A willingness to express emotions in doing scholarly work presents itself in some of the essays. How much does that willingness relate to social status in the church and academy as women are "given permission" in many societies to express emotion in ways that are discouraged for men? Should women lead in helping missionaries and missiologists to become more willing to engage in dialogue that includes expressions of disappointment and anger as well as joy and celebration? As women missiologists and mission workers practice legitimating emotions in their theological work, it may make a significant impact on theologies of mission and their usefulness to the churches.

Listening is another thread that runs through the work of women theologians in this chapter. Listening to third world voices, listening to the marginalized, listening with the intent to respond in love, listening to learn, listening to honor others different from ourselves. Becoming open enough to actually listen to someone that has radically different views from one's own is a task that takes conscious effort to achieve.[59] So here we confront a final question that is not only a research question but also a personal one.

I began this paper with a story of Rev. Carol Rose Ikler and I'd like to close with a reference to her. Doing theology was an everyday practice for Rev. Ikler. She couldn't imagine going a day without reflecting on the work of God in the world and how Christians can be involved in it. Doing this in an academic setting was a new adventure for women in the 1950s and 1960s. Today it is commonplace. Can we utilize that practice

---

58. Adeney, *Graceful Evangelism*, 175–76.

59. Ibid., 166.

of women seminarians, pastors, counselors, and missiologists to a better end than we have in the past? Can we listen?

The next chapter will show how women in this study, including but not limited to missiologists, have used themes of relationality, unity, Christian values, emotions, and listening as well as other themes in outlining their theologies and practices of mission.

PART II

6

Themes in Women's Mission Theology

We must *learn how, what, and when to give* with humility and
compassion in a way that honors, dignifies, and respects others.

—GEORGE, *CALLED AS PARTNERS,* 76

THE LAST CHAPTER ANALYZED various theologies of mission by contemporary missiologists. We uncovered common themes of relationality, unity, values of humility and receptiveness, incarnational witness, using emotions to theologize, and listening to theologies of others. Some of those missiologists were narrators for this study. This chapter explores those and other themes, addressing the question of how those ideas and values influence women narrators across the study. Are they simply academic ideas that missiologists puport? How are those themes known and practiced by women mission workers, church and denominational leaders, and Christian women in congregations?

Relationality

In the last chapter we noted the importance of relationships for contemporary missiologists mainly in the West.[1] In the South and East, relationships have traditionally been at the center of women's lives. Relationships as an integral part of mission theology occurs multiple times in the nar-

---

1. Global contexts and attendant themes are addressed in this and other chapters by women in the International Association of Mission Studies (IAMS), in the history chapter, and in the Brazil Case Study.

rators' accounts. As the most dominant theme among informants, it has a number of dimensions.

Theologies of God

The Holy Spirit's activity in mission across the world is stressed by theologian Kirsteen Kim, a theme that was crucial to missionary women early in the twentieth century as well as becoming a theme in the spirituality movement. Some women theologians, in discussing *Missio Dei*, God's work in mission, focus particularly on the work of the Holy Spirit. At the World Council of Churches Meeting in Canberra, Australia in 1989, Chung Hyun Kyung linked indigenous Korean theologies of spirit with Christian ideas of the Holy Spirit operating in the world. Controversy arising from Chung's presentation of this theology has not prevented women from "re-imagining" God in many creative ways.

Thinking about the sacred and about relationships led Christian women to construct ideas about relationship as part of a theology of God. Chung insists that women use their experience to further their understanding of God. She says, "Only when we Asian women start to consider our everyday, concrete life experiences as the most important source for building the religious meaning structures for ourselves shall we be free from all imposed religious authority."[2] Women working on the Iguassu Declaration on World Evangelization write of the relationality of God as a basic tenet of mission theology. Elizabeth A. Johnson also links experience with the relatedness of God, stating, "Basic trust in the experience of God's threefold relatedness to us suggests that a certain corresponding threefoldness characterizes God's own true being."[3]

Relationship as part of a *theology of God* abounds in women's mission theologies today marking a beginning point for many women. Narrators commented that if God is relational, so humans should relate to others. As God's relationship in the Trinity is one of love and care, humans should relate to one another with care. As the relationships within God spawn creativity, so working with others results in creative actions that serve God.

Dr. Marion McClure, Director of the Kentucky Council of Churches, asserts that "Mission is as concrete as building a house together but

2. Chung, *Struggle to Be the Sun,* back matter quote.
3. Johnson, *She Who Is,* 200.

it is also extremely cosmological. Mission theology occurs at the highest level of your imagination. . . . The endpoint is a comprehensive drawing of all creation back into right relationship with God."[4]

Sarah Rajarigam from India advocates a Trinitarian theology that emphasizes the passion within the Trinity and the suffering of God. Her mother reminds her of God because she gave her life. She can see the work of the Holy Spirit in villages and women's movements in India even though it is not discussed much in the churches. Rajarigam sees a relational Trinitarian theology as a way to solve many problems in ecumenism and inter-religious dialogue. "A Trinitarian perspective could enliven Christianity in India" she said. "Without it, we will hit the saturation point. But with it we can live a more Christlike life."[5]

The Holy Spirit's activity in mission across the world is a strong focus in the theology of God espoused by British scholar Kirsteen Kim. Narrators often spoke of the work of the Holy Spirit directing them into mission:

> At a missions rally at our denomination's annual convention (Christian Missionary Alliance) I heard God saying to me "you've been open to this, but now I want you to pursue it." It was a setting that could be seen as pushing young people to an emotional decision to serve in missions, yet for me, it was a very reasoned, spiritual step of faith that carried a weight of certainty that has helped me in being sure about my call.

> Truly and literally, my greatest encourager has been God.

> I was praying one morning and heard a direct word from God. I actually heard it several times over several days. This happens to me on occasion and I take these quite seriously.

Theologies of Friendship

Relationship in community as a feature of God then becomes a model for mission work among people. It becomes part of the good news of the gospel. Johnson states, "In Jesus Christ God does not wear a mask; the

---

4. Interview, Louisville, Kentucky, May 2, 2007.

5. Interview, Techny Towers, Illinois, June 20, 2006.

power of the Spirit does not hide a deity who is fundamentally cruel and enslaving rather than compassionate and liberating."[6]

In the American film *Fried Green Tomatoes*, a rather frumpy full-time housewife tries desperately to get her husband's attention. Her craving for a real relationship is fulfilled as she gets to know an octogenarian living at a nursing home. Hearing Mrs. Threadgoode's story over a number of weeks inspires this young woman to focus on her own life. She stops lamenting her love for sweets and starts working out at the gym. She stops waiting for her husband to pay attention to her and starts making plans for Mrs. Threadgoode to move in with them. She stops wondering why some people behave badly and asserts her own strength, admittedly sometimes in bizarre ways. She finds fulfillment and direction in a friendship.

Friendship as an integral part of mission plays a huge role for contemporary Christian women. As the World Council of Churches Commission on World Mission and Evangelism prepared to meet in Manila in 2012, Sister Josune Arregrei, a delegate for the Roman Catholic Church, defined mission in this way: "Mission is not a commandment received once and for all. Mission is an *ongoing relationship of friendship and collaboration*."[7]

Contemporary theologian Elisabeth Moltmann-Wendel's book takes up this theme making scriptural and theological arguments that show the importance of relationships for women and for the mission of the church today.

The women in this study show a similar tendency to value personal relationships. Often they are willing to go the second mile to strengthen a friendship. They set aside time to interact with friends, often making this a major part of their professional work as well as their home life. One missionary wife of a mission trainer in Brazil spoke of friendship with local women as the major way in which she was fulfilling her call to work in God's Kingdom.

The author of this study had a warm friendship with a Muslim family in Jakarta, during a time of mission service as a professor at Jakarta Theological Seminary in 1995–96. Ismina, a teacher at the Pakistani International School and wife and mother of two, lived next door. Realizing that I lived alone, she stopped by during the first week with a hot

---

6. Johnson, *She Who Is*, 200.

7. WCC Media Email, March 27, 2012, Accessed on March 27, 2012, Italics mine.

meal for me. "You have no mother here. I will be your mother in Jakarta" she said. Subsequent meals were brought over. I was offered tea in their home. "Pinkie" and I had numerous conversations about our religions. I observed as she taught an after-school Arabic language class to some of her students. Their young girls came over to play with my kitten. Ismina corrected me when I inadvertently left my Bible on the floor—a Holy Book should not be left on the floor. Our relationship was open and mutual. It was a gift to me during a lonely year of teaching in a strange city.

Some mission workers saw friendships with those in their mission context as a major if not *the* major area of service for them. One spoke of her friendship with a Muslim woman as one of her best. That relationship included a giving and receiving of gifts. One of the gifts received by the narrator was an understanding of how her Muslim friend understood God and the connection between her views and Christian understandings of God. Other comments were:

> How blessed I am to have been able to make friends in Africa and Haiti.

> Our friends that visited us the first Christmas we were in Kenya—gift of relationship was priceless.

> When the father-in-law of a physical therapist died in Kijabe Hospital in Kenya, her Masai friends were very upset. The depth of their friendship really showed how deeply they grieved with her.[8]

Theologies of Working in Community

A third area of relationships that was crucial to the women in this study involved *working in community*. Seeing a need, women tended to collaborate with others in filling it. Good paths were forged by people working together. Team building often crossed denominational lines. Ecclesial theologies did not seem to hamper the work while working together fostered the work. Narrators spoke of many ways of working in community.

Sherron Kay George, one of the American Society of Missiology scholars and a narrator for this study stresses working together in her

---

8. Kim Okesson, who helped with interviews of missionaries in many countries, reflecting on the narrative of her missionary friend in Kenya. Email correspondence, September 13, 2011.

theology. As a Presbyterian Church (USA) mission worker in Brazil since 1972, she is committed to working together across the North/South divide. Her recent book *Better Together* follows her book on doing mission work in partnership. She notes that relationships and respect are very important to her. They color the way she works together with others. She asks herself, "Am I treating others as equals with respect for their dignity? Do my attitudes dignify and empower others?"[9]

Working together requires dialogue with those that hold differing views. More than a requirement however, George mentions dialogue and fellowship with professional colleagues as a source of nurture for her life. Other practices that nurture her and involve working with others are teaching and talking with students as well as participating in life in the global south. In this case, requirements for working across difference mesh with nurturing practices.

Retired Professor Eunice Irwin from the E. Stanley Jones School of World Mission at Asbury Theological Seminary in Kentucky also sees working together with women as an important practice that nurtures her and her students. Every year, Eunice hosted a luncheon for women students and colleagues. She met weekly for prayer with women students. She made plans to publish a newsletter with the E. Stanley Jones School of World Mission women students to foster communication among women on the broader campus. Irwin believes that women at Asbury "feel different." And that difference is important. Consequently, during her years at Asbury, she made special efforts to encourage women to "fit in and yet be different."[10]

Unity/Respect

Miriam Adeney's connection between unity and respect for others developed in the last chapter was frequently echoed during interviews. Annie King, a biracial Presbyterian Church (USA) mission worker to Indonesia for more than ten years said that she expressed her mission theology by practicing equality in her work in Indonesia. Rather than take a high position, she worked with people doing what they asked her to do. In her current work as a therapist, she speaks out against injustice in the church

---

9. Email correspondence, June 2006.

10. Interview, Asbury Seminary, Wilmore, Kentucky, November 7, 2005.

and focuses on "whatever brings life, healing, and leads to wholeness in a person's life." That, she said, is her definition of Christian mission.[11]

Roberta Rose King, a professor and ethnomusicologist who worked in Africa, provides an illustration of the connection between unity and respect. While teaching in Kenya she got groups of people together to learn about a Scripture passage. Readers and non-readers worked together to set the passage to music and present it to the church as part of community worship. Rather than "teacher" Roberta described herself as "catalyst" in those seminars.[12]

Carrie Maples, a Baptist health care worker in Africa, struggles to convince men to see their wives as more than property. Many women in the villages have eight to twelve children and still their husbands refuse to use birth control or allow their wives to use it. She said, "It is not my goal to show these people how they are wrong, but . . . to show them the value of a woman as a wife, mother and helper to her husband and not merely property."[13]

Elizabeth Glanville, who guides doctoral students in leadership studies at Fuller Seminary, wrote her dissertation on "breaking down walls." She developed a theology of difference critical for women and for the church, asserting that differences in giftedness, race, and other factors need not be ranked. She argues that accepting differences without ranking them can lead to unity in the church and foster respect for others.[14]

Patricia Sheeratan-Bisnauth from Guyana has spent most of her life working on issues of gender—equality, anti-violence, and leadership. As a young pastor she was barred from doing funerals. Rather than fight that issue, she compromised in the name of unity in the church and sought a male pastor to do funerals. Eventually church attitudes softened and she was able to perform funeral rites. After working in Guyana on political issues and rights for women, she went to Geneva to work for the World Alliance of Reformed Churches as Executive Secretary for Church Renewal, Justice and Partnership. This woman has devoted her life to the issues at the intersection of unity and respect.[15]

11. Interview, Louisville, Kentucky, January 31, 2006.

12. Interview, Fuller Seminary, Pasadena, California, February 4, 2006.

13. Email correspondence, March 30, 2006.

14. Interview, Fuller Seminary, Pasadena, California, February 2, 2006.

15. Interview, World Alliance of Reformed Churches offices, Geneva, Switzerland, April 6, 2006.

Maria Schuller who works as Programme Executive for Combatting Racism for the World Council of Churches, came to awareness of these issues through growing up in Brazil, getting in touch with liberation theology and the black movement, and reflecting on her own history as a black woman. For black people in Brazil and in her own life, issues of gender, race, and class were not theoretical but actual.[16]

Values of Humility and Receptiveness

Humility is required to be open to others and learn from them. A number of women spoke of *kenosis*, the self-emptying of Christ as a model that is perhaps not well understood. Eva Vogel-Mfata, a pastor for fourteen years in northern Germany, has traveled or lived in Europe, Brazil, the United States, Sri Lanka, and India. She identified a crisis of identity and legitimation in Christian mission in post-World War II Germany. "Kenotic structures are spoken of but people are living and doing theology from a different place," she said.[17] She believes that perspectives that could help shift the paradigm from a dualistic intellectual one to a spiritual life and passion paradigm are Latin American liberation theology and feminist theology. The future of the ecumenical movement is not to become stronger against the other but to study cultural expressions and try to merge ourselves into other's contexts. Vogel-Mfata's work for conferences of European churches and ecumenical gatherings puts those convictions into action.

Nancey Murphy, professor of Christian philosophy at Fuller Seminary, defends her "kenotic ethics." "The main criticism," she said, "has been that it may reinforce the capacity for people to oppress others. But self-emptying must be an ethic of choice. One must be aware that they are choosing self-sacrifice." Since every person begins their self-reflection at a different place, Murphy advocates personal attention through spiritual direction to develop that quality. In evaluating her own life, she gives of her time as part of her kenotic ethic. "It is the most precious thing," she

---

16. Interview, World Council of Churches offices, Geneva, Switzerland, April 6, 2006.

17. Interview, World Council of Churches offices, Geneva, Switzerland, April 6, 2006.

said. "A day goes by and never comes back. So doing something for someone else that takes time is an important way of self-emptying for me."[18]

Cultural differences also have an impact on concepts of humility. In societies where women are taught to be self-effacing or are totally under submission to men, perhaps less stress on self-sacrifice and more on self-assertion is appropriate. During my time of teaching social ethics in Java, Indonesia, I thought that different sermons for men and women would be helpful. Since Javanese women were taught to remain "at the back of the house" doing the cooking and care of children, perhaps they needed sermons that stressed their agency and responsibility to God rather than sermons on self-sacrifice.

Marion McClure, former Director of the Kentucky Council of Churches, spoke of her parents' humility as a model for her own life. Her father's preaching against racism and her mother's voracious reading habits impressed McClure as a child. "They showed an attitude of humility that comes with the delight of learning and preparing Bible study classes. They modeled a life of the mind attitude for me."[19]

Incarnational Witness

Theologian Elaine Heath outlines incarnational witness in a broad way that includes experience, emotion, and affectivity. Incarnational witness lies at the heart of Heath's idea of mission and evangelism. "A genuine Christian faith journey," she claims, "will . . . be marked with affective religious experience and will be embodied in ordinary life."[20] Her forthcoming book on the Apostles' Creed advocates living out the Creed as a preparation for missional life.[21] That incarnational life will also include self-emptying and surrendering to God, which does not eliminate experience and emotion, but relativizes their place in theological reflection.[22] Those pathways result in both outward transformation and inner freedom.

18. Interview, Fuller Seminary, Pasadena, California, February 5, 2006.

19. Interview, Louisville, Kentucky, May 2, 2007. McClure tells more of her journey into ordained ministry in "In the Picture" in Lloyd-Sidle, *Celebrating Our Call*, 101–9.

20. Heath, "Quest for Holiness," 399.

21. Heath, "Gospel Bearing: The Theory and Practice of Apostolic Life." Forthcoming with Cascade Books.

22. Heath, "*Via Negativa*," 87–88.

At the 2012 meeting of the American Society of Missiology, Kim Lamberty, Senior Program Advisor at Catholic Relief Services in the Haiti Partnership Unit, spoke of "accompaniment" as incarnational witness. Traveling to a place of conflict and simply being with the people in that place shows Christ's love for them. Lamberty told stories of women in accompaniment groups reducing the risk of violence and strengthening communities in Colombia. She described accompaniment as a mission praxis appropriate for our times, a prophetic dialogue that changes lives and societies.[23]

Receiving gifts comprises another part of an incarnational life. Seeing others as one's equal and being willing to receive as well as give gifts was a theme that came through strongly in many of the interviews. Sherron George notes that in her life in Brazil, "Visiting groups and mission workers testify to gifts they have received: hand-crafted treasures; incarnations of humility, simplicity, joy, and solidarity; demonstrations of relational values; new eyes for reading Scripture and world; renewed meaning and direction in life; an awareness of their need for continued conversion; and questioning of values in their culture."[24] Accepting one's vulnerability and receiving gifts from others contributes to sharing Christ's love as well as nurturing one's own life.

Emotions

Women understand emotions as part of mission practice and theological reflection. Whether a "call for justice," a "passion for souls" or the centrality of relationships in mission endeavors, emotions figure into women's mission theologies. The last chapter described occasions that engendered feelings in mission theologies. Positive and negative feeling both find their place in mission theologies. Anger at deprecation of those from another culture, outrage at women's voices neglected in mission statements, and frustration at encountering difficulties in publishing their views are some of the negative emotions women express. Positive views include an emphasis on gratefulness, love for partners in mission, and appreciation for educational programs and collegial relationships.

Sister Manning, part of the global leadership team of the Union of the Presentation Sisters of the Blessed Virgin Mary, spoke of her work in

---

23. Lamberty, "Christian Mission in Zones of Violent Conflict."

24. George, *Called as Partners*, 76.

life formation: "I have strong feelings about the need for giving tools for growth and life-giving. I am concerned about influencing sisters all over the world. Our organization needs to help them within themselves to be the best possible people they can be."[25]

Sister Manning speaks of having a witness through a life that is worth living. "There is a lot that we can be and do for each other." Sister Manning finds support through good friendship and collegial relationships. She also stresses self-emptying as a positive theology. "Our sisters do not get married or have children—that would be a wasted life if one didn't give it all to life for others. The core meaning of life is living for others."[26] We can see here an integration of themes of self-sacrifice, sustaining practices and mission operating in a theology of relationships.

Dialogue and Listening

For many narrators, dialoging with other traditions and religions played an important role in their lives. Some saw this as an identity building issue—they understood themselves better when they interacted with others:

> As a high school student I loved my French teacher. I had a feel for identifying with someone from another background and place. . . . The stories she told made me feel like I was looking back at my identity and experience through someone else's eyes.

> In Germany I was confronted with my identity—I became more of a Christian Palestinian woman in Germany. I found my identity by being outside my context in dialog with my own context.

> I am a Lutheran in a Catholic University studying a Reformed thinker. This is normal for me.

Some narrators saw dialogue as a cross-cultural issue. They wanted to understand others and be in dialogue with them. At the Council on World Mission and Evangelism Conference in Athens in 2005, members of one sect of the Orthodox Church vigorously protested having an event that brought their members into contact with opposing views. Rather than attend the conference, they stood outside with placards. One participant interviewed in this study sought to understand that protest. She

25. Interview at SEDOS Conference, Athens, Greece, April 24, 2007.
26. Ibid.

wanted to ask questions about difference through real encounter rather than choosing sides.

Other women wanted to dialogue with other traditions to gain theological insights:

> I thought about the difference in thinking about spirit in India and in Korea. In India they speak of one spirit and in Korea they distinguish spirits.

> It is important to study other religions in order to understand one's own religion.

Still others saw dialogue as a way to further mission objectives:

> I want to create space for diverse people, enabling their partici-pation in becoming agents of reconciliation.

> Ignoring indigenous spiritualities leads to ignoring women.

> Valuing differences is an important facet of the integrity of mission.

All of those diverse reasons for dialogue with those of other traditions and religions became an impetus for serious dialogical encounter with people very different from themselves for women in this study.

Of course there can be no dialogue without serious listening. Wom-en understood that listening required opening oneself to hearing others on their own terms. Dr. Marsha Snulligan Haney worked with the Sudan Council of Churches for a number of years. When she found out that four of her friends in a women's group were co-wives, she became intensely interested in Christian-Muslim dialogue.[27]

Mentoring also requires intense listening. Adele Pucci, who works as a team with her husband for the Eagles Ministry in Singapore, recently transitioned into mentoring younger women. "Spending time 'wasting time' with people is the best thing you can do," she said.[28] One of the compliments she gave to a visitor who stayed with her for a month in Singapore was that she was a good listener, warm in relationships.

Another kind of intense listening is described by a Wycliff Transla-tor of the New Testament. She described a summer program in linguis-tics that "opened her consciousness." She said that listening in her ear

---

27. Interview ASM Annual Meeting, Techny, Illinois, June, 2009.
28. Interview, Chiang Mai, Thailand, March 25, 2009.

training class, comparing and analyzing sentences began her journey into Christian mission.[29]

Theologians in the last chapter related listening to respect for others, a necessary ingredient for real dialogue. Examples in this chapter show that listening in relationships, listening through spending time with others, listening across cultural differences, and even listening to sentence structures and the make up of language all contribute to the understanding required for effective Christian mission.

As women relate to God and others, seeking to fulfill their lives in Christian mission, their sense of self grows and changes. How their theologies influence their identity is the topic of the next chapter.

29. Interview, Joann, Chang Mai, Thailand, March 17, 2009.

7

Identity

Inattentiveness to religion has caused women's historians to overlook a
powerful source of women's meaning and identity.

—CUMMINGS, *NEW WOMEN OF THE OLD FAITH*, 14

EXAMINING ISSUES OF IDENTITY is like pouring water through a many-
layered filter. One can begin with coarse broad definitions and sift down
through social and cultural influences to psychological and spiritual
issues. Women and men understand identity differently since in most
societies men are geared to vocational issues and women to family and
relationship issues. Economic status, location and citizenship, culture
and religion all affect how one perceives oneself in the world that they
inhabit.

The women in this study are from Europe, Asia, Africa, Latin
America, Australia, and the United States. Some are scholars. Some are
missionaries. Some are pastors. Some are denominational leaders. Some
are married. Some are members of a religious order. All speak English
and have a country they can call their own. So the voices in this research
project are voices of elite women, however many hardships they may face
in their lives. That limits the parameters a little. The other limit is the
human anthropology they hold and the comments they make in their
writings and interviews. Listening to the identity issues they speak of can
be instructive.

Many women spoke of a crisis in their lives. They had reached a
crossroads and had to determine which direction to take. Or they felt

muddled about who they were. Some felt concern that they could not follow their call and that affected their self- perceptions.

Such identity issues are familiar in societies today. Fast paced change in both the first and the two-thirds world combines with possibilities for individual choice of life direction and career to make identity issues a current concern. Zygmunt Bauman speaks of the uncertainty and fear that characterizes the current global situation. Flexibility is required, "a readiness to change tactics and style at short notice, to abandon commitments and loyalties without regret—and to pursue opportunities according to their current availability, rather than following one's own established preferences."[1]

That hardly sounds like the women in this study. Feeling a call from God, following it if they can, and being dedicated to serving Christ and others marks their lives. They are out of step with the pursuit of individual happiness that more and more becomes a goal of life for many. According to Bauman, We live in a "world where few if any people continue to believe that changing the life of others is of any relevance to their own life."[2]

For women doing mission theology those issues are compounded by a history of exclusion from leadership and theological work in the churches. George Herbert Mead argued identity is built through shared symbols that generate the same response in others as in oneself.[3] H. Richard Niebuhr purported that we know ourselves through another's eyes.[4] No one can take on a role that their community and coworkers deny them. That deepens the identity crisis for women doing mission theology.

Some narrators placed the problem in themselves. They felt confused about who they were. One expressed a battle with self-hatred. Others sensed a disjointedness in their lives—they were moving in one direction but their context, be it church or community demanded something else of them. A sense of inadequacy and confused identity resulted.

The *Cinderella Complex* documented a cultural confusion that American women expressed in the 1970s. At that time women were entering the workforce yet still holding responsibility for most home and childcare chores. Young career women inevitably felt inadequate. That issue has not disappeared from American society. It surfaced in many

---

1. Bauman, *Liquid Times*, 4.
2. Ibid., 24.
3. Mead, *Mind, Self & Society*, 149.
4. Niebuhr, *Meaning of Revelation*, 146.

interviews. Often it was related to the church. Expectations of authorities, theologies taught in denominational doctrines that constrained the roles women could adopt, and pressures from other women and families to conform to a household lifestyle led to pressures from many directions for women called to mission or theological work.

Those pressures presented themselves differently in different church and cultural communities. Catholic women religious in Africa said that they were confined in their roles by Church authorities but also by local church leaders that saw their role in cultural terms that limited options for women. Trappist monastic women at Gedono Monastery in Indonesia felt misunderstood as a cloistered community of prayer. The village nearby expected them to teach, do health care, and serve the community rather than remain in the confines of their monastery.[5] Conservative Protestant women in the United States tried to do both family and church leadership often encountering resistance from both theological and congregational sources. Protestant women working in leadership in ecumenical organizations in Europe separated work life from home life.

For example, the five women narrators from international organizations World Alliance of Reformed Churches (WARC), the World Council of Churches (WCC) and the Lutheran World Federation in Geneva did not mention husbands or children at all in their interviews. In contrast, an email correspondence with Southern Baptist missionary Cathy Maples, written up in the *New York Times* for her work on women's rights in Africa ended with her saying that she was tired and had been up with a sick child much of the night so she "felt a little muddled" in her remarks.[6]

Identity Formation

Identity is shaped by many factors coalescing in different ways in different contexts. Three major influences on identity formation are socialization, philosophy/theology, and biology.

Socialization

Socialization influences some of the attributes of women that we are seeing in their mission theologies. In many countries, girls are exposed

5. Conversation with Sister Martha, Abbess, Gendono Monastery, January 4, 1993.

6. Email correspondence, September 14, 2012.

to cultural forms that exhibit qualities and behaviors expected of girls. Those forms differ in different contexts. Some commonalities across cultures can be identified, however.

Girls are socialized to pay attention to relationships and to notice intimacies. The nineteenth-century novels of Jane Austen and Virginia Woolf illustrate those tendencies. Teenage girls in the United States today spend hours texting their girlfriends. Much of the content of those messages relates to boys and how the boys are responding to them as girls. Human interest stories and "girlie films" about relationships occupy free time. Conversely, for most teenage girls in the United States, interest in political affairs, ongoing conflicts among nations, and human rights rank lower on the list of topics that warrant daily attention. They are socialized into a smaller, yet meaningful, world of relationships. Traditional societies in Africa and Asia show similar tendencies.

Even when a woman's life enlarges to include justice issues and global affairs, relationships may remain at the core of a woman's identity. Women in situations of political unrest, oppressive regimes that discriminate against women, or religious turmoil may speak out against those restrictions becoming active in public life. A fifteen-year-old Pakistani girl shot by the Taliban for her persistent demonstrations against limitations on education for girls provides one example.[7] A former Pakistani student at Louisville Seminary commented in class that she "belonged to Pakistan," a very relational way to describe her dedication to her country. Women called into public service as leaders also enlarge their world of concern. Relationships may still play a large role in their lives and value systems. Presidential Candidate Hilary Clinton exhibits a strong bond with her daughter—a bond that supports her in both public and private ways.[8]

Caring for the needs of others also ranks high among behaviors that girls are encouraged to adopt. "Take a piece of cake to Daddy" a little girl might be told by her mother. In Indonesia, it is considered bad form for a woman to go overseas for graduate studies, leaving her husband and children to fend for themselves. A woman from Salatiga who went to England to do a master's degree in counseling was "abandoning her family," according to neighbors.[9] Of course, many men went to Europe

---

7. *Today Show*, CBS, January 14, 2013.

8. Ibid.

9. Conversation with neighbor, Salatiga, Indonesia, June 1993.

or the United States to study for years without similar accusations. Baby dolls and toy ovens fill the shelves of toys for girls in the United States. Taking care of loved ones becomes a focus for girls from a young age in many societies.

Some of those behaviors are related to the hope, common in many societies, that girls will become mothers. Bearing children, caring for infants, and training children to become acceptable members of society are expectations that most girls are introduced to. The *Today Show* had a segment on seeking happiness on Jan. 2, 2012. One of the young women interviewed stated, "I've always felt that the purpose of my life is to have children." Despite expanded opportunities for women in the work world and public life, socialization toward motherhood is still very strong in the United States.

We find similar attitudes in other parts of the world. In Indonesia, a young woman is asked, "Are you married *yet*?" The need to answer this question on a daily basis stresses the importance of marriage and family. A common idea in Indonesian cultures is that a person is not complete until they marry. Furthermore, mothers are expected to raise their children, teach them good values, and prepare the boys for leadership as they grow into manhood. The Indonesian government sponsors village meetings for women to learn management skills, all of which are applied to life in the home. Although political equality is part of Indonesian national life, marriage and family still rank high among priorities for women. The four wives of missionary leaders interviewed in Brazil each felt a call to have children. Interestingly, none of them felt called to the mission field. Bearing children was central to their identity as women.

George Herbert Mead's argument that the meaning of an action is determined by the response that one receives after making that action makes sense. If someone laughs after a person makes a serious remark, a message that the comment is not taken seriously or causes embarrassment becomes part of the meaning of the statement itself. Telling girls that they need to take care of others and rewarding behavior that steers girls towards relationship strengthens those behaviors. Through coordinating their behaviors with others in those expected ways, a girl's identity becomes centered around relationships.[10]

Aristotle argued that character is formed by repeated actions in a certain direction from the time a child is young. Virtues develop as

---

10. Psychologist Humberto Maturana claims that mutual structural coupling is a key characteristic of communication. "Communication is essentially a coordination of behavior." Quoted in Capra, *Web of Life*, 287–88.

one's character is formed by repeated actions. Applying this wisdom to socialization, we can see that as girls and young women are rewarded for attending to relationships and caring for others, they develop character traits of compassion and other-directedness.

It is not surprising then, that as opportunities for Christian women to engage in mission, their response would be overwhelmingly positive. Mission is about relationships—God's love for people. Mission is about compassion—human hands fulfilling God's work of love in the world. Mission is about service—women's sacrifices for those less fortunate mirrors a Jesus who serves both neighbors and enemies.

The mission theologies of missiologists and mission workers interviewed followed the socialization patterns for girls and women. Women's work for women in the early twentieth-century focused on service to women by women. Socialization influences the idea of relationality that runs through the mission theologies of contemporary missiologists outlined in chapter 5. God's relationality in the Trinity, humans' relational response to God, and the centrality of community are strong threads running through the theologies of narrators in this study. Accompaniment, walking with the poor, empathizing with those who suffer is another theme that arises from the socialization of women toward others. The compassion embodied in accompaniment is one that grows out of cultures that teach girls to care for others.

Life Philosophy/Theology

Socialization doesn't give us the whole picture, however. Christian theologies augment socialization in identity formation. Major theological emphases in contemporary women's mission theology are the Holy Spirit, the relationality of God, the unity of peoples, and the importance of sacrifice. Those themes surfaced in the Christian theologies of women interviewed for this study.

Christian values and theological ideas helped direct women's mission work in the past and today. Christian mission in the United States during abolition included an idea of equality of all people, a Christian notion that is found in contemporary missiologists work, e.g. Miriam Adeney and Cathy Ross. It informs the notion of partnership in contemporary mission theologies of Marion McClure and Sherron George. The temperance movement led by Frances Willard kept justice for women as a center of concern, a theme that predominates in the work of Marsha

Snulligan Haney. The value of self-sacrifice motivated Maryknoll Sisters to face dangers as missionaries in Latin America. Compassion moves Kim Lamberty to do the work of accompaniment in Haiti and informs South Korean scholar Chae Ok Chun's mission theology of suffering. The unity of the human family is a theme that appears in the work of Antonia Leonora van der Meer and Miriam Adeney. Kirsteen Kim's theology of the Holy Spirit's work in the world shows the diversity and strength of the Spirit's work in the world.

Socialization and theology work hand in hand to frame identities of women in mission of the past and present centuries. The themes prevalent among narrators in this study participate in both arenas. Relationships become central. Human equality and respect for diversity display a sense of justice. Service to the poor highlights a need to serve others in ways that show compassion.

Women's ideas of spirituality grow in the soil of local socialization and theologies. Kathleen Sprows Cummings' insight that historians have neglected the role of religion in forming women's identities quoted at the beginning of this chapter can be noted here. As religions develop in local contexts, forming theologies that influence women to attend to spiritual matters, women's identities become influenced by those factors. Women in Christian mission demonstrate that repeatedly throughout history and in today's times.

Biology

A third factor that influences identity formation is biology. Although E. O. Wilson's biological determinism is outside the bounds of a Christian worldview, the impact of biology on identity formation is undeniable. As biology interacts with life/philosophy and socialization, myriad life styles and identities can be formed by women.

Yet, because of biology, women can give birth. Although many women forgo childbearing, it is physically possible for many women to bear children. Because of biology, women are usually less physically powerful in some areas than men. A smaller skeletal frame contributes to that fact. Recent studies show the prevalence of neck injuries in girls that play soccer, possibly because a girl's neck is not as thick as a boy's resulting in more concussions when girls head the ball. A woman cannot usually hit a golf ball as far as a man. Because of biology, women often live longer than men. There are no doubt exceptions to each of those examples. But generalizations based on biological differences in the sexes can be made.

Far too much has been made of sex differences in the past. Perhaps far too much is being made of socialization in the present. The conundrum of the nature/nurture debate has not been solved. But we can confidently assert that a combination of socialization, life philosophy/theology, and biology influences identity formation.

Identity Issues

Issues of identity came up frequently for women in this study. Many expressed concern about the complex nexus of roles, beliefs, status, and relationships that together form a sense of self. Some experienced tension around identity during life transitions, others when roles or status change, either through their own actions or the decisions of others. The main focus of their identity also varied widely. For some, their call to mission was central, for others the role they played in living out that call. Still others focused on their relationships with life partners, children, or community as a central feature of their identity. For all, the grand narrative of Christianity provided an overarching umbrella for their sense of self and themselves as part of a community.

Charles Taylor, in his book *The Ethics of Authenticity*, describes multiple factors that influence identity for educated Westerners. A major dilemma for that group centers in the perception that instrumental reason has become dominant in the West. How to get things done has taken center stage from whether or not what is accomplished is good. Production becomes the focus—the end product becomes incidental. Overcoming this potentially devastating realization has led, in Taylor's view, to a new focus of ethics—the ethics of authenticity. One strives to find one's authentic self, one's true and good center. Authenticity becomes a good in itself. To be "true to oneself" is to be good.[11] That goodness, however, is not found individually but through interaction with communities and their feelings about goodness. Sympathy becomes a value in this system, as does dialogue. The "enemy" is the erroneous view that how one reaches one's goal is more important than the goal itself.

Women in this study don't seem to grapple with the dominance of instrumental reason—how to get something done in the most effective

11. Taylor, *Ethics of Authenticity*, 16.

way. Their identity does not center on effective action as much as on the goodness of the end in view and the way they go about obtaining that end. They are "modern" people in the sense that they all believe that the grand narrative of the Biblical accounts is true. They have a template against which to measure the goodness of a particular path.

And yet, they gravitate toward the ethics of authenticity that Taylor describes. They talk about identity in terms of being true to themselves and to God. They speak of empathy and sympathy with others in how they go about their mission tasks. They enjoy working cooperatively, listening to others, and forging a path through dilemmas in dialogue. It seems they value an ethic of authenticity but for different reasons than Taylor outlines. Rather than an escape from market forces and the un-reason of putting effectiveness first, women doing mission theology value an ethic of authenticity for what it yields. It provides room for dialogue and an appreciation of others. It emphasizes agency and the importance of choice. It gravitates to community for working through problems.

Women add the grand narrative of Christianity to the ethics of authenticity. Christian values keep them from putting the means before the ends. The good end is always present in the gospel. The focus on agency also blends well with the Pauline emphasis on choosing Christ, becoming disciples, and finding direction from the Holy Spirit and the community of Christians. How does the ethic of authenticity as practiced by women in this study influence their sense of identity? It seems there are a number of areas affected: calling, roles, strategies, and inner direction.

Some women working in conservative Protestant settings faced identity issues when the received theologies from their mission boards or denominational authorities came into conflict with their calling and abilities. Insofar as identities are constructed through cultural narratives, including theological narratives, those conflicts can result in confusion and redirection. For example, a medical missionary followed her husband's call to Africa and became a leader with him in their mission work. When he was named director of the mission, she was barred from further leadership activity. Despite her prominence, this led her to question her calling as well as her "importance to God's kingdom."[12]

The marginalization experienced by women in conservative Protestant missions is a "codified marginalization," institutionalized by the organizational culture in support of the received theology. Women are

12. Interview, December 2012, and correspondence about narrator with research assistant Kim Okessen, January 23, 2013.

meant to follow their husband's call and to care for home and family. Sometimes women working within that received theology refocus their own call around their husband's call. Sometimes they redirect their work, developing friendship with women and working with children. That direction is affirmed by many two-thirds world cultures. The direction imposed by the received theology is reinforced by cultural norms.

Many missionary women find fulfillment in this pattern. Others strain at the limitations it imposes. One woman missionary in Brazil discussed her disappointment that she was "not allowed" to teach theology except to native women and children. Although qualified by graduate studies in the U.S., she was limited in her ministry. Not surprisingly, she focused attention on women and children, becoming an incarnational presence in her missionary setting. Another Brazilian missionary breastfed the baby of a neighboring family after the birth mother died from complications of childbirth. That approach didn't work for all of the women, however. One narrator said that she was in crisis for five years after adopting two children in the country where she and her husband worked as missionaries and already had biological children.

Although most of the narrators did theological reflection and some taught theology, few considered themselves theologians. The identity, even of the missiologists interviewed was centered more on education than on theologizing. Manuel Castells identifies three contributors to the process of identity construction: legitimizing identity, resistance identity, and project identity.[13]

Responses to the stigma of limits on action that results in limited identity could also be viewed along those lines. Missiologists that adopt teaching as their main identity rather than theologians find legitimation in the area of education that they do not find in theology. Resistance identity grows as they push back against a non-responsive collegium of theologians. Project identity shapes their lives as they build a career of teaching in academic institutions, serving as missionaries, or working in denominational structures.. The complexities of their identity do not disappear. But they place a major emphasis on themselves as educators rather than theologians.

That identity is displayed in a number of ways. Many narratorss made decisions on the basis of relationships and local needs rather than on the basis of doctrines or ecclesiological organizations. The ecumenical

---

13. Muck, "Dynamic Identity," 1.

cooperation of women in mission in the early twentieth century was based on prioritizing needs over denominational theologies. Much the same is true of the women in this study. Sometimes relationships take precedence. At other points it may be a matter of ethics or the priority of needs. Service trumped doctrine in many cases.

The case studies in Leona M. English's "Feminist Identities: Negotiations in the Third Space" bear this out. That study of the relationship of global civil society, development work, feminism, and Christianity describes how women in this service daily negotiate their identity as fluid and non-static. She uses Homi Bhabha's notion of a third space to describe the complex and moving identities of Christians who work in this area.[14] Although they avoid a traditional missionary identity, they do not identify with a feminist agenda. Instead they reconstruct their identities taking parts of the feminist identity and parts of the missionary identity. They do Christian mission work under a secular guise.

Jennifer Aycock's study of identity formation among *Maghrebian* women in France bears this out. Resistance identity is developed as some women take on the veil, silently protesting the secular orientation of the "common culture" idea in secularized France. Others face the crisis of identity as they enter French society by identifying as secular Muslims.[15] They cannot focus their identity on their religion because the political narrative that shapes identity in France bars their access to many professions as veiled women.

One Algerian woman in Aycock's study showed how she negotiated her multiple identities in order to live in France. She identifies herself as French on government documents in order to receive better benefits. Although Muslim she does not practice her religion because of the cultural expectations of Muslim immigrants living in France. She does not wear the veil. She insists that a woman that feels she should wear a head covering should not come to France. If they do, they must do what is done in France. Muslim women do not need to wear a head covering in France she insists.[16]

That approach meshes with Zymont Bauman's notion of fluid identity. Rather than permanently take up a "Muslim identity" or a "secular identity" Muslim women navigate multiple identities, becoming flexible

---

14. English, "Feminist Identities, 99–102."

15. Aycock, "At the Crossroads," 5.

16. Ibid.

in presenting themselves in various contexts. Thus they avoid fixation and a certain degree of stigma. Redirecting identity in both cases, from a conservative theology to a broader one, or from a secular position to an identity constructed in a third space, is a feature of many women interviewed in this study.

In that "dynamic identity," flexibility becomes a valuable virtue.[17] The case study from Brazil in chapter 11 reveals flexibility as a major quality developed by women that had to delay or reformulate their mission calling because of family obstacles. Catholic misssiologist Angelyn Dries refers to flexibility as a major factor in Catholic religious women's ability to practice and teach liberation theologies in Latin America.[18] Because the theologies were not yet institutionalized in Church doctrines, the women were able to develop curricula and teach those theologies on the mission field.

Identity as Theologian

As we saw in the chapter on sources of authority, some Christian women in mission do not see themselves as theologians. Yet there are many that do.

Dr. Septemmy, a Protestant from Sulawesi, Indonesia, identifies with contextual and feminist/liberationist theologies. As a child she felt called to become a local pastor. Later she focused that call on a teaching ministry. She wanted to become a teacher in a local community—one that worked with the people and spoke to issues of the village:

> My theological method is first to understand reality, then to do theology, and then to communicate with the church.

> I like to work in teams with church leaders. Working with congregations is part of my original calling.

For Septemmy, being a woman is a huge part of her identity as a theologian. She roots her identity in the liberation she sees in feminism:

> While studying at Austin Seminary with Dr. Cynthia Rigby, I personally made the connection between feminist theology and myself as an Indonesian woman.

17. Muck, "Dynamic Identity," 2.

18. Interview and ASM discussion, June 19, 2012.

Septemmy insisted on having a woman committee member when she defended her Master's thesis at Jakarta Theological Seminary as did many of my students in Indoesia. When describing her PhD work she said:

> My doctoral project will be a feminist theology of religious plu-
> ralism. I will become a feminist theologian.

During the 1980s Rev. Dr. Nyambura Njorge became the first woman pastor in Kenya. Her journey is recorded in a film published by the PC(USA). After years of parish work, "I began to doubt the future of my parish ministry. How can I work in a church that cares so little about the daily struggles of its people?"[19] Njoroge looked for answers in theological study at Princeton Seminary. She wrote her thesis on a feminist Christian view of female circumcision. She came to the conclusion that she must "challenge the circumstances that create so much pain and suffering for women."[20] As a theologian Njoroge put her scholarship to work to better the position of women at risk in her country. Yet it was difficult for her to remain in Kenya and she eventually took a leadership position at WARC in Geneva. The pressures of being a feminist theologian in a very traditional male-oriented society influenced her to relocate. "I couldn't stay in Kenya forever," she said.[21]

Njoroge's identity as a theologian influenced her life direction and her actions. Most recently she has taken a position with the World Council of Churches as Programme Executive of the Ecumenical HIV/ Aids Initiative. She models the ecumenical values of many women in this study, putting the needs and suffering of sub-Saharan Africa before denominational theologies. As an ordained clergy in the Presbyterian church, she works with Methodists, Baptist, Anabaptists and congregational leaders of all stripes.[22]

Dr. Anna Marie Kool, professor of mission in Budapest, Hungary, identifies herself as a theologian quite apart from her identity as a woman. She does theology "in the usual way." She worked with a mainly male European group in the post modernism section of the International Association of Mission Studies conference in Malaysia in 2004, later becoming president of that organization. She claims that particular perspectives

19. Njoroge, "Groaning and Languishing," 7.

20. Ibid.

21. Interview, WARC Offices, Geneva, Switzerland, April 7, 2006.

22. TEAG 2012 YouTube video of Njoroge's Contextual Bible Study, accessed August 23, 2013.

she may have as a woman do not come into play in her academic work. She said, "If you want to know how being a woman affects my theology, ask the men."

And yet she is proud of being a woman in her chosen field of mission: "I am the only woman theologian in Hungary. I pioneered the student work here."

Focusing on one or another aspect of one's identity in a given situation can help a woman advance in that area. To self-identify as a feminist theologian or to show how being a woman influences one's theology may help in one context and limit one's options in another.

Ignoring gender in developing one's identity may possibly have negative results. Dr. Kool spoke of an identity crisis in her life: "I am feeling an identity crisis because I am Dutch and have lived in Hungary for seventeen years."

Kool did not relate that crisis to gender. But might it be possible that her male-identified life as a professor, along with her pride in being the only woman theologian in Hungary also led to a sense of crisis?

In contrast to the women discussed in the chapter on sources of authority, all three of these women identified themselves as theologians but in very different ways. Comparing those women, self-identifying as theologians, can be instructive. They each began their ministries serving congregations and students. Septemmy focused her call to the pastorate on a teaching role, later identifying herself as a theologian. Njoroge began her ministry as a pastor, later earning a higher degree and applying feminist theology to issues of health for African women. Claiming her status as a theologian, she was able to influence her cultural milieu on an important issue. Kool began as a cross-cultural student worker, pioneering efforts in Hungary. Her identity as a theologian came later as she studied and gained a post as a professor. Doing radical feminist theology could not aid her in her work as it did for the other two. Instead she consolidated her position as theologian by using European methods and content. Each woman developed her identity in her local context, choosing theological methods that aided their vision and work.

Here we see socialization, life-philosophy and biology working together in identity formation. When disjuncture occurs, as in Kool's long term cross-cultural location, a sense of crisis can arise. Such disjunctures in the lives of narrators in this study resulted in an identity crisis or sense of dislocation and misplacement. Women that went with their husbands to the mission field without a sense of call felt this. Women that had a call to mission but were prevented from pursuing it felt the dislocation. Both of those examples will be explored in chapter 11. Some women that did not find affirmation in seeking leadership in the church found their way into teaching and self-identified as teachers rather than theologians. Many women called to the pastorate had identity issues that centered on not being able to pursue their calling or not finding a place in the church after their training was completed.

For those that resolved those issues, satisfaction and a stronger sense of identity resulted. Dr. Elizabeth Glanville, Director of Leadership Studies at Fuller Seminary, found her vocation after she did her PhD in leadership and began mentoring women doctoral candidates. A sixty-one year old Brazilian began her missionary training late in life. A sense of relief and "being in the right place" gave her much energy for learning the ropes of becoming a missionary in South America. An accountant for a Christian organization in the Philippines told me that her job was not her calling. As a Filipina, she worked with the "McDonald's Church," meeting for worship at McDonald's restaurants in Manila. She described how her husband had come to faith through this group. They provide breakfast for all comers and have a worship service afterward. Her calling was to spread those little congregations across the McDonald's in Manila.[23]

Our current globalized world creates issues of identity as the fast-pace of life and requirements for flexibility combine with dislocation for many. As certain lines of work become obsolete in our world many find themselves working in another country or dislocated by war or political oppression. Cross-cultural issues for people that straddle two cultures and justice issues that have become global all contribute to identity issues. Women in Christian mission have to navigate these "liquid times" as do others. The next chapter tells the story of one of the most influential missionaries of the twentieth century. Dorothy Day revised her identity as she grew in faith, solidified her Christian values, and sheltered the poor in Houses of Hospitality across the United States.

---

23. Interview, Mimi, Bangkok, Thailand, March 17, 2009.

8

Mission Exemplar
Dorothy Day

"Dorothy Day's self-understanding as a radical endured
throughout her life."

—O'CONNOR, *MORAL VISION OF DOROTHY DAY*, 67

DOROTHY DAY PROVIDES AN exemplar of a woman in mission who re-shaped her identity to fit with the gospel in such a way that the gospel and culture, critically evaluated, are both affirmed. Let me begin with a story:

One day, Utah Phillips's four-year-old son asked him, "How come you are *like you are* Daddy?"

"I knew exactly what he meant," Utah Phillips said to himself. He told his son he needed some time to think about that. Later, he tried to explain. He had been a U.S. soldier in the Korean War for two years when he heard one of his comrades refer to the Koreans as subhuman. Part of the good that the war would accomplish was, according to this American soldier, to raise the level of the Koreans to something above the beastial nature he saw in them. Utah Phillips left his unit that very day. The pain of fighting the war, combined with the racist attitudes of his comrade, un-hinged him. "It was all wrong," he said. "The whole system was all wrong."

Utah went to a rehabilitation center run by Koreans in Seoul. On returning to the United States he wandered around the country for nearly two years, drunk most of the time. One day he ended up at a Catholic Worker House of Hospitality in Washington. There he began the journey back to life in society.

From the folks at the house he learned the Christian approach to life and culture taught by Dorothy Day when she and Peter Maurin established the Houses of Hospitality in the 1930s. He listened to the cultural critique that targeted violence as a major evil in society. He stopped drinking. He began to see the racism and violence in American society as facets of his own character. Utah Phillips began the journey to wholeness.

The hospitality house did something for Utah that no church could do because he would never have crossed the threshold of a Christian house of worship. At the hospitality house he received food and shelter. He was given good work to do. He was accepted just the way he was—confused, angry, unproductive. The discussions at the house helped him articulate the roots of his anger. Those discussions helped him discover a road out of anger and despair. That road involved a radical critique of American society, a critique that brought together Utah's problem with racism and the Korean War. At the hospitality house, Utah heard the gospel in such a way that both the gospel and the culture, critically evaluated, were affirmed. He did not stop being an American. But his loyalty to his country was re-channeled into a critique of his culture, a critique that focused on nonviolence.

Utah's journey is not the journey of every American who finds Christianity a balm. But it is one that was suited to his pain, to his problems. He found the heart of the gospel of the love of Christ in nonviolence. The gospel presented at the hospitality house addressed the violence of racism, the violence of gender discrimination, and the violence of governmental constraints as understood by the Catholic Worker movement founded by Dorothy Day.

How did it happen that Utah Phillips' needs were met in such a way that he could begin a journey back to wholeness? Dorothy Day's life story and how her identity changed when she encountered the gospel gives us clues to that question. Day's identity displayed the flexibility of identity that Bauman notes, along with a stability of characteristics that stayed with her throughout her life. For Day, her identity changed yet stayed the same.

Three constant themes are present in Day's life: poverty, transience, and a love for journalism. Those themes arose in Day's childhood but were transformed by her encounters with God, with warm communities she encountered in her youth, and with her colleague Peter Maurin. As her ministry developed, she chose poverty, transforming it into simple lifestyle. She chose transience but instead of it being determined by her father's job moves, she stayed at various houses of hospitality that had been established by the Catholic Worker Movement. Her love for journalism operated in her newsletters and writings rather than in newspaper jobs she held in her youth. Both the Christian gospel and a sensitivity to her culture determined the form of those changes in identity. Looking at Day's history illustrates how those changes came about.

The Context

Dorothy Day's life began in the nineteenth-century American milieu and continued into the twentieth century. She was seventeen when the First World War broke out and twenty-one when it finally ended. During those years, a new century was born.

Dorothy's youth saw the boom of the 1920s and the economic depression of the 1930s. She was part of the intellectual *avant garde* of Greenwich Village and, at the same time she experienced the poverty and unemployment of many of the labor class.

Day's establishment of the Houses of Hospitality began in the 1930s. They continued to grow during World War II in the 1940s and the economic recovery of the 1950s. The late 1960s saw another surge of young people rejecting the middle-class values of their parents just as Dorothy's generation had done early in the century. The Houses of Hospitality addressed those issues on a personal and a public level. The work continued through both the Korean War and the Vietnam War. By the time of Dorothy Day's death in 1980, the Catholic Worker Houses of Hospitality had ministered to people seeking wholeness for nearly fifty years.

The Woman: 1897–1980

Dorothy Day was born in Brooklyn, New York, in 1897, the third of five children. She arrived only ten months after her older brother, Grace Day's first baby. Probably this baby was received into the world by a weary and harried mother. A few years later her little sister Della arrived, and when Dorothy was fifteen, a fifth Day baby came into the world.

Dorothy's childhood was one of transience and insecurity, partly due to the poverty the family experienced. Her father, a journalist by trade, could find work only intermittently. During Dorothy's childhood, he found employment first in New York City, later in Oakland, California, and finally in Chicago. During Dorothy's college years, the family moved back to New York, and Dorothy, although enrolled at the University of Illinois, left school to follow them back.

During the times when John Day was unemployed, the family experienced extreme financial hardship. Added to this was the stress of having the breadwinner at home, pursuing his writing in the middle of the busy household. With a few exceptions, the family lived mainly in small dingy apartments in lower class neighborhoods. Heat and beauty, and sometimes nourishing food became scarce commodities in Dorothy's life.

Perhaps it was those hardships that turned Dorothy's attention to religion. A close friend reported that Dorothy was "hounded by God even in her high school days."[1] Although her mother was Episcopalian and her father didn't have a religious practice, Dorothy visited the Catholic Church to sit quietly and pray. She began to read the Bible, a practice that stayed with her throughout her life.

In her early adult years Dorothy's interest in journalism, her father's trade, grew intense. Dorothy's father was a cold and distant figure who was, nonetheless, demanding and exacting in his expectations of Dorothy. He considered the newspaper world a man's world and tried at every turn to keep Dorothy from pursuing a career in journalism. In this he failed. But when Dorothy, after two years of college, decided on a newspaper career, she moved out of the family apartment and began another decade of transience of her own.

Dorothy's interest in journalism combined with a strong sense of justice to frame her work as a newspaper writer and social activist. She had a sense that the world was good because God created it. That there was so much suffering in the world she loved caused her sorrow.[2] She wanted to have a part in changing that and so was drawn to the people that seemed to be working hardest in causes of justice. She found her first job at a socialist newspaper, *The Call*. Having failed to get employment in any of the major newspapers, perhaps due to her father's influence, she convinced the editor of *The Call* to hire her for five dollars a week. This, she suggested, could be part of an experiment on how little a woman could live on in the city. Her experiences could then be written up for the newspaper.

Having convinced the editor, Dorothy proceeded to live out this experiment, moving from one tenement house to another in an attempt to find safety, heat, and quiet. Her childhood experience of poverty

---

1. Riegle, *Dorothy Day: Portraits*, 79.
2. Ibid.

prepared her to persevere in her experiment. An empathy for the poor resulted that became a central motivation in her life.

The article series itself didn't go far, however, and she soon took another job at *The Masses*. Again, she convinced the editor to hire her, being willing not only to write articles but to manage, type, or do other office work as needed. Dorothy followed her father's footsteps in going from one newspaper job to another, spending time unemployed between jobs.

Although the newspaper world was a rough male-oriented world, Dorothy did find people that she could relate to in the left-wing world of journalism. In fact, her vocational roles suited the early twentieth-century American milieu. Writer, activist, and social critic, Dorothy made friends with Eugene O'Neill and a number of then prominent communist writers. Her unique position as a journalist for left wing newspapers combined with her own experiences of poverty and a spiritual longing for community and justice gave her the foundation for creating a ministry that showed how the gospel could respond to those needs.

Dorothy Day felt like a cultural misfit. But in the critical intellectual world of the early twentieth-century, she found people of like mind. Raised in a troubled family, as a teenager, she found herself estranged from her father, living and working away from home. Her immigrant, lower class background and urban context led her to embrace the communist dream of community and equality for all. Marxism became a religion of sorts for Day, resonating with her concerns for justice for the poor and stimulating her activist yearnings.

Day found her strongest sense of identity was with the working class poor, with whom she had much in common. As the Great Depression dragged on through the 1930s, more and more Americans found themselves in poverty. The American values of equality and freedom, meaningful work and a second chance for all became central in American culture and to the Catholic Worker movement Day began.

Not religiously trained or nurtured spiritually in her home, Day, nonetheless considered herself a religious person throughout her life. During her childhood, she used to attend Catholic mass with a few friends. Later, although considering herself a Marxist, she would go into the church for quiet and solace. Troubling events in her young adulthood drove her eventually to seek solace in Christianity. She fell in love with a man named Moise when she began to study nursing, but the relationship brought her only distress. Moise wanted no part of commitment to marriage or having children. When Dorothy became pregnant, he insisted on an abortion that threw Dorothy into despair. She responded by marrying Barkeley Tobey and living in Europe for a year. But that solution brought little consolation to Day. Her longings for a spiritual dimension were deep, as were her longings for community and friendship.

In 1923 she moved to New Orleans with her sister Della where she practiced nursing and wrote a novel, *The Eleventh Virgin*, which was published in 1924. A friend convinced her to use the money from the book to buy a house. So in 1925, she settled into a beach house on Staten Island, where she spent four years. There she met Forster Batterham and began to live with this nature-loving man. Her cottage was filled with shells and skeletons of the creatures found along the shore. Forster opened up to Dorothy the natural environment of the beach and Dorothy found peace in nature—a peace that led her to begin to pray in gratitude. The house itself provided stability in what had become a wandering life.

With the birth of her first child, Day's religious sensibilities came to the fore. When Tamar Therese was born, the incipient spirituality she had found on Staten Island took on a more definite form. Looking at the fragile and perfect baby in her arms, Day felt that her response of gratitude must be centered in worship of God. Baptizing the baby and then joining the Catholic Church a year later alienated her from Forster, who could not in good faith participate in Christian worship.

That watershed in Day's life moved her into a period of loneliness combined with the nurturing of her child. Summers were spent at the cottage, winters in the city. Her father paid her for caring for her younger brother John but other employment was sporadic. Although Forster still used the Staten Island cottage, she gave up living with him as Catholic mores took hold in her life.

During the winter of 1928, Dorothy contracted the flu while living with Tamar in a rooming house. Unlike one of her previous apartments in an East Side Jewish community, here Dorothy found no succor from neighbors. The next fall she moved to Los Angeles for a movie contract for *The Eleventh Virgin*. Again she encountered a terrible and deep loneliness. She fled to Mexico in January of 1930, telling herself that she would investigate the Catholic Church under persecution. Instead she wrote up her personal experiences with the Church and published them in *Commonweal*. By 1932 she was back in the United States, first to visit her mother in Florida and then to settle into a Fifteenth Street tenement house with her brother John and his pregnant wife Teresa. She had learned something about her need for community.

In December of that year, Day's longing for community was again thwarted as she covered a hunger march in Washington D.C. with some of her old communist friends. They had little interest in her Christian faith and some of them rejected her friendship outright. Because of her Christian faith Day, felt like an outsider in the crowd of socially-conscious protesters. The question that burned in her mind was how to bring Christ, concern for the poor, and the justice that communists sought together. There must be a way.

On December 9th in Washington she prayed that God would show her how to make those connections. Prayer was another spiritual practice that Dorothy continued throughout her life. She had lists of people's names with her when she went to daily Mass. Both intercessory prayer and silent prayer were formative in her Christian life. She believed that since God was not bound by time, she could pray, not only about the future but about the past. She counseled others, "When you are alone, pray."[3] On December 9, 1932, Dorothy felt very alone. And she prayed.

On her return to the Fifteenth Street apartment, she found a shabby but intellectually astute Peter Maurin awaiting her return. He was the answer to her prayer. Peter outlined his understanding of history and the destiny of humanity to anyone who would listen. His gentle ways and love for others soon won over Day's hesitations. The apartment began to fill up with strangers and conversation partners and the Catholic Worker was born.

1933–35 saw an explosive growth of the movement, a "spiritual revolution" that was charted in the *Catholic Worker* newspaper that Day began in 1933. She intentionally designed it as a Christian response to the communist paper, *The Daily Worker*. She worked with Peter who lectured on a Christian understanding of love for the poor, economic justice, and the value of work. She brought in prestigious speakers to augment Peter's lectures. For the fourth issue, she produced 20,000 copies of the paper some of which were sold for a penny and many others that were bundled and sent off to churches and organizations with a plea for funds.

1934 saw the birth of the Houses of Hospitality, an opportunity for the rich to serve the poor as Peter Maurin put it.[4] Every discussion was followed by a meal to which all were invited. The tenement on Fifteenth Street soon became overcrowded and other houses were formed. One of

3. Ibid.
4. Day, *Long Loneliness*, 29.

them was set in Harlem in an African American neighborhood, another was an agrarian commune founded on Staten Island.

Day insisted that love brought healing. From St. John of the Cross she quoted: "Where there is no love, put love and you will take out love."[5] The Houses of Hospitality attempted to put love into action. It was never easy. In her book, *Loaves and Fishes,* Day tells stories of people with "irascible dispositions" that came and stayed at Houses of Hospitality, bringing their problems with them. "How to understand people, portray people—that is the problem," Day insisted. "St. Paul said, 'Are we comforted? It is so that you may be comforted.'"[6] Love, for Day, was the measure of all things.

Peter's ideas and Dorothy's energy worked together to fashion a movement that was exactly what Catholic intellectuals and the masses of poor during the depression longed for. Christian ideals of community and works of mercy combined with American values of dignity, fair practices for workers, and independence for all. Revolutionary aspects added another dimension to the movement that resulted in a complex mix of a Christian theology of love, work with the poor, Catholic ethics, and revolutionary politics. It is not surprising that Day has been known as a social critic, a protester, a dissenter, an anarchist, and a pacifist.[7]

That combination showed itself strongly on a speaking tour in 1936. Day connected with the Southern Tenant Farm Union and she highlighted their work for unionization in the paper. She spoke out on anti-Semitism and prejudice against African Americans. Peter's vision for an agricultural university was channeled into the establishment of a farm commune in Pennsylvania. And in the city, the Catholic Worker was feeding over one thousand men in the bread lines at the Hospitality Houses. By 1938 the anniversary issue of the Catholic Worker put out 190,000 copies. Thirty Houses of Hospitality were active.

But it was also in that year that Day published "On the Use of Force," an essay that solidified the Catholic Worker position of absolute pacifism. With Hitler's regime gathering force and the start of World War II in September 1939, Day's position generated fierce opposition among Catholic Worker proponents and the Catholic Church itself. Here again Day's commitments outweighed her own interests. It was a turning point for the movement.

5. Ibid., 39.
6. Ibid., 57.
7. O'Connor, *Moral Vision,* 11.

During World War II there were Houses of Hospitality in New York City, Boston, Milwaukee, Pittsburgh, Detroit, Houma Louisiana, Chicago, San Francisco, and England. But the spiritual revolution of the Catholic Worker had reached its peak and began its decline. The war boosted the economy and ended the long depression. Men that had been jobless and homeless found themselves conscripted into the armed forces. Day's stringent pacifist views were out of step with the times. The world had changed around her and the movement had to change with it.

During the 1940s the Eastern Farm Commune was changed into a retreat center. By then, spiritual retreats had become a facet of Day's life and a feature of the movement. As a lay Catholic leader, Dorothy received spiritual direction. She attended daily Mass, *compline*, and weekly confession. Day's identity as a Catholic was formed by those practices and especially by the spiritual retreats.

There were other changes as well. In 1945, Peter Maurin became senile and stopped teaching. By 1946 the circulation of the Catholic Worker had dropped to 50,500. Half of the Houses of Hospitality had closed. The opposition to her work became stronger and in 1951, the Catholic Church demanded that she change the name of her publication. She refused.

Although smaller, the movement kept going and picked up new issues in the post-WWII climate of anti-communist feeling. Day and others demonstrated against nuclear arms buildup by refusing to take shelter during frequent air raids in New York City. Frequent arrests and spending time in jail became part of the routine of Catholic Worker folks during the 1950s.

Day's autobiography, *The Long Loneliness* was published in 1952. From her story, one can see that her childhood also influenced the way that she put together cultural and religious strands of thought. As a child, she lived through the San Francisco earthquake, left alone in the house as her parents rushed out with the other children. Frequent and sudden geographical moves of the family and her mother's illnesses were part of the context that shaped both her fears and her ideas.[8] Through those experiences Day developed a resilience along with a sensitivity to the poor.

As she lived through the 1960s Day saw further cultural changes, some of which distressed her. Disappointment with young people's sexual mores and rejection of the Catholic Church put her at odds with a sector of the population most suited to taking up the work of the Catholic

8. Ibid., 23.

Worker movement. While the hippy movement focused on love and freedom for all, concern for the poor and a willingness to sacrifice one's own agenda to support the social and political actions necessary to bring justice to the poor were in short supply.

During the 1970's Day developed cancer and was forced to withdraw from Catholic Worker affairs. Spiritual retreats had, by then, become a feature of her life and the lives of those she influenced. In 1976 she had her last retreat with Father Hugo. On November 29, 1981, Dorothy Day died at her home. Her daughter Tamar was with her. Her biographer William D. Miller articulated her legacy as "A vision of ending time with its evil nightmares by bringing Christ back on earth."[9] Looking at her life and work, it is easy to imagine that, for many of the poor during the depression of the 1930s Dorothy Day's movement did just that.

Spirituality and Practice

Relating the Christian gospel to culture was not an intellectual exercise for Dorothy Day. She believed, first of all, in the importance of salvation. One day she emerged from chapel at the Peter Maurin Farm and said, **"We're all going to heaven because I have asked our Lord every single day of my life that everyone who comes to the Peter Maurin Farm will be saved."**[10] Second, Day believed in the connection between the spiritual and the material. "Everything is sacramental" she would say.[11] The natural and the supernatural were all of a piece in Day's theology.

So it was not surprising that in her loneliness and spiritual sensitivity, she sought answers to her spiritual questions in the culture around her. She longed for community and found it, first in a Jewish neighborhood on the East Side, then in a county jail with prostitutes. The intellectual discussions of writers like Eugene O'Neil and others in Grenwich village stimulated her. Her associates at *The Call* and *The Masses* gave her a chance to look at socialist answers to the pressing issues of poverty, unemployment and oppression she saw around her. The precariousness of her financial condition placed her in situations of poverty and there she empathized with others worse off than herself. The Great Depression caused massive unemployment. Dorothy saw her neighbors furniture put

9. Miller, *Dorothy Day,* 518.

10. Riegle, *Dorothy Day: Portraits,* 80.

11. Ibid., 78.

out on the street. She experienced the discomforts of unheated tenement apartments and the hunger of the unemployed. Dorothy did not intentionally relate the gospel to her context—rather, in a difficult context the gospel found her.

Consequently, the consonance between the gospel and culture, critically evaluated, was part and parcel of her theology. She began with her own experience. She valued her spirituality. From there she moved into action. And that action was based on her critical evaluation of the culture in which she found herself. The hospitality houses were examples of action-theology—a theology focused on action, not words. The test of orthodoxy became the welfare of the persons served; the effectiveness of the ministry showed the cultural appropriateness of her innovative practices.

There are four major areas in which this consonance was most evident: community, economic justice, dignity of the poor, and spirituality.

First, Dorothy's longing for community began in her youth and continued to be a major component of her understanding and practice of Christianity. The pattern of transience due to unemployment that she experienced in her childhood continued in her adult life. She would work at a paper for nearly nothing, sometimes living with others that worked there. Then, when something that seemed better presented itself, she would move. More than once she left friends—to go to Los Angeles for film work, or to go to Mexico to study the Church under persecution, for example. Sometimes she would move house because she heard of a place a little warmer, a little less dingy, or she moved to share an apartment where friends lived. Many of those choices were moves away from the thin threads of community that she had established. So her longings for deeper relationships with others grew.

She satisfied some of those longings through late night discussions with literary or communist friends. That intellectual discourse provided an important community connection for Dorothy that was later channeled into discussions about truth and the unity of history at the Houses of Hospitality that she began with Peter Maurin.

It was Peter that jogged her longing for community into action appropriate to the situation in the 1930s. Peter's vision echoed the vision of the early Marx—every farmer a scholar and every scholar a farmer. The revolution Peter preached was a revolution of workers finding their way back to dignity and ownership of the means of production. But Peter's

vision was not a communist one but a Christian revisioning of the socialist dream.

In the mid 1930s in the United States, it seemed that everyone was
poor. Jobless and often homeless men littered the streets. Women stood
in line for bread, their hungry children clinging to their skirts for warmth
and comfort. Dorothy was enamored with the communist dream of equality but she saw State aid as cold and impersonal. It was Peter's association
of Christian faith with the ideals of communism that enabled Dorothy
to put her longings for community into action. In actuality, Peter simply
began bringing people into Dorothy's apartment to live. In this informal
way, the first Catholic Worker House of Hospitality was founded.

Dorothy's contribution lay in starting the paper, the *Catholic Worker*.
The Daily Worker, a popular communist newspaper, found its Christian
counterpart in the *Catholic Worker*. Creating the first issue with money
from here and there, Dorothy distributed the 20,000 copies and began
seeking donations. The paper emphasized the second concern of Dorothy's life, economic justice. She saw attempts at unionization crushed
by corporate interests. Basic necessities of wages, housing, and humane
work hours were opposed by management. On a visit to the Southern
Worker's Union Dorothy saw families that were ousted from their jobs
because they attempted to unionize. Mothers and children were living in
tents in seventeen-degree winter temperatures. Children suffered from
flu, colds, and malnutrition. Dorothy was incensed enough to phone
Mrs. Roosevelt whose investigation led to the governor's response that
those people were simply ignorant folks that refused to work. Dorothy's
passion for economic justice fueled many articles in the *Catholic Worker*.

Protests and demonstrations also became part of the practice of
hospitality and work for the poor that Dorothy created. She joined a national march on Washington in 1932 and was jailed for her participation.
Unionization as a path to economic justice for the poor was supported
both by Day's words and by her actions.

The Houses of Hospitality that she and Maurin began exemplified
a way of life that allowed the poor to feel their human dignity. Peter
stressed the importance of work as a creative endeavor that was not only
productive but also chosen. There was always meaningful work available
at the Houses of Hospitality. To study and to work were two of the lynch-
pins of Peter's philosophy of Christian humanism. If persons could do
both of those, they could experience their dignity as human persons. So

the houses and later the farm communes were organized around study and work.

That framework addressed one of the most serious problems of the depression era, the hopelessness of unemployment. Thousands of people found themselves jobless, and then homeless. Their sense of dignity was accosted daily as men and women found themselves unable to care for their families. Communism offered a solution that was hugely popular in Russia and much discussed in the United States. The Third Reich offered a solution that young people were flocking to in Germany. But Day and Maurin offered a solution that was small and communal, a concrete solution that people could benefit from immediately.

That solution, however, was linked to a spirituality that grounded and motivated it. For the hospitality and creative work offered by the Catholic Worker was connected to the church, and thus to the God of the universe. Dorothy believed that personal sacrifice was necessary to reform unjust systems of power. Peter taught that personal sacrifice was the basis of Christian community and the motivator for justice. Their innovative practice linked Catholic faith to the longings for community and justice that were rampant in the depression of the 1930s.

That connection between longings for community and justice and the ongoing crisis of the great depression gave both relevance and urgency to the Catholic Worker movement. Neither Day nor Maurin would have termed their efforts a "movement." Their work was, to them, simply a result of linking the gospel of Christ to the needs of society. That connection, however, resulted in a movement that caught the imagination of willing volunteers and aided thousands in their time of need. Community, justice, dignity of the poor and Christian spirituality blended together in their efforts. Consonance between the gospel and the culture became a reality in the Catholic Worker movement.

Results

For a critical time in the 1930s, the Catholic Worker movement grew like a spiritual revolution. Maurin's lectures on the meaning of history, the importance of work, and the Christian call to works of mercy moved many to serve the poor. Day's focus on putting into practice what she believed about God and justice for the poor set a new standard for the centrality of action in theology. On the first page of her book *Loaves and*

Fishes, which tells the story of the Catholic Worker, Day put a quote from Matt 14:16–20, which begins with the words, "But Jesus said to them: They have no need to go. Give you them to eat," and ends with the words, "And they did all eat and were filled." People were hungry. Feed them in the name of Jesus.

It was the right combination for the times. At the height of the movement, its effectiveness and visibility demonstrated that the gospel and culture could and must be connected in Christian mission.

However, as the times changed, Day's message became less relevant to the masses. World War II brought prosperity back to the nation. Absolute pacifism seemed hopelessly idealistic to many who saw Hitler's raging dementia dominating more and more of Europe. While active well into the 1960's the heyday of the Catholic Worker movement ended with World War II.

The decline of the movement demonstrates the effectiveness of consonance as a central practice of Christian mission as much as the rise of the movement. Shifts in the culture and economic situation in the United States called for a shift in mission methods. To stay in touch with the changes in society presents obstacles to an established Christian mission. The challenges of changing with the times often require new mission works. The practices of the Catholic Worker remain an important way to show the love of Christ to the poor. But as mainstream society moved from depression to economic growth, new ministries grew up with practices that were meaningful to times of growth and prosperity.

Day's single passion was concern for the poor, whether that took a political, a religious, or a social form. The practices she developed to implement that passion have been reinvented in later ministries. Many of those ministries have followed the contours of the houses of hospitality as they evolved. Shelters for the homeless and battered women are one example. Food pantries and meal programs for the poor sponsored by churches are another. Community projects like Habitat for Humanity not only provide shelter for poor families, they also give opportunity for volunteers to discuss the relationship of their spirituality to the physical tasks of building homes.

The Peace Core is another example of a ministry that takes poverty seriously, providing shelter and services to those who have long been without basic necessities of life. Day's idea of works of mercy has influenced the American mainstream in programs like the Peace Core, and in welfare initiatives that utilize the energy and compassion of Christians through church and community-sponsored programs.

Although Catholic Worker influence has diminished over the past half-century, the creation of these and other programs display the diffusion of the innovative practices that Day and Maurin began. From a small group of Christians that caught the vision to a few hospitality houses that sprang up in the early thirties, to an explosion of the movement later in that decade, the vision of putting the poor at the center of Christian mission has spread. Equality and dignity of all, the rights of the poor to food and shelter, and the spiritual rewards of works of mercy have found new expressions since the Catholic Worker was founded. The movement raised consciousness of the culture about poverty, showing the value of the working class, and anticipating the government's use of church structures for hospitality and welfare programs. Dorothy Day's theology of action for the poor showed that the gospel and culture, critically evaluated, can both be affirmed in the presentation of the Christian gospel. "If I have accomplished anything in my life, it is because I wasn't embarrassed to talk about God," she once remarked.[12]

Day's innovations in mission began with herself. Day shifted her identity by choosing to change behaviors and develop habits based on the commitments that grew out of her spiritual experience. Her choices were unlike the flexibility Bauman speaks of which is based on individual preferences and a low passive view of tolerance. That is—I am doing right by not "interfering" with anyone else's lifestyle. Instead, Day chose to live out her Christian values of radical hospitality and non-violence—values rooted in her commitment to God. Those choices cost her much—her long-term relationship with Forster, the father of her child, the stability of place, the economic improvements she might have gained had she put her skills to serving herself. Hers was a true sacrifice in Nancey Murphy's terms—a choice to serve others and give up an advantage to herself.

The values that Day displayed in making those choices centered around integrity, care for others, and sensitivity to her culture. Newspaper work had prepared her for a clear-eyed critique of American society based on Christian values as she understood them. Poverty had given her a heart of compassion for those without food and shelter. Her own search for community had led her to build communities of care where transients

12. Riegle, *Portraits*, 77.

could stop and rest, discuss important life issues, and begin a journey to wholeness.

Not everyone that stayed at a Catholic Worker Hospitality House found wholeness. But the path to salvation lay open before them because of the exemplary mission methods and theology of Dorothy Day.

Day Timeline

b. 1897–d. 1980

1897   Born in Brooklyn, NY, third of five children (two older boys 10 months apart, then sister Della and last in 1912 little brother John).

1904   Moved to Oakland, CA.

1906   After Earthquake moved to Chicago, 37th St.
Lived in tenement above saloon. Father wrote at home, no job.

1907   Dad gets job at *The Inter Ocean* (Chicago newspaper)

1910   Moves to Webster Ave. near Lincoln Park (age 13). Better home.

1912   "Fell in love" (15 yrs). Imagination only. Married musician that lived nearby.
Little brother born, John. Her responsibility to care for him.

1914   Graduates from Robert Waller High School.
Wins scholarship competition and goes to U. of Illinois at Urbana in Fall.

1915   *InterOcean* goes under. Father jobless again.

1916   June left university after 2 years. Went to NYC with family.
Father got job at *Morning Telegraph*.
Dorothy got job at *The Call* (living in poverty as experiment).
Leaves home.

1917   Posters and protests against going to war. Mar. 29 Washington Peace Trip.
Apr. 13: quit *The Call* and went to *The Masses*, Apr. 23.

Sept.: government closed down *The Masses*.
Nov. 10: sufferage demonstration in Washington. Arrested and abused by police.

1917–1918 Village winter. Eugene O'Neil. Both left after Holladay's death.

1918 Worked for Liberator. Began nursing school with Della
Apr.: descent into darkness. In love with Moise. Moved to his apartment.

1919 Pregnant in May.
Abortion in September.

1920 Marries Barkeley Tobey and goes to Europe.

1921–3 Tries again with Moise.

1923–4 To New Orleans with Della.

1924 *Eleventh Virgin* published. Receives $2500.
Meets Forster Batterham.

1925 Buys cottage on Staten Island and lives there until 1929.
Connects with nature through Forster and beach.
Pregnant.
Begins to pray.

1926 Mar. 3: Tamar Theresa born.
April: takes on little brother John (father pays her for care).

1927 Dec. 28: baptism and confirmation in Catholic Church.

1928 Summer: beach experience of community and transformation
Winter: moved back into New York City West 14th St.
Isolated and ill with flu in rooming house with Tamar, nearly three years old.
(not like East Side Jewish community)

1929 Fall: goes to Los Angeles for movie contract. Lonely. Realization of need for community (Miller 212).

1930   Jan.: Mexico City. Lived with poor. Went to investigate Church under persecution. Wrote of Church experiences for *Commonweal*.

1931   Winter: left Mexico because Tamar ill. Spends time in Miami with mother.
Summer: beach cottage on Staten Island.

1932   April: returns to NYC, Elizabeth St. tenement then 15th St.
Fall: invites brother John and pregnant wife Teresa to share her flat.
Dec.: covers hunger march in Washington DC. Feels like an outsider because of faith (M225f). Her question—How to bring Christ, the poor, and the justice that communists sought together.
Dec. 9: prayer. Returns to NYC. Peter Maurin at her house—answer.

1933–1935 Birth of Catholic Worker.
Explosive activity. Catholic Worker "spiritual revolution." (Miller265).

1933   May: First issue of *Catholic Worker*
Fall: Worker's School inaugurated. Brought in prestigious speakers.
Fourth issue of *Catholic Worker*, 20,000 copies.

1934   First houses of hospitality besides Day apartment on 15th St.
Dec.: paper reaches 60,000 circulation.
House in Harlem Black neighborhood begun.

1935   Moved from 15th St. to 144 Charles St. for more space.
Agrarian commune on Staten Island begun.

1936   Speaking tour.
Southern Tenant Farm Union Work.
Picketing German-American Bremen Nazi Anti-semitism.
Matthew St. House opened.
Farm in Pennsylvania begun.

1937   Bread lines at houses of hospitality reached 1000 men daily.
Dorothy works with labor movment.

1938   Anniversary issue of Catholic Worker puts out 190,000 copies.
30 Houses of Hospitality active.
Dorothy publishes "On the Use of Force" solidifying Catholic Worker Pacifism stance. Causes much opposition in Catholic circles.

1939   Dorothy and associates form "Committee of Catholics to Fight Anti-Semitism"
Sept.: World War II begins.
During World War II there were Houses of Hospitality in NYC, Boston, Milwaukee, Pittsburgh, Detroit, Houma Louisiana, Chicago, San Francisco, and one in England.

1944   Easton Farm Commune changed into Retreat Center.

1945   Dorothy with mother at her death.
Peter Maurin becomes senile.

1946   Circulation of *Catholic Worker* drops to 50,500
Half of Houses of Hospitality had closed. Still eleven houses.

1948   Spends four months with Tamar and family at West Virginia farm.

1951   Catholic Church asks Day to change name of *Catholic Worker*. She refuses.

1952   *Long Loneliness* published.

1950s   Demonstrates against nuclear arms buildup by refusing to take shelter during air raids. Arrests and jailed numerous times.

1963   Trip to Vatican. Disappointment with young people's sexual mores and rejection of Church.

1970s   Failing health. Develops cancer.

1976   Last retreat with Father Hugo. Withdrew from Catholic Worker Affairs.

1980   November 29. Died at home. Daughter Tamar with her.

Legacy: "A vision of ending time with its evil nightmares by bringing Christ back on earth." —William D. Miller

9

Overcoming Obstacles

I am best known for my work with the anti-lynching campaign. I began my activist work at the age of twenty-two, when in 1884, I successfully sued the Chesapeake and Ohio Railroad Company after being forced from my first-class seat, in favor of a white man, and moved to the "Jim Crow" car. The verdict was later overturned on appeal by the Tennessee Supreme Court.

—IDA B. WELLS-BARNETT (1862–1931)
SMITHSONIAN BOOKMARK

AS THEY ENTER MISSION or academic work on mission theology women encounter many obstacles. This chapter outlines some of those obstacles and shows how contemporary Christian women work to overcome them.[1]

The catalog of obstacles ranges from internal obstacles of identity, body image and responses to family through relational obstacles such as non-supporting spouses, and responsibilities for children, to economic obstacles that prevent women from pursuing education or mission work, to social obstacles of perceptions of women as weaker or less authoritative and customs that reinforce those perceptions, to professional obstacles such as lack of education and exclusion from academic or professional leadership, to theological obstacles of limiting received theologies and theological frameworks, to institutional obstacles such as exclusion from academic teaching, pastoral work, and ordination.

---

1. Names of some contemporary women and organizations have been modified to protect the identity of women narrators in this chapter since it could affect their work and status.

The ways those obstacles manifest themselves include active resistance to women's inclusion and leadership and passive resistance—ignoring women's abilities and accomplishments in an attempt to render them marginal or invisible. Furthermore those obstacles do not operate in isolation but form a matrix of perceptions, customs, and institutionalized patterns that limit women in mission. Although customs differ across cultures, overt and sometimes covert resistance to women in mission occurs wherever Christianity is found. Often that resistance meshes seamlessly with perceptions and customs that limit women's activities in society.

Perhaps the most significant thing to note in this complex context is that women in this study focused not on the obstacles but on finding pathways through obstacles to realize their vocation in mission and theology.

Resistance to Women's Flourishing

Active Resistance

The history of discrimination against women is well documented and briefly reviewed in chapter 13 in this volume. Land ownership and divorce laws have favored men resulting in poverty and lack of opportunities for women in many areas of the world. Health care and education for girls and women still lag behind.[2]

Discrimination against women in religious matters is not new. A sense of the otherness of women pervaded European cultures in medieval times. Simply by being female one was considered different and less than men since men had established themselves as the measure of humanness.

In the thirteenth century, Mechthild, who joined the Community of Beguines in Magdeburg, Saxony, and Lalleshwari, a Hindu woman, took different paths to deal with their otherness and the fear engendered by it. Mechthild chose to identify her marginalization as redemptive suffering, claiming that God willed the difficulties that doing mission theology led her into. Lalleshwari claimed nonattachment as her response. Through her meditative practice she transcended the sufferings of otherness.[3]

2. See statistics compiled by World Vision, "The World in the 21st Century" at the back of Muck, *Faith in Action*.

3. Roberts, "Fear and Women's Writings," 27.

Michelle Voss Roberts notes that "the otherness of Mechthild and Lalleswari emerges at the point when they attempt to tread the path of the insider of their religious traditions."[4] Both women chose to follow the highest ideals of their religious traditions—ideals that they were barred from pursuing because of their femaleness.[5]

Similar views of women occur today in churches and theologies that deny women's equality and abilities to lead. Simply by being female some women are barred from vocations of priesthood, evangelist, pastor, and teacher of the church. The Southern Baptist Convention provides a recent example of active resistance to women leadership. After becoming the largest denominational missionary-sending force in the world in the late twentieth century, the SBC's revised "Baptist Faith and Message" statement limited the office of pastor to men.[6] Some interpreted that revised statement as barring women from any leadership in the church or denomination.[7]

Sister Rose Uchem's work on the Igbo culture of Nigeria and the influence of the Catholic Church in that area provides another example. She brings together the original egalitarian ethos of Igbo tradition and shows how the church denies that ethos and reinforces aspects of the Igbo culture that are oppressive to women.[8] Dr. Uchem then proceeds to offer an inclusive vision that would overcome that oppression in the Church and Igbo culture.[9]

Passive Resistance

Many contemporary churches, seminaries, and mission societies ostensibly affirm women's gifts and leadership abilities. However, a passive resistance to women's leadership sometimes becomes apparent.

Since the leadership in most denominations and mission organizations is predominantly male, women's talents can be undermined in a number of ways. Usually women that become leaders orient themselves towards men in the group. "Men are the real people" is a perception that

---

4. Ibid.

5. Ibid., 29.

6. Allen, "Shifting Sands," 113–14.

7. Ibid., 114.

8. Uchem, "Overcoming Subordination," 20–21.

9. Ibid., 21–24.

pushes women to act and think in ways that preserve male authority even if a woman is the named leader. Women may also be prevented from assuming leadership roles by a subtle ignoring of their presence in mission groups. A third way that passive resistance operates is through a kind of "gentle violence" that sees women solely through the eyes of men.[10] Repeated instances of such passive resistance occurred in this study.

"Men Are the Real People"

During participant observations in national and international organizations of missiologists and mission workers over the course of seven years, I noted behaviors that exhibited a male-orientation among women leaders.

A woman we will call Doreen Archer was eager to chair a committee on internet publications in an association of missiologists. She offered numerous suggestions about how that committee could be organized and what could be accomplished. Subsequently, she was selected to organize the committee. Doreen wanted to have the final say on who would be on the committee and what activities they would undertake. However, when she gathered the new committee together she spent a good deal of time asking who she should ask permission of for every kind of decision about changes in the web page, future plans and their implementation.

Her sense of authority seemed geared to the men. She invited no women to be on the committee. I came to the first meeting as an observer and was the only woman present. She did not acknowledge my presence. During the meeting she kept asking different men, e.g. the publisher, the journal editor, the chair of the publications board, how they would like to be involved, what authority they wanted, etc. Some of this showed a good understanding of her role as committee chair of a committee working under the publications board. Since it was rather extreme, however, and repeatedly expressed, it became clear that a gender component was operating. (I am a woman and am willing to do a lot of work but want to make sure that I have permission from all of you men to do it.)

Earlier in the conference I introduced myself to Doreen saying I wasn't sure if we had met. "I'm sure we have" she replied curtly. "I've been coming to this meeting for three or four years." Then she moved away. She was the only regular woman attendee of the conference who did not

10. Woolf, *Room of One's Own*, 81.

join the women's luncheon, the one event that gathered women together at the conference.

Doreen reminded me of Ava Martin at an international meeting of missiolologists a few years earlier. Ava was very male-focused and wanted very much to have a position of importance in the organization. She resisted being interviewed for this study of women's mission theologies. At the meeting Ava was delighted to be chosen as the vice president. Over lunch I asked her how her being a woman affected her theology. She said she didn't know. I should ask the men she worked with. She did theology in the "normal way," she said. It had nothing to do with her being a woman.

These two women appeared cheerful, energetic, hard working, and competent. They appealed exclusively to men for affirmation and direction. In relating to women, both were irritable when the gender issue came up and didn't want to discuss it. They appeared competitive with other women rather than cooperative.

In a study of evangelical women, narrators reflected similar attitudes. One said, "I would bypass the table of women . . . to get to the table of men where I felt they were talking the real stuff."[11] Another said that to avoid being labeled a "pushy broad" she allowed herself to be ignored, becoming invisible.[12] Sometimes women were silenced or shamed. Many simply absorbed those gender injustices.[13]

Those women display a male focus that ignores both their own embodiment and the presence and role of other women in their world. They see men as "the real people." Women do not get on their consciousness screen in their professional world. At some level they realize their gender is an obstacle to their professional goals so they ignore it completely. Their male mentors, although encouraging their scholarship, also encouraged male-identified thinking.[14]

A "men are the real people" attitude surfaced in another participant observation session at a meeting of scholars and missionaries. Despite the fact that women spoke of gender-related obstacles in their work, they showed little interest in gender issues as a topic for future meetings. When someone did suggest gender as a topic at an informal gathering of

11. Creegan and Pohl, *Living on the Boundaries*, 77.

12. Ibid., 78.

13. Ibid., 86–89.

14. Ibid., 82.

women, the response was that the incoming president decides (in other words, we have nothing to say about this). She turned to the upcoming president, a woman at the meeting. The incoming president replied that although we could do this "gender has never been my thing. I haven't studied it."

In this case also, the women ignoring gender as an issue were very cheerful and insisted that they had faced few or no gender-related obstacles in pursuing their professional goals[15] Most of those women attending the meeting were succeeding in their chosen mission or academic post. Perhaps they downplayed gender issues because they were doing well professionally. They may have realized that men in the group didn't like addressing issues of gender that affected women's advancement. And men held the keys to success. Alternatively, I wonder if they saw discrimination against women at all, if they felt exempt from it, or if they were just ignoring and suppressing their bad experiences with obstacles they faced because they were women? Maybe by refusing to recognize disempowerment, they simply hoped it would go away.

Women Ignored

Since the 1990s it has been a tradition of the women in one missiological association to gather for lunch on the second day of the meeting. That meeting became a part of the formal program in 2004. Reasons for going formal were 1) space was not arranged for the meeting and for two years running women had to carry trays from the basement to the fourth floor to have a room to meet in. This was time consuming and difficult for some less mobile women. 2) Women new to the group didn't know about the lunch and sometimes made other plans. Women in the group would check repeatedly to see if the lunch was scheduled. 3) As a leaderless group, it was hard to know who to ask about the luncheon. It seemed best to formalize the gathering as part of the formal program. That was done at the business meeting that year.

15. Five women interviewed from this association said they had encountered no gender-related obstacles. Yet in the women's meeting most of the twenty attendees spoke of obstacles in their work. Facing difficulties in job acquisition, publishing, or advancing in mission organizations were some of the obstacles mentioned in this and other annual meetings of the women in this group. Identifying a gender component to some of those would not be difficult. Some of the women did mention gender as a family or institutional factor that hampered their vocational work.

Yet, for the next two annual meetings, the women's lunch meeting was not printed on the meeting schedule. Women had to request that it be announced. In 2005 no meeting room was scheduled and participants again had to carry trays to the fourth floor. In 2006 the lunch was announced only a few hours before the scheduled time. An alcove had been made as part of the remodeling of the facilities so a place became available for women to meet that didn't include special arrangements or carrying trays to the fourth floor.

Formalization of the women's luncheon had no effect on the planning and organization of the conference. Each year it was "forgotten." That situation persists at this annual meeting until the present day. It is evident that there is resistance to a women's meeting although verbally there were reassurances to the contrary. Despite official formalization the lunch meeting still has not been put on the program. The meeting is not announced without reminders to the planners. Those reminders have been limited to Saturday morning after the meeting has been "forgotten" in the list of regular announcements. This way of handling the women's luncheon has been ongoing since the luncheon was formalized in 2004.

Ignoring women and their meetings in that way disempowers both women and men. Leaders, both men and women, hesitate to give the lunch a scheduled place since it has not been done in the past. Women may be reluctant to attend, fearing being branded in a negative way. When verbal announcements are finally made, they usually invite "women missiologists" to attend the luncheon. Wives and mission workers in attendance may feel excluded. The connections women make at the luncheon are crucial for women in mission and the spirit of camaraderie at these meetings is much appreciated by all in attendance. But the climate of disempowerment continues.

Another way to ignore women is to insist that they cover their hair, their faces, or even their entire bodies with loose clothing or veils. Despite theological "warrants" the societal effect of those practices renders women's bodies invisible and reduces their humanity and their status in society. This complex issue will be discussed further in this chapter when we talk about women's bodies and body image.

Women Idealized

Oddly, an opposite practice has a similar effect. In another association of mission academics, my husband gave the first plenary address at one annual meeting. Although I have no recollection of being approached by the planners, when introduced, it was stated that I had been asked if my husband could accept this invitation and I had said yes. So the joke was that without me my husband would not be giving the address. A good laugh was had by all and my husband graciously said that because marital bliss was a top priority for him, he was happy to give the address.

As such this was not offensive. But no less than six times during the course of the conference persons thanked me for "letting" my husband give the address because it was really good. All of those comments were made by men. No woman complimented me on "letting my husband give the plenary address." In a way, the men's comments were indirect compliments on the address and given in a warm spirit. Unfortunately such behavior reinforces the gender stereotype that acts as if women are in charge of men—a joke of course because everyone is aware that the woman does not make those decisions for her husband. "Behind every successful man is a wonderful woman" is the idea. And the emphasis is on the "behind' and that is why it makes for a good joke. Here is another disempowering practice that discriminates against women while appearing to idealize them.

In one international group of missiologists, the women's track is becoming marginalized. Emails circulating on certain scheduling conflicts for the last meeting did not include the chair of the women's track although their meetings were affected. Informal discussions among leaders about canceling the women's track altogether occurred at the last meeting. After all, the argument goes, women are now fully involved as mission workers and academics so there is no longer a need for studying them or for women meeting together to discuss common concerns. If held at all, the women's track should be changed into a gender track.

However, although gender studies have become popular, they lack attention to women's particular issues as an idealized and yet oppressed group. Women hesitate to speak up about injustices in a mixed group for fear of becoming a marked "feminist" that will never be able to achieve a leadership position in the group. There remains a pressing need for a women's track at an international meeting that includes women from Asia, Africa, and Latin America as well as Europe and the United States.

Gentle Violence

Virginia Woolf speaks of "gentle violence," the kind where not much needs to be done or said but somehow a coercive message gets sent and received. Postmodern feminist critiques point out that sometimes "trust is used as an excuse for keeping others in states of bondage or in unacceptable danger."[16]

That phenomenon occurred in a mild way according to a number of interviews of women married to conservative, charismatic, or evangelical men. Those women worked in missionary or seminary contexts that held a male oriented gender theology, i.e. men were the leaders, had the authority and held high positions in the institutions. Women in those contexts usually named their husbands as encouragers and mentors. They felt supported by them but felt held back by institutional pressures or by internal barriers. Some of their revealing remarks were:

> I didn't want to become more educated than my husband.

> Expectations at the seminary were that I would always be with my husband.

> Students said I was almost as good a professor as my husband.

> My husband was hired and I was offered a job within a month.

I had a similar experience when my husband and I taught at different seminaries. Despite repeated corrections, dinner invitations always came to me with his name on them. People expressed surprise whenever I accompanied my husband to faculty events, usually saying how seldom they saw me. In conversations, his colleagues assumed that, since I worked at a seminary ninety miles from my husband's workplace, I was commuting. They expressed amazement when they learned that it was my husband that commuted and we lived in the town where I was professor at a different seminary. That conversation was repeated whenever I attended faculty events over the course of twelve years. In addition, male colleagues in my field limited conversation with me to family matters, rather than discussing academic issues of common interest with me. Those subtle pressures added up. Although I continued attending events and doing occasional seminars at the seminary, I began to feel less

---

16. Creegan and Pohl, *Living on the Boundaries*, 140.

comfortable visiting campus. As one of the other narrators expressed in her academic situation, I felt they wanted me to be "only a wife."

Internal Obstacles

Virginia Hearn, editor and longtime mentor of younger women remarked to me early in my mission and writing career, "I've never met a woman that didn't have an inferiority complex."[17] Young and brash as I was, I retorted that I certainly didn't have an inferiority complex. Over the years I have come to understand the wisdom in Hearn's remark. Internal obstacles must first be recognized before they can be overcome.

Body image, gender stereotypes that diminish self-confidence, inclination toward self-sacrifice, response to marginalization, and naivete about discrimination are some of the gender related internal obstacles women face in mission today.

Body Obstacle

The female body has been an obstacle for women doing mission theology since the inception of the church. The early church offered women a wide range of leadership activities.[18] But as the early church fathers institutionalized the church, older prejudices against women found in Roman, Greek, and Hebrew cultures took root in the church.

Those prejudices included not only Aristotle's notion of women as incapable of moral reasoning, but also ideas of the inferiority of a woman's body itself. The capability of the female body to arouse sexual desire in males also played a part in the re-limiting of women's roles. By the medieval era, women, because of their bodies, were denied the prerequisites for doing theology: education and ordination.[19] A woman's body necessitated her subjection and was synonymous with it.

Women overcame this obstacle in part by simultaneously claiming and rejecting their authority to do theology. By claiming authority directly from God and at the same time humbly declaring their unworthiness

17. Conversation, Berkeley, California, September 9, 1974.

18. See Gundry, *Woman, Be Free*, and Scanzoni , *All We're Meant to Be*, for analysis from the late twentieth century, and the website of Christians for Biblical Equality for current writings on gender equality.

19. Holmes and Farley, *Women, Writing, Theology*, 53.

to do theology because of their female bodies, a few women overcame this obstacle.

It remains, however, an obstacle for women into contemporary times. Even today, a complex dance to negotiate the authority to do theology must be played out.[20] A part of that dance includes figuring out how to be in the pulpit in a female body.

In 2011, a seminar for women in the MDiv program at Louisville Presbyterian Theological Seminary was held to discuss how an ordained woman should dress. What forms of modesty should female pastors exhibit? What kind of clothing was appropriate to wear during preaching? That seminar caused some stir at the seminary. Some professors thought it inappropriate in the twenty-first century to even discuss issues of the female body and how to camouflage it for ordained women. Others thought that the issue itself should be discussed so women could find the best way to dress for their ordained profession. It seems we are still negotiating the "inappropriateness" of women's bodies for church ministry.

Women in this study addressed that issue. One said that when she preached she tried to dress in a way that made her body invisible, but in social setting she allowed her feminine, even flirty qualities to resurface. While teaching graduate school in Indonesia, I felt it necessary to fully cover my slight frame so as not to offend Muslim neighbors who covered their bodies fully and colleagues at the Christian university. Ignoring the body in that way influences self image. Is the female body something to be ashamed of? How important are cultural norms for missionaries? It was interesting that undergraduate students at the university often dressed in blue jeans and tee shirts. Can a balance be struck?

Other issues with the female body arise in Western societies in which the ideal female body is slender, beautiful, and young. Socialization in those societies sets an unattainable goal for women that can lead to obsession with the body or distancing oneself from it. That can lead to spending inordinate amounts of time on one's appearance, or neglecting bodily appearance and health altogether. Some women have found that a larger body can be imposing and claim more authority than a more diminutive appearance. Academics sometimes neglect their bodies claiming that time does not allow them to exercise or eat properly.

Sorting through those issues is a task for women doing mission theology today. How does a woman experience her body as a mission

20. Ibid., 54.

worker? What health issues related to the body arise for women in poorer societies? What cultural issues arise for women crossing boundaries into other societies? How is interaction with men affected by one's body and correspondingly how does a woman's body affect her work? Study and reflection on those issues is crucial for women doing mission theology today.

Writing Theology

The obstacle of a woman's body has contributed to a lack of claiming women's place in mission theology today. It is not surprising, then that some women feel conflicted about writing theology.[21] Because of a strong desire to do theology in settings where it has been prohibited, women sometimes feel shameful about it—as though they have no right to write theology. A number of women missiologists interviewed claimed that they were not theologians. Historians yes, educators, yes, but not theologians.

Frameworks for writing theology have traditionally been male. Access to education required has been denied women. Relationships with male colleagues as women theologians are sometimes difficult. Ignoring theological work done by women or censuring it has also deterred women from writing theology.

In 1989, Chung Hyun Kyung caused a stir by giving a verbal and visual presentation about the Holy Spirit at a World Council of Churches meeting in Canberra, Australia. She showed connections with spirits in popular culture in Korea through a dramatic presentation. Censorship was immediate and harsh. The text of her presentation was circulated without the completing aspects of the dramatic presentation. That alone changed the message of her presentation.

At a gathering of Presbyterian Church (USA) women explored the theme of re-imagining theology. The figure of Sophia as a symbol of God was connected to the wisdom literature in the Psalms. Again, the constructive theology developed was criticized by church officials and a long and bitter battle began. Professor Johanna Bos of Louisville Presbyterian Seminary and other women scholars continue to use Sophia imagery, focusing on the importance of female understandings of God.

21. Ibid.

Because of such incidents, women may be hesitant to develop theologies based on female images, cultural sources, or their own practices. Menstruation, childbirth, and women's aging process are a few of the rich sources women can draw upon in developing theology specific to women's experience. Marianne Katoppo has used women's experiences of mothering as a resource for doing theology in Indonesia.[22] Sallie McFague develops the metaphor of mother earth for doing theology on care of the planet.[23] But much more can be done.

Some women avoid censorship by working mainly from male theologians to develop their theology. Women writers in the volume on the Iguassu Declaration usually developed their thought from male missiologists. Antonia van der Meer used South African missiologist David Bosch as a model. She did go on in the middle of her article to develop her own creative ideas. She presented them almost as an afterthought, yet they contained original ideas developed from her experience and biblical understanding.

Some women theologians build theologies that use stereotypes of women to a good end, arguing that women by nature are compassionate, hold high moral values, and are dedicated to practical service. "Women are more apt for demonstrating a love that is ready to give our lives for others, a love that reflects God's love. Women are created for motherhood and have a greater capacity for suffering because they suffer in childbirth. Women have a greater capacity to love, listen, and care because of that natural inclination to motherhood. This is the greatness of women, to love without asking for anything in return."[24] Other women theologians find those idealized views of women simplistic and limited, reinforcing stereotypes that oppress women..

Women doing theology may fight back against censorship or mainly use male sources for doing theology. The constructive female-based theologies mentioned above are another response that can be used to further mission theologies in our world.

---

22. Katoppo, *Compassionate and Free*, 67.

23. McFague, *Abundant Life*, 210.

24. Comments made by Sister Wisnelda Castro from the Pontifical Office for Migrants in the Vatican in a Synaxeis Panel at the CWME Conference in Athens, May 11, 2005.

Gender Stereotypes

Although gender stereotypes may differ from society to society, they nonetheless occur in some form in contemporary societies. Hence, they are not absent from the church and mission societies in those contexts. In Indonesia men are credited as having more *akal* (intellectual reason) than women.[25] In Nigera, the Igbo culture insists that men are in charge.[26] Devolution in the Church in Madura India saw the power of missionaries handed over to Indian men who maintained traditional cultural assumptions.[27] Those examples can be multiplied from facts in churches around the world. Often women internalize the gender stereotypes from their context, sometimes accentuating them even more.

Mothers as keepers of the home exerts a strong influence in many U.S.A churches. A woman attending a Reformed church in Berkeley CA while doing her doctoral studies at the Graduate Theological Union had three children. The youth group planned a fundraiser and requested each family to provide three dozen brownies for the bake sale. Knowing how busy her mom was with her studies, the middle daughter went ahead and baked the brownies herself.

About a week later the mother received another call requesting the contribution of brownies. The mother explained that her daughter had already donated them. To which the organizer replied, "Yes, your daughter did bring in some brownies, but the mothers are supposed to bake them." Needless to say the relationship of this mother with the leaders of the youth group did not continue on a friendly basis. The pressure to "do it all" intensified as this member sought advancement in her work and good relations with members of the congregation. Although the church was near the university and filled with highly educated members, traditional gender roles were still the expectation for women congregants. Frustration with the double burden of work and home added to the traditional roles expected of women in the congregation caused this woman to exclaim, "Must I do it all?"

---

25. Adeney, *Christian Women in Indonesia*, 53–54.

26. Uchem, "Overcoming Women's Subordination," 89.

27. Heim, "Standing Behind the Looms," 59.

Relationships: Obstacle or Asset?

Families can be very supportive of a woman doing academic work in theology or mission or following a vocation of becoming a mission worker. On the other hand, relationships can impair or prevent a woman from pursuing a vocation related to mission. Some of the obstacles for missionaries created by relationships were practical, others were attitudes held by family members:

> My grandmother didn't want me to go and laid a big guilt trip on me. My brother was only ten and it was hard to leave him and have him grow up while I was so far away.

> My parents didn't want my husband and I to go. We are in U.S. right now because of needs of elderly parents.

> My husband is disabled so I need to remain in the United States.

> I have a child with medical condition.

> The thought of leaving the U.S. was stressful. And the thought of uprooting our family was stressful.

Singleness

Because motherhood is lifted up as an ideal in many churches, singleness can also be obstacle. Or, it can be an asset.

In the early days of the nineteenth-century mission movement, single women were not accepted as missionaries. When they did become eligible to go overseas as missionaries, it caused problems in cultures that thought women should be married. A single woman ministering in a congregation could be seen as a threat to married women's families. The culture may not accept women as leaders or pastors leaving the status of the single woman missionary uncertain at best.

Single women in those situations sometimes move into ministry with other women. Social mores prevent male missionaries from relating personally to women in some societies in Africa and Asia. Although most marry, women and men lead separate lives in many ways, spending their day with persons of the same sex. In those settings, women can be reached only by other women. In such instances, being a single woman missionary can be an asset.

Dr. Bonnie Sue Lewis tells of her work with Native American Indians of the Owjiba tribe. She documents that her lower status as a woman in the society enabled her to support and affirm the men as they became pastors. As a woman she was not a threat to them as a male missionary would have been.[28]

Singleness presents obstacles to women called as pastors in many societies. Rev. Nyambura Njoroge became the first woman pastor in Kenya. She overcame the prejudices against her through flexibility and creative non-confrontation. When elders barred her from doing funerals, she graciously sought male pastors to perform them. When she was challenged because she was a woman she simply did her work as a pastor, eventually breaking down hostility in the congregation.[29]

Even though women may be ordained in many denominations, finding a congregation that accepts a single woman pastor may be difficult. In Sumatra Indonesia, women cannot be called to the pastorate without being married. The idea is that without being married themselves, they cannot relate to the difficulties of marriage that their congregants may face. Yet many women studying to become pastors in Indonesia do not marry because they say that once married they will have to follow their husband's call to ministry and become a pastor's wife. This catch-22 hampers women called to become church leaders in Indonesia.[30]

Support of Husband

A husband's support is crucial for a woman to follow her calling into mission work or doing theology. Men are instructed in Eph 5:25, "Husbands, love your wives, even as Christ loved the church and gave himself up for it." Many men want to support their wives in their God-given calling. Without his support, a wife can begin to feel that she is causing dissension or dividing the family. So both may see her calling through the eyes of a husband's support:

> My husband did not feel called to missions as I did. After he died from a heart attack while surfing I began to seriously investigate missions and what it would be like to take my daughter to

28. Lewis, *Creating Christian Indians*, 121.

29. Interview, Geneva, Switzerland, April 7, 2006.

30. Adeney, *Christian Women in Indonesia*, 88.

the field. The doors to Africa Inland Mission and especially Rift Valley Academy just swung wide open.

The difficulty comes with theologies of male authority in the church and home that seem to conflict with a husband following his wife's call to ministry or even supporting it. If a man believes that he should always walk ahead of his wife, taking decisions into his own hands, and following Christ by leading his household, his wife's call into a ministry of her own can seem threatening. Other men in the congregation or seminary may not appreciate the leadership or assertiveness of another's wife. One narrator spoke of how important it seemed to men in her congregation that a woman not be named a leader. Another described the ecology of her seminary as one that discouraged wives of professors even if the wife was also a scholar.

Sometimes the obstacle to following one's call can be labeled an internal obstacle. In one interview a professor of Christian leadership said that she found it difficult to follow her calling into Christian education and leadership. She spoke of the support her husband gave her to pursue a calling to Christian leadership. Yet she had felt held back by internal obstacles, believing that she had her husband's support. Years later when she asked him about it he said that he probably was resisting her call to ministry but just wouldn't verbalize that. His ambivalence had come through to her but she had thought it was her own hesitancy unrelated to his attitude toward her dreams of Christian leadership.

Self-Sacrifice

Kenosis, the idea that Christians must empty themselves as Christ emptied himself and became "obedient even unto death" has been an important doctrine for many centuries.

According to some theologies, self-sacrifice is a worthy goal of Christians—perhaps the central goal of Christian life. Jesus' admonition is invoked: "Whoever finds his life will lose it, and whoever loses his life for my sake will find it" (Matt 10:39). Some Catholic theologians have linked that giving up of one's life in sacrificial love to Mary, Jesus' mother, thus crafting a theology of self-sacrifice for women.[31] Anabaptist theology has emphasized the self-emptying of Jesus, "who, being in very nature God, did not consider equality with God something to be grasped, but

---

31. See Bellagamba, "Mary as Inspiration," in *Mission and Ministry*, 142–43.

made himself nothing, taking the very nature of a servant, being made in human likeness. And being found in appearance as a man, he humbled himself and became obedient to death—even death on a cross!" (Phil 2:6–8). As women follow Christ, they often feel a call to self-sacrificial giving.

Narrators and theologians in this study show the importance of self-sacrifice in the Christian life. As long as a woman is not forced to live sacrificially it can be a holy path. Catholic evangelists at the 2005 World Council of Churches meeting on evangelism in Athens argued that women have a particular gift for self-sacrificial giving. Women operate more from the heart, the seat of emotions and therefore can focus their service to God in a devotional way by giving of themselves.[32]

Mother Theresa provides an example. She lived very simply, ministering to the dying, establishing communities for lepers, accepting gifts from others, even Hindus that wanted to help with her work. Her attitude of humility combined with a giving attitude in every situation to exude a self-giving love that has greatly benefited many. Be kind even when kindness is not returned, give of yourself even when others take advantage, love even those who refuse to love you.[33]

Yet, this is a theology that presents much ambiguity for women since the idea of self-sacrifice can be used in oppressive ways. It then becomes not a source of holy living but an obstacle to be overcome. Gender stereotypes are read into admonitions toward self-sacrifice. And preachers that emphasize self-sacrifice don't usually make gender distinctions in their preaching. I heard a sermon in the Protestant Church (GKME) in Salatiga, Indonesia in 1993 that called on all Christians to sacrifice themselves for Christ. Yet it was the men in the congregation who led, held authority, and benefited from the women's self-sacrifices.

In her study *Masters and Managers*, done in Java, Indonesia, where this congregation was located, Norma Sullivan documented how women made sacrifices of their time and money to benefit the family. They managed the money but were not at liberty to decide how the money was allocated. Often it was the country market wife's money that paid for school uniforms and food while the husband's salary was spent in discretionary ways.[34]

32. Sister Wisnelda Castro. Synaxeis Panel, CWME Conference, May 11, 2005.

33. See ch. 13, "Charity," in Muck and Adeney, *Christianity Encountering World Religions*, 185–97.

34. Sullivan, *Masters and Managers*, 34.

If men call on their wives to sacrifice in those ways, calling it a Christian virtue, the balance is tipped toward male privilege. Women do not choose self-sacrifice but are coerced into it. Or they "choose" self sacrifice because they have internalized cultural expectations in their context. Such expectations can hurt a woman's ability to follow her own calling or develop her spirituality.

Response to Marginalization

A marginalization occurs when women consistently choose others over their own goals. Mary Stewart Van Leeuwen identifies a kind of emeshment women are prone to that make self-sacrifice easier yet not always healthy.[35] How Christian women respond to many forms of marginalization makes a difference.

Women's responses to marginalization can present an obstacle. Perceptions of marginalization can be quite subjective, leading a woman to feel hurt and disenfranchised when other reasons for decisions that exclude her may abound. Remaining in a situation in which one feels marginalized can lead to a level of anger that reduces or even annuls her effective work in that setting. Recognizing marginalization requires discussion with others, prayerful humility, and a clear recognition of the facts in a given situation. Only then can a helpful response be articulated.

Some women saw marginalization as an asset—something that gave them an empathetic position with women in the mission setting, an entrée into deeper relationships with women, and opportunities to act that those with public power may not have. A delicate balance is required—a perspective that recognizes discrimination without becoming so focused on it that it hampers one's ability to see and opt for positive directions that are available.

One narrator said that although she was marginalized in many ways as a professor overshadowed by the fame of her husband, she intentionally thanked God for opportunities she did have and moved into areas that were open to her. Rather than focus on her marginalization, she made use of opportunities available to her. At the same time, an underlying sense of ambivalence pervaded her remarks. She spoke of counseling a recently married young woman about how "sex hurts." She said that

---

35. Van Leeuwen, *After Eden*, 170.

women needed to "make do," recognizing the limitations that the gender roles of her community imposed.

Pathways

No one can totally reject the roles society places upon them. When George Herbert Mead in the 1930s postulated that the meaning of a person's action is known through the response one receives can be applied to women. H. Richard Niebuhr argued the converse—no one can fulfill a societal role without support from the community. Peter Berger's notion of world construction echoes those ideas.[36]

The obstacles women faced through stereotypes that they were more emotional, more practical, and more nurturing bounded women's activities in the late nineteenth and early twentieth centuries in the U.S. and Europe. Society purported those values. Women accepted them. Whether or not those stereotypes were born of nature or nurture does not concern us here. What is important is how women turned those obstacles into pathways for mission.

Women were quick to find a place among the expanded opportunities they saw for mission. The temperance movement and anti-slavery work both called on women's "higher moral sensibilities." Overseas missionary work to China, India, and Africa demanded great sacrifice—sacrifices that women were eager to make. The care women took on the mission fields were tied to those stereotypes. Women helped other women with health and hygiene, built relationships with women that could never have been established by male missionaries, served practical needs of husbands, mission boards, and congregations in the field. Women's character as understood in this era was particularly suited for such sacrifices. And they did much good.

Women also made a pathway of the focus on relationships that the stereotypes about women generated. Virginia Woolf argued that women may have chosen the novel as a form of fictional writing in the nineteenth century because middle-class women were socialized to become experts at the intricacies of everyday social discourse.[37] They wrote about what they were good at. And they were good at analyzing social situations,

---

36. Berger, *Sacred Canopy*, ch. 1.
37. Woolf, *Room of One's Own*, 66.

figuring out how women could survive in a society that based their value and economic status on the choices of the men around them.

Clifford Geertz describes ideologies as maps that guide people to focus on what is important in their social world.[38] Because no one can pay attention to everything, an ideology directs attention to what society will laud or condemn. The ideological map of women's nature created obstacles for what they could do in society. But women used those maps to create pathways to service that gave meaning to their lives and spread the gospel.

Contemporary women in mission sometimes follow an updated ideological map of this sort. At the World Council of Churches conference on world evangelization in Athens in 2005, two Catholic women presented papers on women as nurturing and spiritual after the model of Mary. The differences between women's and men's character was emphasized. At the Iguassu Dialogue of evangelicals in 1999, two of the articles by women emphasized the special gifts of compassion and service that women can bring to mission. Others emphasized relationships as a major way that women outlined their call to mission.

Ideological maps can be used in a positive way by Christians by helping to formulate categories for morals and a standard of ethical critique.[39] In their study of evangelical women and feminism theologians Nicola Hoggard Creegan and Christine D. Pohl argue that many women choose to live on the boundaries of two ideological maps. That position allows them to bring different questions and experiences to light that might provide insights into the difficulties they experience in institutions.[40]

The fear of becoming estranged in one's deeply held religious tradition sends some women underground in a real sense. The internalized voices of the dominant male culture admonishes them to stay within certain boundaries in doing mission theology. And most do. The few that cross the boundary and seek insider status risk rejection both by the institutional church and by other women and men. Creegan and Pohl state, "The separatism that is born of a profound alienation from disappointing institutions may begin as prophetic; however, it can become sectarian

---

38. Geertz, "Ideology as a Cultural System," in *Interpretation of Cultures*, 220.

39. See Adeney, "A Framework for Knowledge."

40. Creegan and Pohl, *Living on the Boundaries*, 178.

and closed in the long run, hence the boundary, the unclear maps and the sense of unease when crossing these boundaries in both directions."[41]

For instance, why didn't the women in the luncheon group organize themselves and choose a leader? That path is fraught with dangers in a group that, although supporting women's theology on the surface, also fears feminist theologies and avoids substantive interaction with all but the most male-oriented women's theologies. Why don't the women resist being marginalized? As one internalizes the fear of one's own otherness a person begins to see *through* one's marginalized status rather than looking *at* it. To many, therefore, there is no problem. Creating tension by bringing up the marginalized status of the women's lunch isn't an option, not because of the risks involved but because the problem is simply not perceived.

Today, women doing mission theology choose that path or another. The ways women may do mission theology can aid them in recognizing and dealing with the inherent marginalization engendered by their choosing to do mission theology. Marianne Katoppo said that her perception of her own otherness fostered *independence* in her life.[42] Women can describe their suffering as *intended*, using Mary's "Magnificat" as a proclamation of inclusion. Or they can rise above the fray, continuing to do mission theology but separate themselves from the need for recognition or full inclusion. Women in this study have chosen each of those paths.

Alternatively, women can insist that they *are* included. Appeals to the authority of the Holy Spirit, actively seeking pastorates, writing books, finding opportunities to insert themselves into positions or events that normally exclude them are some ways to do that. Alternatively, voicing theologies that *support* women's marginalization, identifying with men that have power—those paths too have been taken by women doing mission theology today.

The conclusions are multifarious. Certainly there is not one way to approach the obstacles of exclusion. Many paths are chosen by women—paths that embrace exclusion as well as paths that deny it. Women's multifaceted responses to exclusion show creativity and persistence in overcoming gender obstacles. Women continue to follow God's call into doing mission theology. They continue to work with the obstacles

41. Ibid., 149.

42. Adeney, *Christian Women in Indonesia*, 86.

presented by exclusionary church dogmas, being ignored, and their own fears of otherness. The next chapter shows how women facing those obstacles find a way into leadership in the church and academy.

10

Leadership

Because really, let's be honest, the Lord Jesus Christ would not
get ordained . . . if he were to come and carry out his earthly
work today.

—HEATH AND KISKER, *LONGING FOR SPRING*, 43

DO THE VARIOUS RESPONSES to obstacles documented in the last chapter tell us anything about leadership in mission theology? Margins and center discussions are popular in mission studies. Who is leading? And are they leading from the center, by definition, perhaps? Or can there be leadership from the margins?

We can learn from the diversity of views of narrators in this study. Some claim women have been barred from leadership and their contributions ignored or forgotten. In the United States in 2006, only 5–31 percent of pastors in liberal Protestant churches were women. In fundamentalist churches 52 percent objected to women clergy.[1] Nonetheless many women have founded churches or movements. Over half of the missionaries in the great missionary movement of the nineteenth and twentieth centuries were women. More than half of the church today is comprised of women around the world. So, according to mission historian Dana Robert, Christianity is a women's movement.[2]

Leadership for women in this study builds on relationships in community. Women focus on empowering others, finding ways to pursue their

1. Putnam and Campbell, *American Grace*, ch 7.

2. Robert, *Christian Mission*, 118.

157

vision with or without the status of a leader, and developing character qualities of perseverance creativity, and flexibility. Dana Robert stresses the partnerships between indigenous and Western women during the late nineteenth- and early twentieth-century missionary movement.[3] Do those efforts put them on the margins or at the center of Christian mission?

Anna Marie Kool, a Dutch theologian, spoke of her initiative to organize the youth movement in Hungary in the early 1990s. Claiming to have begun a movement is definitely a statement made by someone that believes she is at the center, not the margins of leadership.[4] Chun Chae Ok from Korea argued that women are at the center of the mission efforts in Korea. She also said that women's contributions haven't been recognized and that single women were often barred from becoming missionaries. That sounds very marginal. Yet Chun suggested that women are at the center of the mission movement in Korea, doing most of their work *from the margins*—in local communities and family settings.[5] So here is another way to look at leadership.

Cultural divergences may contribute to the discussion on women at the margins or at the center of mission. It is clear that women have not been in top leadership positions in institutional settings in mission. With important exceptions, most women in mission have been part of the rank and file. That does not mean they have not been at the center of the movement however. Chun convincingly argues that women have moved Christianity into Korean society in a huge way. The Bible women of China did much the same thing. In their cultural settings, it would be awkward for a Korean or Chinese woman to claim honor for this work. Nonetheless it is work that leads the church. African and African American women educators also claim a place in mission history. European or American cultures allow for claiming a legitimate leadership role so it is not unusual that women narrators from those regions were more likely to claim credit for work accomplished.

Whether claiming status at the center or seeing their work as coming from the margins, it is clear that women have had a huge impact on mission itself as well as on mission theory and theology. This ability of women in mission to "make lemonade out of lemons" has served the church well over the last century.

3. By 1909 the women's missionary movement had 441 missionaries but 6154 Bible women and native workers. Robert, *American Women in Mission*, 169.

4. Conversation, IAMS Malaysia, August 4, 2004.

5. Interview, Port Dixon, Malaysia, August 4, 2004.

Concept of Leadership

As in so many other areas of mission, women in this study center their idea of leadership around a number of practices. Rather than define leadership in terms of power or decision-making, directing others or being in charge, they focus on the relationships and contextual factors in outlining their understanding of leadership. Encouraging others, finding support in collaborative work, and aiding those in positions of power were some of those practices:

> Weekly faculty prayer meetings and monthly staff meetings were important to me. Professional development days and challenging each other to improve our teaching made us better leaders said a teacher at a residential mission School in Africa.

> I find support through continuing education and consultations with professionals in my field.

> I think about how life is mission/mission is life. Fellowship is important.

> I value good training and have a genuine heart for the host country and the people there. The integrity and honesty of the sending organization and accountability in all things as well as faithful prayer partners and like-minded relationships sustain me in my work.

Women speak of empowering others in leadership. Bonnie Sue Lewis, missiologist at a Presbyterian seminary in Iowa describes the leadership style of women missionaries to Native Americans in the early twentieth century. She notes that the women missionaries could be accepted by the Native Americans because rather than compete with the male tribal leadership, they encouraged Native American pastors to lead, stepping aside to do so.[6]

Presbyterian Church (USA) periodical *Horizons* illustrates that method. Between 1988 and 1994, that women's journal published over sixty articles about Presbyterian women in mission. Yet the magazine published only four articles on leadership. Barbara A. Young's article entitled, "A Moderator—Who Me?" may illustrate a low

Concept of Leadership

Cooperative

Empower others

Nonpermanent

Flexible

Humble

6. Lewis, *Creating Christian Indians*, 121.

expectation of attaining leadership positions in the church. Alternatively, it could indicate a humility that recognizes leadership without self-aggrandizement.[7]

Empowering others was part of mission practice for women in this study:

> Sustaining practices for me have been contributing to my husband's professional work as a counselor by praying, sitting in on meetings and counseling sessions. I also enjoy hosting guests, praying and encouraging those who come. Many stay overnight so we have the opportunity to be good hosts.

> With computers we can stay in touch with those who need ongoing encouragement and help.

Some women were concerned about the lack of voice of women serving in leadership in mission. One mission worker spoke at length about that issue saying, "In theory, our mission is open to women and leadership. In practice, however, married women are rarely, if ever, a part of field leadership and often communicate through their husbands. I don't think the men realize that our voice is not as easily listened to. I find this frustrating at times. I sometimes voice questions or ideas nonetheless, and think these are received generally, but I get the impression it is seen as a bit out of the ordinary. I don't see other married women often doing this. When I brought this up to our team, several of the married women agreed with me, and the men were totally unaware that we as married women might experience this *lack of voice*.[8]

Cultural issues may heighten the lack of voice that women missioners experience. Missionary Terry Althaus elaborates on that dynamic. "Living in a culture where women's opinions are not respected can be challenging. That cultural context has sometimes required living under cultural constraints related to my work: how I dress, what's appropriate as a woman, etc. I find this not nearly as difficult to accept as limitations that come from my compatriots! In general as a woman I have been free to pursue some interesting avenues of service. However, our placement has given priority to my husband's role/placement or ours together, not mine as the primary one."[9]

7. Young, "Moderator? Who Me?," 34.

8. Email Interview, September 10, 2011.

9. Ibid.

Mary E. Hunt speaks to that issue, relating the lack of status and the emphasis on service. She titled her 1989 article "Priests, Priests Everywhere and Not a One Ordained."[10] By 2006, the 50th anniversary of women's ordination in the PC(USA), the situation had changed somewhat. Women were celebrating their success in struggling for the recognition of their leadership in the churches.[11] In general, however, the emphasis in *Horizons* was still on service rather than leadership. A servant leadership model is operating here, but recognition for that leadership still presents issues for women.

American society reflected similar priorities for women during the last fifty years. During the 1970s the feminist revolution listed work, childcare, and public life as issues for women. Women sought equal opportunities in the workplace and equal division of labor in the home. American religion adapted to those revolutionary changes in gender roles according to Robert Putnam.[12] Religious women joined the workforce, adapting to changes in gender roles with little dissent.[13] They influenced the norms about gender roles in all but the most conservative churches. Women were leading from the margins.

That was not easy, especially for women in churches that advocated traditional gender roles. In order to fulfill the service they feel called to, however, women in this study show perseverance in pursuing their vision. They don't quit. If doing the job requires status as a leader, a status they were not entitled to by the organizational standards, they would seek another way through that dilemma. In *Leaning In*, Sheryl Sandberg describes leaning in as "being ambitious in any pursuit."[14] Part of being ambitious is not giving up. Sandberg notes that only 17 percent of countries are run by women. But many women are still pursuing leadership in the political arena.[15]

A similar state of affairs affects women in ministry. Rev. Jamesetta Ferguson, an African American woman that earned a Master of Divinity degree from Louisville Presbyterian Seminary, illustrates that persevering mindset. During her time as a student she participated in a trip to South

10. Hunt, "Priests, Priests Everywhere," 10–12.

11. See Lloyd-Sidle, *Celebrating Our Call.*

12. Putnam, *American Grace*, ch. 7.

13. Ibid.

14. Sandberg, *Leaning In,* Part I.

15. Ibid.

Africa, experiencing first hand both white privilege and black oppression. She gravitated to leadership when the group visited ministries and were invited to teach. She maintained her sense of independence, listening to newly elected United States President Obama's first inauguration speech while the other students visited with church people. After graduation, she found a call to a dying Caucasion church in an African American neighborhood. She turned that church around, starting new ministries, putting old ones to rest, and including others in her leadership style. She persevered in her ambition to lead a congregation and she achieved it.

Making way for other leaders, as missionary women to Native Americans sometimes did, shows a cooperative style that marks women in mission leadership. Edwina Gateley, founder of the Catholic Volunteer Missionary Movement persevered in gaining support for her ideas yet gave up her leadership position after years of service. Her reason? No one, she believed, should establish themselves as a permanent leader—leadership should be shared, passed around, and not reside in a sole person.

Edwina Gateley

An Idea That Could Work!

She was sure she had an idea that could work. Edwina Gateley grew up in the Roman Catholic Church in Lancaster, England. Born in 1943, she experienced an overwhelming sense of awe as a fifteen-year-old one day during the liturgy at church. As a young woman she felt a call to missionary work, beginning a school in Kyamaganda, Uganda. But lacking support from the Church and suffering from Malaria, Edwina returned home to England after two years.

Her circumstances changed. Her vision did not. She believed that lay people could contribute much to the missionary effort in the two-thirds world. She didn't think one had to have a call to the life of a priest or woman religious. God could use anyone to build what she termed the "Kindom." Lay people could form and lead their own volunteer missionary societies.

Edwina tried in a number of ways to realize her vision. She advertised for lay missionaries and found support for their journey to Africa. She simply sent them off to Africa. Many returned home disillusioned. Loneliness, malaria, and an inability to relate to the people were a few problems experienced by those "Lone Ranger" missionaries. Edwina realized that proper selection, preparation, and ongoing support would be necessary for this experiment to succeed.

Although discouraged, Edwina did not give up. Vatican II documents "The Apostolate of the Laity" and "The Missionary Activity of the Church" affirmed her dreams. She sought support from Church authorities but was told that an order needed to be set up for the purpose of sending missionaries. Edwina didn't want an order, didn't see the need for vows, continued to believe that God could call lay people to missionary service.

After a short period of time during which Edwina tried to live a "normal life," she returned to Uganda. It was there, amidst the collapse of her vision that she received word that the Church would help her establish the ministry that became the Volunteer Missionary Movement, a movement that serves the God's "Kindom" throughout the world.

Sources:
Angelyn Dries, OSF, *The Missionary Movement* (1998)
Edwina Gateley, *Psalms of a Laywoman* (1999)

Cooperative leadership became a theme in the interviews. Gateley set up a community for the Volunteer Missionary Movement. Pastor Ferguson brought on Teresa Walton, another Louisville Seminary Graduate, to help with ministries of her new congregation. A Protestant male pastor brought on women at every turn, building a cooperative style of leadership that empowered the congregation.

Those examples show both creativity and flexibility that become effective tools of leadership. For Catholic women developing curricula for priests during the pre-Vatican II era, doing the job at hand seemed more important than having a title or a position from which to work. Catholic religious in South and Central America were learning liberation theologies from Gustavo Gutierrez and other Latin American liberation theologians. The Sisters formed base communities and began using liberation methods with the people. Without waiting to attain leadership positions in the church, those women educators influenced the next generation of priests with the powerful ideas of liberation theologies.[16]

16. Dries, *The Missionary Movement*, 219.

Working With Resistant Churches

Many obstacles to women doing leadership tasks that are part of their work arise as women follow their call into mission service. Those obstacles take different forms in various parts of the church.

Catholic women experience obstacles to leadership since leadership by male priests is the norm. Women religious may not lead in certain areas of church life and theology without endangering their position in the church. Lay leadership of both women and men has only recently been accepted in the Catholic Church and is still limited. Women meet the challenges that prevent them from leading in a number of ways.

According to mission historian Angela Dries, times of transition in the church offer opportunities for developing innovative forms of leadership.[17] It was before Latin American liberation theologies were accepted formally by the church that Catholic women educators wrote school curriculums that put forward those ideas, thus influencing a generation of Catholic leaders in new ways of thinking about theology and the poor.

Help from established authorities also paves the way for women in leadership. Seeking support from Bishops, Cardinals, and men in religious orders has often resulted in opening women's paths to their vision of leadership. Edwina Gateley, founder of the Volunteer Missionary Movement sought help from John Cardinal Heenan of Westminster in 1968. Although initially discouraged by his response that the Church was not ready for her creative idea of a Catholic lay missionary society, Gateley received word while in Uganda that the Church would offer a house and support for the establishment of a lay missionary movement.[18]

African American Protestant women in mission experience a different kind of opposition. In Black communities, the struggle for equality in society often takes precedence over the call for women leaders. Since African American men seem under siege already by inequities, prejudice, and lack of opportunity, seeing women take charge may add to the sense of oppression already experienced by African American male leaders.

African American women called to leadership must address that situation in creative ways. One response is the formation of women's ministries that empower women in the home and in the workplace. Pastor Hawkins of Shawnee Christian Church in Louisville, Kentucky, advertises her ministry of the Good Friday service on Facebook. Each year

17. ASM Meeting, Wheaton, Illinois, Discussion Session, June 20, 2012.

18. Gateley, *Psalms of a Laywoman*, xviif.

on Good Friday seven women dressed in red preach seven sermons on the seven last words of Christ. Pastor J. Alfred Smith Sr. at Allen Temple Baptist Church in Oakland, California, began this ministry years ago with seven women preaching on Good Friday. Pastor Hawkins perpetuates that practice in her local congregation. In so doing she both follows an established tradition and avoids competition with male pastors. Women are given voice, the congregation is edified, and the gospel is preached.

Another response is to lead mixed congregations in changing neighborhoods. Establishing community ministries that reach out to the neighborhood as currently configured bring new life to old congregations. Pastor Ferguson does this well at Beuchel Presbyterian Church in Louisville, Kentucky. Cross-cultural divides are overcome and women's ministries are affirmed as the congregation renews its life and commitment to the gospel, demonstrating equality and love for all.

For some conservative Protestant Caucasian women, a theology of limited roles keeps women out of leadership. A common theology that women should be first of all assistants to their husbands and under the leadership of men in the church dominates some Baptist and independent Protestant churches. Overcoming that obstacle requires women to study the Scriptures, reinterpret them, and gain confidence for the leadership role that they are called to.

Two examples can be helpful here. Dr. Elizabeth Glanville, a narrator in this study, shared her call and her struggles to affirm women in leadership. She now works as a professor of Leadership at Fuller Theological Seminary in Pasadena, California. Carrie Maples, a missionary with Africa Inland Mission felt called to take the gospel in to Kurungu a small village in Kenya. Home-schooling her children and working with her husband, Carrie found herself addressing human rights for women, especially female circumcision. That turn of events surprised her. Yet she felt she was preaching the gospel in a new way, leading women to value their bodies and assert their God-given rights. She and her husband Rick "had become progressive social activists, champions of female emancipation and sexual fulfillment"[19]

19. Bergner, "The Call," 10.

Internal Barriers

In discussing leadership in American society Virginia Valian's book *Why So Slow?* describes internal barriers not unlike those faced by women in mission. Highlighted on CBS in March 2013, Valian questions the idea that barriers to women's attaining top leadership positions in American society is related only to external factors. Although women have made great gains since the 1970s in business, politics, and educational institutions, they still fall short of attaining the top positions in those fields. Valian argues that invisible barriers may be operating. She suggests that gender schemas, unacknowledged and unarticulated beliefs we all—male and female—hold about gender influence our evaluations about the worth of contributions made by women and men. If a woman makes a contribution it is subtly devalued. If a man makes a contribution, it receives added value. The accumulation of those evaluations lead to more advancement for men[20]

The sacrifices made by women in top leadership positions reflect factors experienced by women in mission. Women interviewed by CBS on the topic of "leaning in" suggested that those sacrifices may be too great for some. Family commitments, relationships with children, household chores, responsibilities for engagement with extended family, and church responsibilities have not diminished proportionately to the amount of time demanded by top leadership positions. Women may be choosing to "lean out," staying in midlevel management positions because they do not want to give up those other areas in their lives.[21] In that same discussion on CBS, Sheryl Sandberg countered that idea by offering common sense solutions to those dilemmas facing women in the workplace. As the chief operating officer of Facebook, married and the mother of two children, Sandberg has experience with juggling the pressures of work and family. She says that the expression "You want it all" is perhaps one of the worst adages of the women's movement. Yet she encourages women to lean in, saying that we move closer to the larger goal of true equality with each woman who leans in.[22]

Christian writer Bonnie J. Miller-McLemore echoes those sentiments. "When 'having it all' really means 'doing it all' it is a dubious

---

20. Valian, *Why So Slow?*, 2–3.

21. CBS News, March 10, 2013.

22. Sandberg, *Leaning In*, Part I.

honor at best."[23] "Yet the endeavor to 'have it all' dares to suggest that women, like men, are created to love *and* to work."[24]

In the film *Out of Africa*, the protagonist wants her lover to spend more time with her on the coffee farm. "You want it all!" she explodes. He wants the freedom to come and go as he likes, the lack of commitment to one single relationship, and yet the benefits of a stable partnership. Perhaps women in today's career world face a similar dilemma. They want close family relationships, they want to be first in the eyes of their children, they want community involvement. Sheryl Sandberg points out that choices must be made.

In recognition, perhaps, of those dilemmas, *Horizons Magazine* increased the number of articles on leadership from four articles between 1988 and 1994 to seventeen articles between 1995 and 2004. The tensions around Christian women in leadership were definitely on the radar of women in Presbyterian church life and mission.

Putnam in *American Grace* applies those trends to religious entities. In the 1970s, churchgoers were more likely to see women's main role in the home and support of her husband. Although the feminist revolution spread in religious sectors, including evangelical Christianity, as fast as it did in secular realms, changes in churches themselves have not kept pace. Gender roles may have changed somewhat in the family setting but leadership positions in the church—pastors, mission directors, and denominational leaders—are still largely in the hands of men. Women also find affirmation in congregations for fulfilling traditional gender roles. Internal barriers are set up as women seek affirmation from the church and yet feel a call to mission or academic leadership.

In a church I attended in Louisville, Kentucky, the pastor's wife made it very clear that she was not tied to traditional gender roles. Nor was she the main assistant for the pastor. She came to church dressed informally, didn't sit near the front, play the organ, or do childcare. Her career as a lawyer demanded her time and her choice to put her energies there was very clear.

It is not that easy for many women. A kind of double bind sets up women to seek affirmation by the church community by following traditional gender roles and still follow their calling to leadership in secular

23. Miller-McLemore, "Work and Family," 5.

24. Ibid., 4.

or religious realms. For women seeking to become leaders in Christian mission, that dilemma is real.

Societal Barriers

Women in mission face not only barriers set up by churches, and internal barriers created by balancing multiple expectations, but barriers set up by our society. Sheryl Sandberg reports that thirty years after women became 50 percent of college graduates in the United States, men still hold the vast majority of leadership positions in government and industry. Sandberg suggests that women are rewarded for achievement whereas men are evaluated on the basis of potential. Progress has stalled, she says, for many reasons. Sandberg's book analyzes root causes and suggests common sense solutions to the barriers that society sets up and the ways that women also unintentionally hold themselves back.

Ideas of women's roles are held generally, not only in the churches. Victorian ideas of women in the home as a mark of attaining middle-class status have been perpetuated, sometimes in new forms, into the twenty-first century in the United States.

In the Victorian era, certain areas of artistic endeavor, e.g. drinking tea, domestic activities, and even the artistic painting of children, were seen as part of women's domain. Excluded from the academy because they were thought to be less intelligent and more emotional then men, women took up embroidery, piano playing, and forms of crafts to occupy their time and energy.

Time-consuming and not very challenging activities for women today abound. Many contemporary women take up scrapbooking or creating greeting cards. Precut materials and stamps provide an easy pattern while limiting creativity. American middle-class women devote significant amounts of time and money to those crafts. Coupon collecting also occupies women. Advertising, email coupons, and affirmation for taking good care of one's family lure women to make binders of coupons that they take to stores, spending time searching for particular brands or brand combinations in order to use the coupons. Saving a dollar on a pizza or twenty-five cents on a can of soup becomes a near obsession for many.

On the one hand, women struggle with prejudice, satire, and exclusion as they move into leadership in the church or workplace. On the other, activities that receive commendation are often time consuming and trivial.

A Third Way?

Elaine Heath in her book *The Mystic Way of Evangelism* suggests a third way to lead. Sensing a decline in American society and in the church, she suggests leading by example. An incarnational presence of prayer for society and the church may become a leadership style with influence. That leadership would be egalitarian, with a preference for new church starts in disadvantaged areas.[25] Simply beginning somewhere else, not with barriers to leadership, not with desire for advancement, but with prayerful presence in society may have results that we can scarcely imagine.

The mission practice of accompaniment shares some of the spirituality of the contemplative approach to evangelism. To simply *be with* people that are oppressed or suffering makes a powerful and prophetic witness. Kim Lamberty, Senior Program Advisor at Catholic Relief Services Haiti Partnership Unit, works with Christian Peacemaker Teams in Colombia and Palestine accompanying rural communities at risk of violence from armed groups. She suggests that Christian Peacemaker Teams present a mission praxis that is effective in reducing the risk of violence and strengthening communities in conflict zones. Lamberty notes that accompaniment is a growing phenomenon practiced by numerous religious and secular groups. Here is a leadership style that goes around barriers to women's advancement in leadership while having an impact on reducing violence.[26]

Changes in traditionally structured congregations can also empower women as leaders. During the 1970s a Protestant pastor began to catch a vision for involving women more fully in the life of the congregation. He began teaching what he saw in Scripture about women serving in the early church. He then took two steps: he allowed women to serve communion and serve on the boards.

The results astounded him. Women felt a new sense of worth as they served communion along with men. Young girls began to see new role models for them as they grew. Women's contributions brought a fresh life to the boards. And there were now more than double the number of

25. Heath, *Mystic Way of Evangelism*, 161.
26. Lamberty, "Christian Mission in Zones of Violent Conflict."

potential deacons, elders, and trustees. Taking their new appointments seriously, women began asking different questions, coming up with new ideas. The men were challenged to take their own positions more seriously. A new excitement grew in the church, a sense of expectation of what they could do together. They listened to questions and input from women, they devised new programs, they created new opportunities for women in areas of leadership.

Not long after this, the church hired a new intern, a woman from the local seminary. Never having had a female pastor before, this presented challenges to the congregation. But the pastor declined to put her into traditional gendered roles as assistant. Instead, she was given opportunites to preach, perform weddings and funerals, and to participate in hospital visitation. Her assignments were geared not to gender roles but to her gifts and interests.

As the pastor and intern worked together, they found they could serve a broader spectrum of people. They modeled diverse leadership styles for the congregation. Other barriers began to fall—race, class, and ethnicity no longer seemed the dividers that they once had been. The benefits of working together as pastors and as men and women in leadership changed the congregation. They were better together!

Theological Barriers

Women may be barred from leadership in mission and in the churches by theological barriers. Elizabeth Glanville, Senior Assistant Professor of Leadership at Fuller Theological Seminary in Pasadena, CA describes the effects of two different theologies on the leadership activities of women. The first is a traditional gender roles view that takes from the New Testament epistles the idea that women should be confined to home and family activities. Although not so much a factor in the early church, limited gender roles became the norm during the second and third century process of institutionalization of the church. Since notions of women's limited roles coincided with Greek and Hebrew ideas, they soon became dominant in the churches.

The second model for women in the churches that Glanville outlines is one of giftedness. She points to the priority of the Gentile mission over local cultural ideas of women's roles.[27] She points to the give and take

27. Glanville, "Breaking the Dividing Walls," 3.

between Gentiles and Jewish believers—a give and take that builds relationships and models a unity of fellowship and gender equality. Glanville goes on to show that the new creation Christians become in Christ breaks down cultural barriers, allowing for new forms of relationship as heirs of the Kingdom.[28] Women and men can learn to work cooperatively, listening to one another as equals, bringing their unique gifts to the mission of the church, and valuing the different life-experiences and perspectives that women bring to the church.[29] As Glanville trains doctoral students for leadership in churches and mission organizations using a model of gifts, she helps the church expand its mission more effectively.

Glanville did not come by this theology without struggle. She had been taught a traditional gender role theology for women in the church. In her interview she also described the impact of gender schemas on her life. Although she and her husband felt called to ministry together, he became ordained and she did not. That did not seem abnormal during the 1970s. When the opportunity to do a PhD at Fuller arose, she felt "subconsciously" not ready to do a higher degree than her husband who was working on a Doctor of Missiology degree. She did recognize her giftedness in the area of teaching. That knowledge along with relationships with faculty at Fuller helped her break through her internal barriers. After presenting a project in a research methods class, she felt like God was shouting at her, "Do the PhD on this!" She "felt pushed" to do the PhD, revisit the scriptural issues on women in leadership, and take a position developing leaders at Fuller. Glanville said that a combination of calling, support from other people, providential circumstances, and an inner sense of God pushing her through the doors as factors that led her to training women and men as leaders in the church.[30]

Glanville's model has much in common with the model of "giftive mission" presented in *Christianity Encountering World Religions*. Rather than seeing themselves as only the givers of good news, mission workers can encounter those of other religions as receivers of gifts as well. Professor Glanville is training leaders in mission in a cooperative leadership in that style can bring much to the church and the world.

In the next chapter, a case study from Brazil will show how cooperative leadership from the margins can be an effective force in church and society today.

28. Ibid., 4.

29. Ibid.10.

30. Interview, Pasadena, California, February 4, 2006.

11

Case Study
Leading from the Margins

"But I am born," I said with firmness, "To walk another way than his."

—ELIZABETH BARRETT BROWNING,
"AURORA LEIGH," LINES 579–80, 49

MISSIONARIES ARE DISPLACED PERSONS, entering a strange society, adapting to a new culture, and experiencing the joys and disappointments of sharing life with strangers. They are marginalized in many ways. When Christian mission went from North and West to South and East, women learned to lead from the margins. Themes of calling, ecumenical cooperation, and service influenced their practices and theologies of mission. Today Christian mission is from everywhere to everywhere. What influence do those ideas have for women in mission today?

This case study draws connections to those ideals of the last century and illustrates many of the themes, identity issues, and obstacles that women face in mission work today as described in this study. The case uses participant observation and draws on interviews with nine women missionaries in Brazil. The women come from the United States, Brazil, and Mexico, and represent both leaders and mission trainees. Theories and theologies of women missiologists as well as the voices of the women interviewed suggest that women can lead from the margins, continuing to work with strengths of women in mission from the last century and developing new ways to approach mission in the world today.

In the May 2012 issue of the international journal *Monocle*, Nyamko Sabuni, Minister for Gender Equality in Sweden, answers the question, "How equal is Sweden?" She replies, "In an international perspective we're more equal than others but I'm not satisfied. Women earn less than men, there is segregation in the labour market and women still do most of the work at home. We're working to change that."[1]

Women in Christian mission are working to address gender inequalities as well. As Professor Rose Uchem, MSHR cogently pointed out in a paper delivered at the International Association of Mission Studies in 2012, gender inequality is an enduring problem in Christian mission. It seems that it is an enduring problem on the whole planet. Working to change that as Nyamko Sabuni is doing is Sweden is an ongoing project that both women and men in IAMS are working on. But, in the meantime, women in mission need to be leading from the margins. How do we do that?

We find an example in the character Katniss, protagonist in Suzanne Collin's trilogy *The Hunger Games*. Katniss is thrown into a battle for her life when she volunteers to stand in for her little sister who was randomly chosen to fight to the death in the arena, a staged battle in which only one of twenty-four contestants can win. Almost without realizing it, Katniss leads from the margins. Her integrity, her love for her family, and her friendships guide her choices, bringing her into prominence as "Mocking Jay," a symbol of revolution in an unjust world. In standing up for what she believes, in holding dear those she loves, Katniss finds that many others stand with her. She receives help from the most unlikely sources. Perhaps she can serve as a model for women doing mission and mission theology from the margins in our own unjust world.

Katniss doesn't start out with the intent of becoming a hero. Quite the contrary, her main goal is to save the life of her sister Prim and her friend Peetra who is her partner in the games. Until the final battle demands that she kill even Peetra. Katniss' approach is to act on her values and do her work diligently. She continues her everyday practices of hunting for game and looking out for the weak even in the death battles of the arena. She discerns who the enemy is but mercy rather than vengeance guides her decisions. Katniss lives in a dangerous world. Her anchors are the conviction that she is the right one for the job, the cooperation she seeks and finds with others in the arena, and the service she renders to

1. Sabuni, "Q&A," 58.

both Peetra and Rue, a young girl who must also fight in this battle, during their times of weakness.

Those practices sound startlingly like calling, cooperation, and service, major foci of women in mission during the last century. Since most denominations did not recognize women as leaders in the late nineteenth and early twentieth century, many women argued that their calling from God to leadership and missionary work was a calling that superseded organizational prohibitions. Women missionaries believed they were right for the job. In *Sisters of the Spirit*, William Andrews recovers the stories of three African American woman evangelists that heard and followed God's call despite opposition.

Cooperation across denominational lines characterized women's missionary work around the world. Rather than focus on doctrinal differences, women banded together to serve the needs of their constituencies.

Service to others has been a major focus of women's missionary work for over a century. Women's work for women, healthcare, education, and work with the poor were hallmarks of women's mission work. Education provided an important avenue of service for women missionaries. Catholic, Presbyterian, and Methodist women overcame tremendous obstacles to establish both coeducational institutions and schools for girls. Catholic women in religious in Latin America received in depth training and then set up college level educational programs for women, most notably Regina Mundi in Lima, Peru.[2] In *Our Spirits Walk Beside Us*, Barbara Savage recounts stories of Mary McCloed Bethune and other African American women that gave their lives to educational efforts. Calling, cooperation, and service—those themes, among others, have characterized women's mission work over the past one hundred and fifty years.

What influence do those themes have for women in mission today? Can those everyday practices and the Christian values that source them provide a basis for leading from the margins in mission and mission theology today? What other issues present opportunities for women in mission to lead from the margins?

This case study covers a two-week missionary training session of The Mission Society at Tereopolis, Brazil in 2008. The Mission Society for United Methodists was founded in 1984. Controversy surrounded the organization, seen by some as a step back in missionary methods rather than an advance. By 2008, however, the United Methodist General

2. Dries, *Missionary Movement*, 207.

Conference praised the society for its perseverance and urged denominational agencies to cooperate with it. Historian Dana Robert argues that the path from controversy to acceptance characterizes many developments in Methodist history.[3]

During my stay at the training session I acted as a participant observer, attending sessions, engaging in numerous conversations, and doing in depth interviews three wives of mission leaders and six women training to be missionaries with the Mission Society. The women ranged in age from twenty-eight to sixty-two. The youngest was an unmarried trainee, four were married, including the wives of the training leaders, and four were divorced. Five were Caucasian Americans, three were Brazilians, and one was a Mexicana.

General observations revealed that for the duration of the training program, women were relegated to learning from the lectures and taking on structured roles of caring for children. The Brazilian man in charge of the training seemed overworked as he took on administrative, teaching, and translating tasks although his wife was an expert translator herself. She participated in childcare instead. The wife of the American leader curiously declined to participate in childcare although she held a high view of motherhood.

The men in the group seemed to be "the real people." They saw themselves as the decision-makers and power-holders in the group. Men frequently shared derogatory jokes about women in relaxed informal conversation with women present. The skills of the wives of leaders included one with a master's degree in literature, one with missionary experience both in Brazil and Katjistan, and one with extensive experience as a missionary in Southeast Asia and the South Pacific. Some of those women taught and translated in other settings.

The lack of use of women's skills was evidenced on the first day when the arrival of one of the teachers was delayed, leaving large blocks of teaching time vacant. None of those women was called upon to stand in. I volunteered through my husband who was part of the teaching team so I was scheduled to do about four hours of teaching. My presentations were much appreciated by participants and leaders alike.

When I told the wife of the Brazilian leader about my research on women and mission, she immediately set up an office for me in the administration building and began talking to women about my project.

3. Robert, "Innovation and Consolidation," 127.

That gracious response allowed me to augment my participant observation, hearing from narrators in a private air-conditioned office. That gesture on the part of the leader's wife gave status to my presence and project. Women offered to be interviewed and enthusiastically shared their journeys into mission.

My findings surprised me. My hypothesis was that some major strengths of women in mission during the twentieth century (sense of calling, ecumenical cooperation, and dedicated service) as documented by William Andrews, Dana Robert, and Angelyn Dries would be confirmed. Those foci were present but they were complicated by social and theological factors that I did not anticipate.

Mission Leaders' Wives

Calling

There were surprises in the accounts of the wives of mission leaders. Of the two Caucasian Americans and one Brazilian wife of the mission leaders, none of them felt a call to mission. Each felt a stronger call to marriage and childrearing. One of the women decided to marry and then talk her husband out of going into mission. She ended up following him since he went ahead by himself. Another was engaged for two years while her fiancé took a mission post overseas. The third spent time doing youth and pastoral work in the U.S. before finally hearing a mission call and going overseas as a wife and missionary in her own right.

As a call to mission was a flexible calling that could be pursued anywhere, two of the women decided that following their husbands to the mission field was a valid path. They reasoned that serving their husband's call was a way of following God's will. The third refused to go overseas until years later when she and her husband each felt a call to mission.

Each of those women faced difficult times in their missionary settings. Fear of villagers, trouble with health and hygiene, attacks on their husbands, and general dissatisfaction with their lives pervaded the stories of those women. One had a *kairos* experience—a vision or awakening that confirmed that God had placed her in that setting. Another left the most difficult situation and returned to a former post in a country where she felt comfortable. The third stuck it out unhappily, finding ways to balance her life and serve God in her dislocated setting.

Cooperation

Those same women did not mention ecumenical cooperation, either as a strategy or a reality in their lives as missionaries. What did come out as a strong theme was friendship with people from other cultures. That approach fit in well with the mission theory of the Christian family, used by Baptist missionaries in Hawaii in the nineteenth century.[4] Those one-on-one friendships were based not on paternalism but on a deep respect for the other culture. These women understood that God was using them in their mission setting even though they had not chosen it. One of them taught village women about hygiene. One of them said her best friends were Muslims. One of them, after hating her missionary placement, became attached to the local people and didn't want to leave. Each of them stressed the importance of friendships with people on the mission field. So the cooperation was less with other mission organizations and more with people in the culture.

Community, another form of cooperation, also played a significant role for these women in following God's way for their lives. Whether based on an intense desire to get a job done, as one woman and her husband worked for economic gains for the poor, or based on a sense of the Body of Christ as crucial to any mission effort, as another articulated, working together in community was a value that was important to those women.

Service

The narratives of these women abounded with examples of service. Two taught in seminaries in their mission placements, a curious fact considering they were not invited to teach in the mission training sessions at Tereopolis. All of the training sessions were led by men except for my own volunteer lectures. Both women stressed teaching the value of the indigenous cultures and the dignity of the people that they served, an important distinction from the nineteenth century missionary model that taught a superiority of Western culture. One of the women said

4. Robert, "Evangelist or Homemaker?," 130.

that she shared the loving emotional nature of God in the friendships she developed with local people. She augmented that with serving local women by teaching cooking classes and other homemaking skills. One missionary wife took on the care of infant twins whose mother had died in childbirth, even breastfeeding them along with her own baby.

Dislocation and Sustaining Practices

Dislocation was a major factor in the way that wives of mission leaders understood their calling and lived their lives. Each had to deal with the fact that they did not have an initial calling to mission work. They did this in various ways.

One woman expressed that mission happened everywhere. It was not necessary to go to a "mission field." So her idea of mission work did not include a special sense of calling to overseas mission. Rather, her curiosity about other cultures turned into a love for what she termed "international people." It was the friendships that she built in new cultures that sustained her and focused her work. In that case, a sense of dislocation was overcome by a focus on relationships.

One long-term American missionary posted in Brazil felt loathe to leave that setting after years of struggle had resulted in deep friendships with people there. An assignment to another country (again following her husband's call) resulted in years of distress as she attempted to fit into a Muslim setting in which foreigners were targeted with hatred and violence. After her husband was nearly killed in an attack, the couple returned to Brazil, a setting in which the woman's friendships formed a strong base for ministry with the poor. This woman had a strong sense of the need for economic justice and her teaching skills were crucial in training Brazilian missionaries to work in this important area.

Others highlighted worship, both personal and in community, as sustaining activities in their dislocated setting. One talked about incorporating worship into her everyday housekeeping tasks. Another focused on Bible study. A third mentioned the giving and receiving of gifts from women she came to care for in her mission setting. Mission, for her, was as much about receiving as it was about giving to others on the mission field.

In each case, dislocation resulted in two things: First, a subsequent experience or discovery of practices that allowed each woman to accept her location and find fulfillment in work and worship in that setting. And second, a focus on friendships with women in that culture that led both to work with the people and also to an ability to give and receive gifts from the women there. Susie Wiggins, a student at Louisville Seminary told a moving story about the women she worked with one week of every year to help them build their church building in Oaxaca Mexico. At the end of her third visit, the women of the congregation gave her a warm farewell, presenting her with a hand made traditional dress. Wiggins then understood in a deep way the idea of giftive mission.[5]

Leading from the Margins

How were those women leading from the margins in their situation of dislocation? Rather than struggle to gain ascendancy and leadership in a male-dominated society and Christian subculture, the women focused on valuing the other culture and forming friendships with other women. Two found opportunities to teach the value of the other culture. One found a niche in working with women. Dana Robert highlights this tactic in her section on "Women's Work for Women" in her study of American missionary women.[6] These missionary wives entered the society where they were accepted—they related to other women. In so doing they identified needs, affirmed local women, and worked for positive change. The ones that had opportunity to train male leaders used their teaching gifts to emphasize the necessity of helping women in their economic development. Many worked directly with village women, training them in health and hygiene and learning from them the ways of the culture that allowed the gospel message to be interpreted in their setting.

Mission Trainees

The missionary trainees represented a very different demographic. Four of the six were women of color—one African American, two Brazilians, one Mexicana. Two were Caucasion Americans. That two to one ratio is the opposite of the ratio of the three mission leaders wives two of whom were Caucasian American and one of whom was Brazilian. Four were divorced, one was single, and only one was married as opposed to all

5. Adeney, *Graceful Evangelism*, 175–176.

6. Robert, *American Women in Mission*, 130–33.

being married in the first group. Their age range was younger, mainly in their 30s and 40s rather than the late 40s to 50s range of the mission leaders wives.

Noting similarities, their denominational affiliations were predominantly Methodist as were the mission leaders wives—two were Methodist and one was Southern Baptist. Each of the women in the mission trainees group, except for the twenty-eight year old single woman, had two or more children, as did each of the mission leaders wives.

Calling

Surprises occurred in this group too. It is striking to note that all six of the women in this group had a strong calling to mission, most from a young age, exactly the opposite of the mission leaders' wives, none of whom felt an initial call to mission work. It is also striking to note that of the five married or divorced women not one had a husband that was supportive of her mission work. Each of the divorced women began their mission training after they were divorced. One married woman with previous missionary experience had a husband who was called to mission but "made it difficult" for her to pursue her own mission work.

Cooperation

There was a strong emphasis on cooperation in each of the life accounts of these women. Becoming active in Christian communities, supporting missionaries financially and with their work, and working cooperatively in churches was a major emphasis in the accounts. One woman is secretary of a church congregation and has served as secretary to the regional Methodist Bishop. Another supported a woman missionary in Bolivia from the times she was seventeen years old, even traveling to Bolivia to visit this woman and then write a book about her ministry. The single woman was interested in cinematography and planned to do films on mission work that could then be used for fundraising for the missionaries. One woman went on several short-term mission trips with the Mission Society and described how community developed between the mission workers and the local people as they tore down inadequate houses and replaced them with new ones.

Service

The idea of service dominated each of the interviews. The sense of call to serve God through serving others ran like a strong thread throughout the accounts. There was no mention of hardship on the field other than the strenuousness of building homes. One woman was interested in prison ministry, especially doing a film that would show the hardships of prison life and engage the church in service to prisoners. It was axiomatic in each account that the calling of Christ on their lives was to service of others. No distinction was made between spiritual work, e.g. Bible study, and social justice work such as micro financing projects, healthcare, and building projects.

Dislocation and Sustaining Practices

Rather than being pushed into working in another culture, this group of women *wanted* to be doing mission work in a culture different from their own. Their sense of dislocation arose mainly in their past experience, sensing a call to mission that they could not follow. At this time, each was looking forward to being sent to a new location to do mission work so they were not feeling a distinct sense of dislocation in the present. As they related their past experience, most of them found strength in worship and Bible study. One mentioned that everything in her life seemed to strengthen her, even her struggles. Another, who had past missionary experience, spoke of playing with children as a way of reviving herself spiritually. A third spoke of self-care, specifically exercising and losing weight, a topic that she wanted to share with others.

Putting the Two Groups Together

Despite differences among the women, individually and demographically, one can inquire whether or not these women emphasize calling, ecumenical cooperation, and service as late nineteenth and twentieth century women missionaries did. The answer is yes, with some major differences.

Calling

The wives of mission leaders did not exhibit a strong call to mission initially but followed their husbands to the mission location. They each came to accept their situation of dislocation and work with it as time went on. On the other hand, the missionaries in training each felt a strong calling to mission work although their husbands were not supportive of that call. In both groups non-supportive husbands created a sense of dislocation.

That dislocation itself became a factor in pursuing God's will. Some women waited until after divorce to pursue mission while others developed a sense of call when in the mission situation of dislocation. The marginalization of gender inequality was compounded by the dislocation of the women, having to not go out to do mission or having to go out when not called. Each of the nine women developed skills in leading from the margins that were at least partially a result of their specific dislocation.

Cooperation

One of those skills was an ability to identify with the culture in which they found themselves. Women that wanted to do mission but could not go overseas found mission venues where they could do mission work in their locale. Women who were dislocated to an overseas place found ways to identify with women in that culture, value them, and develop friendships with them. Cooperation based on gender oppression itself may have been a factor in some of those friendships.

Although the word ecumenical was not used in any of the interviews, a strong emphasis on cooperation runs through the accounts especially the mission trainee accounts. Cooperation was not stressed as much by missionary wives, perhaps because of their sense of marginalization. However, they did lead from the margins in specific ways. One found a way to value women as mothers which she saw as her primary calling. She also found opportunities to teach cooking classes to village women. Another found ways to teach in a seminary, stressing Christian values of human dignity and worth in a culture that she thought didn't value its own roots. A third found a way to offer me administrative assistance in my own research on women, making my work easier and raising the status of women at the conference.

None of the women fought the male-dominated system of authority but found creative ways to assert their own values with integrity and use the authority of their husbands to gain access to teaching posts, office space, and opportunities to lead.

Service

All of the interviews stressed service. Trainees spoke of service opportunities in the past and were excited about the service they would be able to do as missionaries. One informally taught hermeneutics, helping women in the society to interpret Scripture in culturally attuned fashion. Another found mission opportunities in her local church, enlisting her pastor to help gain support from her husband. A third financially supported a missionary to Bolivia. Missionary leaders wives, although discouraged about service in their dislocated mission settings, nonetheless all found ways to do it. Serving God through service to others was seen as a major part of being in the will of God.

Dislocation and Sustaining Practices

Tension around gender issues pervaded all of the interviews. Mission leaders wives were pushed into service they didn't feel called to. Missionary trainees had husbands who rejected their call to mission. Both experiences led to a sense of dislocation. The practices that sustained the women varied but showed no significant difference between the two groups. Finding out how to follow God's will, immersing oneself in worship and Bible study, discovering everyday practices that provided balance in their lives, and developing friendships with local people were a few of the sustaining practices of the women in this study.

Leading from the Margins

Despite the gender inequalities and dislocation, these women developed and exercised leadership capabilities. Eight of the nine women had college education and some of them had professional careers in physical therapy, teaching literature, and speech therapy. Some had goals to write books or make films. Others used homemaking skills and knowledge about health and hygiene to train women in rural areas. In all of those cases, three qualities characterized their leadership: perseverance, creativity, and flexibility.

Perseverance

In the book *Outliers*, the author speaks of talented people that don't quite fit in to society. He argues that success in those talents depends more on perseverance than on the talent itself. He uses the example of the classical pianist, saying that if a person that loved the piano put in 10,000 hours of practice time, they could make it to the top.[7] Whether or not that is actually the case, the women in this study definitely persevered, overcoming incredible obstacles to pursue mission work or to serve God despite their dislocation into a mission field that they did not feel called to. Like the Mission Society itself, these women persevered, overcoming obstacles to their missionary calling. Some sustained their vision through years of opposition. Even the missionary leaders' wives, who felt no call to mission, found ways to serve God in the situations in which they found themselves.

Creativity

The women creatively found ways to serve, build friendships, and give and receive with the people they were serving. One missionary trainee published a book about a missionary on the field despite her own lack of education and money. She has another book project planned. A missionary wife developed a hermeneutical method to teach the Bible in culturally sensitive ways and trains church leaders to do that, thus working herself out of a job. She sees training the local people to study the Bible as an essential tool in spreading the gospel in that culture. One leader's wife found ways to affirm motherhood while rejecting the pressure to do childcare at the conference. One trainee has plans to make a film to help support mission work and another about prison ministry despite difficulties of being a woman doing research in an all male prison facility. One wife of a leader procured an office for my project on women in mission. And I used my husband's connection to the leadership team to gain an opportunity to teach at the conference. In these and other ways, the women in this study creatively led from the margins.

7. Gladwell, *Outliers*, 34.

Flexibility

Those creative efforts required flexibility. Missiologist Angelyn Dries emphasizes flexibility as a strong attribute of women religious on the mission field. When church work is as yet unstructured, women have an opportunity to lead, doing pastoral as well as educational ministry. Once more formal Catholic structures are in place, women's opportunities for leadership are often curtailed. Dries speaks about flexibility as one of the most important qualities of Catholic women in mission.[8] The women in this case study utilized that skill, finding ways to lead in situations in which much of the focus of mission work was geared to men.

Although none of the husbands supported the callings of the wives, each woman found ways to sustain her life, find balance, and serve others. One woman that could not become a full time missionary because of her husband's objections joined several short-term mission trips. She did everything from tearing down clay houses and rebuilding them with wood, to teaching vacation Bible study. Another woman who couldn't become a missionary despite her calling, kept track of a woman missionary to Bolivia, eventually making the journey out to visit her and write her story. A third, that could not pursue her dream of teaching literature, found ways to work with women missionary trainees.

These women show that mission happens everywhere. Mission support can happen without going overseas. A woman can find ways to serve even if she doesn't feel called to a particular place. A woman can teach cultural values in informal ways even when leadership opportunities are denied her. Life can take a new direction into Christian mission even at age sixty-two.

It was a privilege to hear the narratives of the women in this case study. The interviews were not based on academic questions about gender or dislocation but queries about the lived experiences of ordinary yet exceptional women. Some faced physical dislocation, others a dislocation because they could not follow their calling. Each faced issues of gender inequality. Yet they did more than survive. They led from the margins.

In speaking of Methodist mission history, Robert says, "The people whom we honor as missionary pioneers often challenged the system. On the other hand, without organizational support for the experiments of

---

8. American Society of Missiologists Annual, Meeting Panel Discussion, Techny, Illinois, June 17, 2012.

the Spirit-led enthusiasts—many of them lay people—there would be little sustained work for us to remember today."[9]

"Spirit-led enthusiasts" include the women interviewed in this case study. Some felt called to mission work. Others felt dragged into mission work as they felt God's Spirit leading them in another direction. In both cases, the opposition they felt to their calling led to a sense of dislocation as they could not follow the path that they saw God calling them to. Despite those obstacles, the women in this case study continued

the twentieth century foci of women doing mission: calling, cooperation, and service. They also developed character virtues of persistence, creativity and flexibility. In so far as those efforts are not supported organizationally, they will be forgotten. The focus and character qualities of missionary women need to result in changes in organization that reduce or do away with gender discrimination.

This case study graphically illustrates Uchem's assertion that gender inequality is an ongoing problem for mission, a problem that causes dislocation, personal pain, and the under-use of women's talents. Like Sabuni in Sweden, We will continually work to change that. But, in the interim, there are ways to lead from the margins. Like Katniss in *The Hunger Games*, the women in this study asserted their values, honored their friendships, and led from the margins through perseverance, creativity, and flexibility. The model of Christian mission resulting from that combination of emphases and virtues can cogently inform mission theology and mission work for women and men in our time.

Women's creativity in using art and beauty and a love for nature in their mission theologies and self-nurturance can also become part of leadership as the next chapter will show.

---

9. Robert, "Innovation and Consolidation," 127.

1 2

Art and Beauty

"In the Grove: The Poet at Ten"

She lay on her back in the timothy
and gazed past the doddering
auburn heads of sumac.

A cloud—huge, calm,
and dignified—covered the sun
but did not, could not, put it out.

The light surged back again.

Nothing could rouse her then
from that joy so violent
it was hard to distinguish from pain.

—JANE KENYON, *COLLECTED POEMS*, 149

ART AND BEAUTY PROVIDE resources for women doing mission theology. Poetry, hymns, singing and playing musical instruments, drawing, painting, sculpture and calligraphy offer opportunities for women to express theologies of God and God's mission in the world. Growing and arranging flowers, gardening and collecting wild plants and flowers are ways of embracing the beauty of nature. Participating in outdoor sports give women another kind of chance to revel in God's creation. Camping, kayaking, canoeing, fishing, skiing, walking, jogging, volleyball, tennis, baseball and other sports offer the pleasures of enjoying the outdoors. Knitting and other home crafts along with the products of other artistic endeavors can beautify the home and worship space in satisfying ways. Such activities often become sustaining practices that energize and sooth women in mission. In addition, theologies of mission can be developed in many of those artistic endeavors.

This chapter outlines some of the artistic work that leads to theologies expressed by women. Poetry and hymn writing offer creative outlets for developing theologies. Creating through the visual arts and enjoying the beauties of nature express theologies, incipient or articulated. We will explore theological themes expressed by women through poetry in particular. Finally, we will outline a *method* for developing theologies through poetry, discovering sources of authority that augment those described in chapter 2.

Hymns

In her book *Music in the Life of the African Church*, Professor Roberta Rose King recounts something of the history of music in the church in the West and in Africa. She cites the Victorian era as an influential period in both.

For Europeans and Americans it was a time of singing in the church, in the streets, in the pubs, and in everyday life. Hymns became the folksongs of Britain and gospel songs penetrated popular music in the United States.[1] The emotional appeal of hymns linked with their theological content gave Christian music a powerful voice in society. R. W. Dale, a great congregational preacher of the time, remarked, "Let me write the hymns of a Church, and I care not who writes the theology."[2]

In Africa, traditional music strongly linked life cycle stages and was used, along with drumming and dancing, at important life passages in community and individual lives. When missionaries brought their beloved Christian hymns to Africa, they encountered those diverse and deep associations of music to life practices and rituals among Africans. In Africa certain instruments and types of drums were associated with religious ideas and spiritual powers. The use of Western instruments avoided those associations. For the missionaries, it was not just the words

1. King et al., *Music in the Life*, 33.

2. Ibid., 35.

and their meaning that was crucial to Western hymnody, but the cultural associations of the music itself.

Music became a contested site for political and social dominance by colonizing forces.[3] The missionaries may have had good motives but they unwittingly contributed to that conflict. Music in African cultures spoke truth as people understood and practiced it.

The theologies brought by Western hymns both aided the spread of the gospel and resisted associations of African music. "To sing is to theologize" King insists.[4] So the churches used Western hymns to avoid associations with African religions and the spirits that were dominant in those religions. Western hymns written by women, including "Beneath the cross of Jesus" by Elizabeth Clephane and "Take My Life and Let it Be" by Frances Havergal were among hundreds of hymns that influenced Christianity in Africa. Those women hymn writers brought new truth to the African continent.

African Christian women also became songwriters. "Faith Is Like an Egg," by a contemporary Christian woman named Nonyime in Côte d'Ivoire, begins with a cultural proverb and develops ideas from Heb 11:5.[5] Nonyime taught the song to choirs and it soon spread widely. Women's theology in this case widely influenced the church in that context. Although neither Western nor African women held positions of authority in the churches, women's theologies became incorporated into the life of the church through their hymns. After all, how one sings is how one believes.[6]

Appreciating African cultural forms occupies a strong place in the musicology of the churches in Africa today. Theological reflection through songs promotes knowing God in context according to King.[7] King's hermeneutical method for theologizing through song helps African musicians become grounded in biblical knowledge and spiritual disciplines. It sets up a "dialogue of listening" that enables Western Christians to listen to African cultural and religious themes, learning to appreciate them and integrate them with Christian theologies.

3. Ibid., 49.

4. Ibid., 128.

5. Ibid.

6. Ibid., 117.

7. Ibid., 142.

In some African cultures, music negotiates among various spiritual realities.[8] Africans were doing theology through their music well before Christianity came on the scene. Today, all four streams of African Christian music (Western, African-based in independent or mission churches, and music influenced by contemporary media sounds) offer opportunities to "talk about God." "The singing of Christian songs and hymns offers hope, protection, and renewed strength to survive."[9] Many of those songs are written, taught, and sung by African women.

Mission as an Art

Professor Chun Chae Ok from Ewha Women's University in Seoul outlines a mission theology practiced by women of South Korea. Its major tenets are emptiness, comfort, and beauty. Since Korean women work mainly in the home and local community, that theology fits their context. In her interview she made these comments:[10]

> In defining mission theology I looked inside of myself to see what my experience was teaching me. Three words emerged— emptiness, comfort, and beauty. Out of those three words I developed my theology of mission.

Chun calls her theology one of mission of the poor to the poor. She recognizes the importance humility and the mission women do in comforting others:

> Women's approaches are hidden and veiled but the church is made up mainly of women and youth. Korean women have spread the gospel through relational work in their families and communities. The ideal of emptiness, being receptive to God's use combines with the activism of comforting those that suffer.

In a paper that Professor Chun delivered in Malaysia in 2004 she states, "The reality is that women in mission without names and in most cases without writings have been vehicles of the gospel in the Korean churches and in Asia. Their roles have been just giving, life giving without any demand for receiving and for recognition"[11] Women spend time com-

8. Ibid., 137.
9. Ibid., 146.
10. Chun Interview, Port Dixon, Malaysia, August 4, 2004.
11. Chun, "Integrity of Mission," 3.

forting others as a mother comforts her child. "Women give faith, love, and hope to the people of the church and to the people of the world."[12]

The element of beauty and relating praise of God to both art and nature rounds out Chun's holistic and accessible mission theology. She says, "I would like mission to be seen as an art rather than politics, economy, expansion, power, ruling, and managing."[13] In her interview, Chun describes art and compares it with Christian mission:

A Korean artist may make two strokes of bamboo that can become a well-known work of art. It is very quickly made, usually on a small canvas. Another artist may take many hours, even days, to paint a huge canvas with mountains, many pine trees, a river, and a boat. It is also valuable but not *more* valuable or artistic than the simple two-stroke bamboo painting.

Women trying to do mission with men's mission structures may feel they are wearing someone else's clothes. It is not wrong, but it doesn't fit.

In my garden I planted violets, cosmos, and sunflowers. The sunflowers are most valued because of their many seeds that are used for food. Also, they are very tall and imposing, brilliant in color and strong in appearance. But sometimes when I look at my garden, I think the tiny violets are more beautiful than the sunflowers.

So mission is like art—it doesn't matter if it is a large or small canvas, if the painting took many hours and has many strokes, or if it is just a few well-placed lines on a simple background. And mission is like flowers— the small and simply grown violet is as valuable as the large productive sunflower. So mission takes many forms—none are more valuable than the others. Korean women are most comfortable in small forms of mission, mission in their homes and communities. It is as valuable as large institutional forms of Christian mission.

Chun's theology of mission as emptiness, comfort, and beauty is not limited to use in Korea however. Neil Young's song Jesus of Rio shows its universal appeal. The song speaks of Jesus standing on top of the world—just as the grand statue of Jesus of Rio stands above the city of Rio in Brazil. Jesus stands opens his arms with grace to people searching for freedom and love in their lives. The statue high over the city draws hundreds of tourists daily. It comforts and gives hope to us all.

---

12. Ibid., 5.
13. Ibid.

A Historical Perspective

Because theology has been the domain of men, women's theological reflection on many topics was not recognized as theology for centuries.
The business of doing theology went on in church councils and academic
institutions. Women were excluded from participation in both. Women
themselves often had no self-consciousness that their ideas fit under the
rubric of theology. The universe of theology was closed to them, except
as followers—therefore, it followed, their ways of understanding many
topics that were not "counted" as theological by the reigning paradigm—
could not be theology.

Exceptions to this pattern occurred during the first century of the
church's life. The story of Mary, Lazarus' sister, who sat at the feet of Jesus
with the disciples rather than helping her sister Martha prepare food for
their guests, showed that Jesus favored women's engagement in theological work. Junia, the first woman apostle, and other women leaders in the
early church such as Lydia who had a church in her house, and Priscilla,
who trained younger disciples, were examples of women doing theology
in the early church. This was mission theology as a main focus of the early
church was to spread the good news that Jesus had come into the world
to reveal God's love to people.

Exceptions to the exclusion of women in theology also occurred in
places were women focused on the religious life and governed their own
affairs—monasteries. Over the centuries of Christian history, women
have written theology from within the safety and solitude of monastery
communities. Writings by Hildegard of Bingen, Teresa of Avila, and Juli-
ana of Norwich, monastic women of the 4th and 5th centuries influenced
theological discourse in their own time and in centuries to follow. Evelyn Underwood, a mystic who lived centuries later influenced an entire
movement. Antinuclear Christian activist Daniel Berrigan showed how
the writings of Julian of Norwich can be relevant to contemporary Christians. In the 1970s he wrote a poem intertwining her themes of revelation, the beauty of nature, humility, and experience:

> **Vision**
> (after Juliana of Norwich)
>
> then showed me he
> in right hand held
> everything that is

the hand was a woman's
creation all lusty
a meek bird's egg

nesting there waiting
her word and I heard it

newborn   *I make you*
nestling   *I love you*
homing   *I keep you*[14]

During the nineteenth and twentieth centuries, women influenced the direction of religious movements through their theological work. Mary Baker Eddy founded the Christian Science movement, Phoebe Palmer influenced a generation of Pentecostal Christians, Catherine Booth developed a following among wealthy Londoners, and Dorothy Day developed the Farm Worker movement in the U.S. in the 1930s. Missionaries Lottie Moon in China and Ida Wells in India also had great influence.

In the 1960s in the U.S. something new began to happen. The second wave of American feminism was sweeping the nation. Women moved out from the 1950s domestic ideal and called for equality in the workplace. Christian women decried the inequalities of power in the church. Many found their voice. They spoke and wrote of things that mattered to them, connecting their ideas with their views of God, their understandings of justice, and their notions of beauty and truth. Women began doing theology in new way.

As with Korean women, the topics they worked on were topics close to them—their daily struggles, the birthing and nurture of children, their sensitivities to the injustices they encountered, their celebration of life. Taking up their perspective as women in a new way led to a self-conscious owning of women's thoughts and an emphasis on their importance to the world. Organizing some of those reflections resulted in works such as *The Feminine Mystique* and anthologies of feminist thought. Publications of women's history like Rosemary Radford Ruether's *Encyclopedia of Women in the U.S.* also appeared. The reclamation of women's history and the importance of women's thoughts on topics centered in their experience began in earnest.

14. From an advertising poster of the Christian World Liberation Front in Berkeley, California, 1974.

This movement to reclaim and focus women's historical contributions and reflections on ordinary life expanded the domain of theology. The immanence of the sacred, the importance of the body, the crucial dimension of relationships in knowing God, and the necessity of justice across genders became themes in women's theology.

Appreciation of Nature

The beauty of nature makes another contribution to women's mission theologies. Chun Ok Chae's love for flowers, narrators appreciation of the beauty of the natural world, love for pets, and the creation of natural beauty in the home are some examples of how nature functions for women in mission.

For me, I can't remember exactly when wilderness began to becken. One early memory sees me filling my new green wicker doll carriage with milkweed pods from the field beyond the chicken coop. Gleefully I brought them onto the lawn, freeing the feathery wisps from each pod. Age five or six found me sitting up in the mulberry tree down the road feasting on the dark rich fruit. Then there are memories of walking down the lane with Mom to visit our wooded lot, crawling under the brambles of the huge blackberry patch in the field across the street to find the biggest and best. In middle school I used to take long bike rides stopping to climb a pear tree along the road, studying rocks in a creek down the lane, or tramping through fields along the highway searching for soda bottles.

Maybe it's a "nature gene" calling me to "wildness and wet," an unforgettable phrase by Gerald Manley Hopkins that has adorned my home for decades. Whether nature or nurture played the larger role, I don't pretend to know, but I do say that the urge to get outdoors began early and stayed with me into high school. A love of nature can become a source for theological reflection, especially in poetry and hymns.

Poetry as a Medium for Theology

Marilyn Sewell's *Cries of the Spirit: A Celebration of Women's Spirituality* provides an example of the integrated themes of women's theology as developed during the thirty years following the "awakening" among women during the 1960s. Sewell, a Unitarian Universalist pastor, developed an anthology of women's poetry, to be used as a religious resource for church leaders and lay people. Her practice of using poetry as a resource during worship services led her to gather poems that had theological significance. The result was a book that organized and exemplified the new topics of women's theology.

Sewell's method in gathering the material is worth noting. First, she noted the lack of women's perspectives in works on spirituality. Then she began gathering examples of women's poetry that touched on their views of spirituality. Rather than organizing categories and searching for poems on certain topics, she let the typology arise from the poems themselves. This inductive method resulted in a list of topics that displayed a "female aesthetic of the sacred that is clear and identifiable."[15]

Sewell's Twelve Categories: Sources of Authority for Women's Theological Reflections

1. Oneness of spirit and flesh (3–5)
   start with the body
   refuse separation of matter and spirit
   body is one with the sacred
   sexual relationship transformed – invitation, reception, renewal
   body not feared and avoided
   body as joy
   body as source of knowledge

2. Nature as metaphor (5–6)
   natural world as source, sacredness, fertility, connection, unity
   body
   life
   power

3. Writer herself as authority (6–7)
   internal source of truth, meaning, identity
   daily experience – the ordinary
   inner experience – linked to systemic injustice
   her "no" leading to her "yes"
   identifying wholeness in midst of fragmentation

15. Sewell, *Cries of the Spirit,* xvii.

4. Feelings (6–8)
   expression of life force of writer
   anger, revenge – emerge into a yes
   longing for union that brings life
   place of love and belonging in life
   honoring feeling as prophetic act

5. Intimacy as imperative (8–9)
   vision of friendship
   need for trust

6. Language that is honest and direct (9–10)
   heart, earth, common speech
   direct style
   breaks down emotional barriers

7. Owning of self (10–11)
   self definition
   framing own vision
   refusing male definitions of self
   taking life into own hands
   distance and closeness
   centrality of agency
   finding self as prerequisite to finding God

8. Unity of life (11–12)

9. Relationship (12)
   primal unity demands relationship
   promise and danger
   illusion of autonomy

10. Prophetic voice for justice (12–13)
    moral and political commitment
    call others to action
    salvation tied to well being of all creation

11. Revising cultural myths (14–15)
power in retelling
challenge the canon

12. Revisioning the Divine (15–16)
immanent
incarnated
vulnerable
female images
one who receives
protects
holds
brings forth life

That view of the sacred focused on the embodiment of women and ways of knowing through that embodiment. Sewell found herself nourished by the wisdom, courage, and love of the women's words.[16] Her perspective from the late 1980s gave her a clearer vision of themes that were developing since the 1960s, making her topical organization of women's theological themes reflective of the direction of women's theology at that time.

Sewell organized the sources of authority that women used in their theological reflections into twelve categories. Taken together, those categories result in a new starting point for women's understanding of themselves and the divine.

She begins by objecting to the traditional Western body/spirit dichotomy. Beginning with Pauline theology, Western theological work has followed the Greek body/spirit dichotomy, idealizing the spirit and denigrating the body. Paul, like Aristotle and Plato before him, stressed the necessity of disciplining the body and keeping it under control, lest one's physical appetites get the better of one's spiritual sensibilities.[17]

The body and its weakness have also been identified with femaleness. Women have been portrayed as weak in themselves. In identifying women with the body and men with the spirit, women, by definition, are inadequate. Aristotle's view of function led to his belief that women

16. Ibid., xvii.

17. 1 Cor 9:23–27.

could not engage in moral reasoning.[18] Biblical interpretations of women as temptress, the cause of men's moral downfall is a related and common theme in Western theology and literature.

In her collection of women's poetry, Sewell reports that women clearly reject both the mind/spirit dichotomy and its implications of feminine weakness. Instead women understand the spirit and the flesh as an integral unity.[19] They begin with the body, refusing a separation of matter and spirit. The body, in fact, is one with the sacred.

That positive view not only elevates women but transforms the sexual relationship. No longer seen as a struggle to dominate, the goals of sexual intimacy become invitation, reception, and renewal. No longer is the body to be feared and avoided, battered into submission and eternal youthfulness. Rather, the body is seen as a source of joy and a fountain of knowledge. In knowing our bodies we know ourselves and connect with God who created us.

The integration begun by rejecting the body/spirit dichotomy expanded as women used nature as a metaphor in poetry.[20] The natural world becomes a source of authority for women. Its sacredness is recognized intuitively. The fertility of nature and its connection with humans lead to a perception of a kind of unity that links the body with life and power. The natural world is seen, not as something to be conquered, but as an integrated whole with women's bodies, knowledge, and understanding of the sacred. Father Daniel Berrigan picked up on that connection in his poem "Revelation."

Along with nature as a metaphor, Sewell notes that the writer herself becomes an authority for theological knowledge.[21] There is, for these women an internal source of truth, meaning, and identity. Their daily experience of ordinary life becomes a source of truth for them. Those insights stand in stark contrast to the Western enlightenment tradition that understands truth "revealed" through intellectual reason and science.

Judith Shapiro, in *Sources of the Spring: Mothers Through the Eyes of Women Writers*, provides an example of the integration of women's thought with embodied practices. She tells a story of Margaret Mead's

18. Aristotle, *Nichomachean Ethics*, 290–91: "Men could reach for the divine through exercising practical reason because man's highest nature is rational. Women could not hope to participate in such a quest."

19. Sewell, *Cries of the Spirit*, 33–36.

20. Ibid., 5–6.

21. Ibid., 6–7.

mother walking fifteen miles to a book sale and then painting the ceiling of her kitchen. She stepped out of prescribed role activities and nurtured both body and mind in diverse ways despite the criticism of others.[22]

Here the inner experience of women becomes authoritative, not only for what they may choose to do but also for evaluating larger systems of injustice. Speaking from her conscience, a woman can critique systemic injustice without allowing intellectual arguments to unbalance her.

An example from my own life came when in my study of social ethics I was presented with a manuscript that argued that an atomic bomb could be dropped on a city as an act of love. The argument went back to Augustine's idea of sin as lodged in motives rather than acts. In short, the argument stated that if one's motive was loving, e.g. to protect the establishment of justice in the world so that humans could flourish, then dropping an atomic bomb was not only justified by just war theory, it could be considered an act of love. It took me about five seconds to reject this argument. However rationally defensible, it was self-evidently nonsensical. Later I read works of the critical theorists and Jean Bethke Elshtain's critique of Hegel, gaining a better intellectual grasp of how such reasoning can go so badly wrong.[23] But I knew it intuitively immediately.

The fragmentation of the Western intellectual tradition, in which reason can lead to incredibly unreasonable ethical dictums, needs a revision that can identify wholeness. The focus on ordinary experience and the inner life as sources of authority in knowing can become part of that revisioning. Zygmunt Bauman argues that post-modern ethics may begin to correct the "search for universals" emphasis in modern ethics by sweeping away modern Western "universal ethics" and allowing individual conscience to resurface as a source of authority in ethics.[24] The women writers of the 1960s to 1990s brought together by Sewell have made this move.

Expressions of women's inner experience through feelings now becomes a source for theological reflection. Avoiding sentimentality, Sewell's poets pour out their feelings as an expression of the life force. Anger, for instance, can direct a woman to identify her objections to a situation.[25]

---

22. Shapiro, *Sources of the Spring*, 18.

23. Elshtain, *Public Man, Private Woman*, 176–77.

24. Bauman, *Postmodern Ethics*, 14–15.

25. Harrison, *Making the Connections*, 25.

The "no" of her angry feelings can lead her to a "yes" by directing her to an alternative action or life style that is more true to herself.[26] Rather than denigrating feelings as the Western intellectual tradition has done, relegating them to a less valuable stance than thoughts, women elevate feelings, listening to them, finding wisdom in them, and using them as an authoritative source for action in their lives.

As feelings relating to the place of love and belonging in life thus become a focus for women.[27] Women see the longing for union not as something that puts them out of control of their lives but as something that can *bring* life.[28] Separating themselves from others because relationships often involve pain is not an option for women who believe in the integration of all of life. Instead, women honor feelings as a prophetic act.[29] Feelings become an authority, leading one to take a course of action that, were those feelings suppressed, would not appear as an option.

Woody Allen's comedy *The Curse of the Jade Scorpion* gets laughs by portraying a woman who listens to her head not her heart. She becomes an efficiency expert, but at the same time, she comes to all the wrong conclusions about truth and love. Eventually, she changes her course, trusting her feelings to direct her life. Who benefits? Woody Allen, of course. But Helen Hunt, who plays the silly woman in the story, also finds her way to happiness.

Feelings are complicated. Following them and can result in disaster as well as productive outcomes. Psychologists continue to work on the complex arena of feelings. But, beginning to trust feelings and use them as a source of authority for seeking truth and goodness, can aid women in critiquing their socialization and finding new paths for seeking justice and finding fulfillment. We have seen the use of emotions in theology as a theme in this project.

As inner experience and feelings become authorities for women, intimacy as an imperative becomes an authoritative source for women. The hero of the solitary warrior, so prevalent in Western literature, gives way to an alternative vision of friendship.[30] Elisabeth Moltmann-Wendel, in her book *Rediscovering Friendship*, argues that women's experience of

26. Sewell, *Cries of the Spirit*, 6.

27. Ibid., 7–8.

28. Ibid., 7.

29. Ibid., 8.

30. Ibid.

friendship is an important step in breaking old patterns of domination, hierarchy and violence.[31] The autonomous thinker, the self-sufficient individual, the one who stands against others, can be set aside for a model of friendship that is life-giving. Sallie McFague points out that in Hebrew thought, the opposite of friend is not enemy but stranger.[32] God can also be understood as a friend, "a sisterly companion, who helps us to cope with life in its complexity."[33] Sewell speaks of the need for developing trust, finding the wisdom of choosing intimacy as a source for life.[34]

Trust can be developed through honest communication, so it is no surprise that the next authoritative source for women brought out by Sewell is the use of language that is honest and direct.[35] Speaking honestly from the heart, using common speech in a direct style gives others the opportunity to trust the speaker. It does this by breaking down emotional barriers and opening others to the heart of the speaker. In this way, a direct style, Sewell asserts, speaks essence, breaking the ladders of hierarchy.

Jürgen Habermas in *The Theory of Comunicative Action* argues that in communication geared to understanding, persons have three expectations: truth, rightness, and sincerity.[36] In using honest and direct language as an authoritative source for knowledge, women are claiming those expectations as they communicate. Habermas sees those expectations operating in the life world, the cultural and interpersonal arenas of life. In the lifeworld the desire for understanding outweighs the search for power and money, goals that govern the systems of economics and politics. It is within the lifeworld that women have traditionally lived. It is there that art and beauty thrive. However, as women move more and more into the systems of economics and politics, they can carry those expectations of truth rightness and sincerity in communication into those realms.

Inner experience, feelings, intimacy, and honest communication cannot be utilized as authoritative sources for knowledge and theology

31. Moltmann-Wendel, *Rediscovering Friendship*, 5.

32. Quoted in ibid., 7.

33. Ibid., 5.

34. Sewell, *Cries of the Spirit*, 9.

35. Ibid., 9–10.

36. Habermas, *Theory of Communicative Action*, 1:398.

without an owning of self.[37] Unless a woman frames her own vision, refusing male definitions of who she is or should strive to become, her inner experience is muddled. She cannot communicate honestly because she does not yet know herself. Like Helen Hunt in *The Curse of the Jade Scorpion*, she thinks a lot, charts her course coldly, but has little understanding of either herself or others. In the owning of self, a woman stops defining herself in terms that others give to her. She takes her life into her own hands.[38] She becomes the decider in her life. In other words, her own agency becomes a primary source of authority, not only in her thoughts or feelings, but in her actions.

In many cultures, both Western and Eastern, women are socialized to fulfill the expectations of others. Family priorities and structured religious roles often define life for a woman. Having children, supporting her husband, caring for aging parents, and becoming a model of morality for society go a long way in defining a woman in Indonesian society, for example. When women begin to allow their sense of agency to become a source of authority in their lives, they often chart a different course. In my own study, *Christian Women in Indonesia*, women changed drastically as they asserted their agency in their families and their society. As in this study, change often began with a sense of calling from God.[39] Owning of self and theology are linked from the beginning.

The owning of self does not imply an individualistic autonomy but rather a mediation of distance and closeness that can help a woman discover the unity of life, another source of authority for women.[40] Moltmann-Wendel argues that the closeness of friendship must be balanced by a detachment that respects the mystery and strangeness of the other.[41] In discovering her own unique power, a woman becomes able to appreciate the mystery of the other, seeing both sameness and difference in the other. In that way, finding self as a distinct and powerful agent prepares a woman to grasp the unity of life, a theme brought out by contemporary women missiologists in this study.

It may also become a path to finding God, the creator of life in all of its intricate connections. Loving our neighbor as ourselves presupposes

---

37. Sewell, *Cries of the Spirit*, 10–11.

38. Ibid., 11.

39. See Adeney, *Christian Women in Indonesia*, ch. 4.

40. Sewell, *Cries of the Spirit*, 11–12.

41. Moltmann-Wendel, *Rediscovering Friendship*, 6.

knowing and valuing ourselves. Because of socialization that denigrates women, adult women in need to learn to value themselves, to own their uniqueness, opening the way to appreciating the God who created women in love.

The unity of life can then become a source of knowledge for women. Centering ourselves in the web of life gives women wisdom as we see ourselves as part of an intricate unity that does not obliterate our distinctness but honors it. This understanding of the unity of life is not emeshment, an inability to distinguish self from others. Using the unity of life as an authoritative source for knowledge assumes that women have gone beyond emeshment to an understanding of unity as being a part of all that lives.[42]

If life is a unity, relationships become necessary to exhibit and dwell in that unity. The illusion of autonomy gives way to an understanding of primal unity that demands relationships.[43] Those relationships become crucial to a woman's artistic development and moral choices.

Sallie Sinclair, wife of a highway patrolman in Texas began to do calligraphy before she married. The busyness of life overtook that hobby until her husband needed some calligraphy work done for his job. His encouragement to get back into her artistic endeavor reinvigorated Sallie who began to use her calligraphy art to highlight Christian themes in church publications, engrave wedding invitations and illustrate Biblical themes. She credited her "dear husband Burt" for making it possible for her to do calligraphy and engrave.[44]

Carol Gilligan, social psychologist, showed that women making moral judgments use relationships as a major source for their decisions.[45] Rather than rely on independent choice or autonomous action, women see the web of their relationships as an important source of authority for moral action.

That path includes both promise and danger. There is the promise of sustaining relationships and making moral choices that make sense for the family and community, and not just to advance the interests of the individual. Danger lies in the possible loss of boundaries of the self, opening women up to the emeshment that destroys a sense of ownership

---

42. Sewell, *Cries of the Spirit*, 12.

43. Ibid.

44. Gum, "Designing Woman," 14.

45. Gilligan, *In a Different Voice*, 105. See a cross-cultural analysis of Gilligan's theory in Adeney, *Christian Women in Indonesia*, ch. 9, 154 and 163–64.

of one's self. Despite that danger, women in Sewell's anthology as women in this study understand relationships as central to life. Women face the dangers of relationships, holding out for the fulfillment and well-being that they promise. The choice of relationship as a source of authority for women is a reasoned one, connected to all of the sources that have been described, especially feelings, intimacy, and unity.

As women understand their lives to be connected in significant ways with the lives of others, a prophetic voice for justice becomes a source of authority for them in their lives.[46] According to Sewell, moral and political commitments are common among women owning their own lives in these new ways. A call to others to act on behalf of those that have no voice becomes a feature of women's poetry and theology. For example, widowed Dalit women whose husbands had been killed by their landlords in 1985 protested against that injustice by refusing to return to their homes. They sang a song as an appeal for justice: "In distress and at all times We will praise you, mighty God, O, our Redeemer and Salvation."[47] They appealed to the church to aid the many women of India living in poverty. For those women and many others, a woman's own sense of well-being is tied to the well-being of others. Sallie McFague expands that notion with her theology of abundant life. For her, as for Sewell's poets, there is no individual redemption—redemption is tied to the well-being of all creation. "We must see ourselves as both radically dependent on nature and as supremely responsible for it."[48]

It is evident in the above descriptions that women are viewing their lives in new ways. They are grasping their own power and agency as persons of value; yet at the same time, they are asserting their connections with others. They are seeing the need for justice, not only for women, but for all of creation; and they are speaking out about it. The form of their communication in Sewell's anthology is poetry.

In order to do these things, the cultural myths women have been taught must be revised. Women are finding in those revisions, a source of authority for their lives [49] They find power in retelling stories of women from the past. Although much of women's history has been lost, there is much to be rediscovered and celebrated. Clarissa Pinkola Estés retells

46. Sewell, *Cries of the Spirit*, 12–15.

47. Devi, "Struggle of *Dalit* Christian Women," 136.

48. McFague, *Abundant Life*, 210.

49. Sewell, *Cries of the Spirit*, 14–15.

many myths that empower women in her book *Women Who Run With the Wolves*. She laments the depth of the struggle women often go through simply to do what they long to do in the world. Estes finds that retelling archetypal stories can help women break out of cultural stereotypes and move from inaction to empowerment.[50]

Women writers and theologians are challenging the Western canon, questioning the choice of classics that shape our cultural myths. They are reevaluating the dearth of women scholars in the vast collections of great thinkers in the Western world—philosophers, theologians, scientists. Women scholars are rediscovering and including women in the wisdom literature of the Western world.

Finally, women are re-visioning understandings of the Divine.[51] God has been pictured in classical Western theology as transcendent, omniscient, and distant. Women are discovering other qualities in God that are also present in the Bible and tradition. God as immanent, incarnated, and vulnerable become themes for women's theologies. God can be pictured as one who receives, protects, and holds, Sewell points out. Cynthia Crysdale's theology of the cross in *Embracing Travail* stresses the suffering of Jesus as a point of relationship with suffering women everywhere.[52]

Female images of God became a focus for women during the late twentieth century. In the 1970s *Christa*, a sculpture portraying Jesus on the cross in female form, toured seminaries in the U.S. Hymnals began to change masculine language to inclusive language for people and sometimes for God. Metaphors for God as One who brings forth life, biblical references of God as a mother that cares for and nurses her children began to be more commonly used in preaching and writing.

Those themes began to be preached in churches by women pastors. A sermon I once gave at a the Berkeley House Church for an Easter sunrise service during the 1980s was titled "Rainbow Maker, Fire Bringer." It used biblical passages to bring out aspects of the resurrected Christ that were not often stressed in traditional services. At the end of the sermon, the children of the congregation released helium balloons, as a visual picture of Christ as rainbow maker, healer of the universe and lover of children.

---

50. Estés, *Women Who Run*, 56.

51. Sewell, *Cries of the Spirit*, 15–16.

52. Crysdale, *Embracing Travail*, 76.

Advantages of Poetry as a Medium for Theological Reflection

As this chapter shows, women are branching out in their theological reflections, utilizing history, art, myths, experience, and relationships. Sewell brings out the sources of authority women can utilize in using poetry as a medium for theological reflection.

Poetry does indeed make an excellent medium for women to express their theological reflections for a number of reasons:

Reasons for Using Poetry as a Medium for Theological Reflection

Ordinary: Topics can be small and focused on ordinary life, not necessarily large or abstract.

Freedom: Women can use free expression, not bound by usual conventions of theology.

Universal: Anyone can write poetry, not necessary to publish.

Personal: Poetry focuses on personal experience, a major source of authority for women's theology.

Feelings: Focus on expression of feelings in poetry advantages the integration of the affective domain into theological reflection.

Integration: Integrated, non-linear, uses right brain and allows artistic expression, acceptable for women.

Ordinary Life

Many women turn to ordinary life in their theological reflections. Women's days are often filled with caring for family and home, attending to the needs of others. Even women in workplaces or careers participate in the details of ordinary life. Experiences in that realm make excellent topics for poems. Either inadvertently or purposefully, women use those topics for theological reflection. Mary Bednarowski in *The Religious Imagination of American Women* shows how contemporary women in the U.S. express the immanence of God through a focus on ordinary life.

Jane McAvoy's edited book, *Kitchen Talk: Sharing Our Stories of Faith* describes women meeting together to share their everyday efforts to live with integrity. The women that share their stories in this book are doing theology. Their situations, their issues, their faith, and their struggles become grist for the mill as they construct local theologies of pain, of comfort, of healing, and of reaching out to others. This is theology on the ground and we see the struggles up close and personal. The influence of everyday practices in developing their theological ideas is crucial for our work with women doing mission theology, as many mission women have done theological reflection through taking action, writing letters, having conversations, or other informal means.

Poetry offers a mode of expression to women that does not confine their ideas. Unlike traditional theological writing, poetry is not bound by topic, e.g. God, humanity, sin, salvation. Writing poetry allows women to express theological ideas about topics that have not been considered theological at all. Instead writing poetry offers a blank palette upon which women can express their thoughts. Women may write poetry about topics considered theological—God, humans, sin, salvation. Or they may write poetry about other topics.

Anthologies of poetry such as Sewell, Jane Kenyon and Emily Dickinson exhibit very theological results. God's presence or absence in the everyday may delight or startle the reader. Ideas that may have escaped the notice of traditional, male oriented, theological writing come into play in women's poetry. Those ideas may express deep theological truths about God's action in the world and relationship to people that can broaden understandings of the holy and benefit contemporary Christians.

Freedom

The freedom of writing poetry extends beyond choice of topics. Although writing poetry is usually not discouraged, no pressure to publish or exhibit their poems comes from society. Women are free to write their thoughts and feelings without censorship. Sometimes it is in the writing of thoughts that clarity emerges. Writing poetry offers women the freedom to explore their experiences and feelings. New insights may be discovered through the freedom one senses in writing not theology, but a poem.

Universal

Another reason poetry provides a good medium for women doing theology is the universality of writing poetry. One need not be a writer. One need not consider oneself a poet to write poetry. Anyone can do it. One need not share their poems with others but keep them as a private journal. The writing itself fulfills a longing in a person. And so young and old people alike write poetry, for themselves. Women express longings, describe experiences, formulate meanings, and question the anguish and joy of life in their poetry. A woman's theology comes out in her poems even when she hasn't intended the poem to be an expression of theology.

Personal

The medium is both artistic and personal. It requires no references to theological writings of others. The criteria for poetry focuses on expression and aesthetics rather than content. One's personal ideas become valid in this medium. Women can communicate on theological themes without fear of censorship since it is the personal and aesthetic that judges a poem, not the "theologically correct" in anyone's view.

Feelings

As women write poetry, they bring out their feelings about whatever topic they are writing about. The affective domain of feelings has not been a part of some sectors of Western theological writings for a long time. Feelings become a major focus in poetry, as one aim of the poet may be to stimulate certain feelings in the reader. Using inner experience as a source of authority for their beliefs, writing poetry about their feelings can unlock that inner experience, bringing it to expression.

Integration

Through those efforts integration occurs, both in the theology and in the life of the woman herself. She becomes more whole and experiences the uniqueness of herself. She clarifies relationships with others, with society, and with God. She wrestles with questions of meaning and belief as well as experiences and feelings.

My own sensibilities about prayer were clarified at a visit to Gedono Women's Trappist Monastery in Indonesia. As I waited on the steps of the chapel listening to the Sisters singing, I watched a frog sitting in the pond and composed this Haiku poem:

The frog sat on the lily pad, not waiting. Later reflection led to an article about meditation that was published in *Buddhist-Christian Studies.*

Those multiple reasons for using poetry in theological reflection form an invitation to women to struggle with and express their theology through poetry. The medium is universal, there is a freedom in writing poetry that escapes traditional confinements, and women are empowered to give thoughtful attention to their feelings about ordinary life. The integration of the affective arena with the cognitive process of expression through language encourages a holistic form of theological reflection. This integrated non-linear medium allows artistic expression, acceptable for women that may feel limited by their socialization or received theological method. Topics can be small, not necessarily the large abstract topics of theology proper but ordinary things that bring a woman to reflect on the big picture. Poetry breaks through the usual boundaries of theological reflection, making it an excellent tool for women doing theology.

Contributions to mission theology from using poetry as a medium for theological reflection can be many and varied. Writing hymns, poetic essays about experiences with nature, and poems about ordinary life each contribute to the richness of contemporary mission theologies.

The next chapter takes a look back at Christian history to set this and other themes of women's mission theology and practice in a broader framework.

Part III

13

Women Doing Mission Theology
through the Ages

Precisely because of their grip on the popular imagination of church
people, the memories of leading women missionary "saints and martyrs"
have been sites of power struggles in the churches.

—ROBERT, "INFLUENCE OF AMERICAN MISSIONARY WOMEN," 80

THE CHURCH HAS A long history of women doing mission theology.
Although the lineage has been broken in places, records of how women
did mission and what they thought about it are available for those who
would seek them out. This chapter explores theologies of women from
New Testament times to the present day. Some were written. Some were
spoken. All were lived. All of those theologies had consequences in the
contexts in which they were practiced. Societies were influenced. Women
doing theology were sometimes lauded. At other times they were pun-
ished. The history of women doing mission theology reveals diverse attitudes and impacts of women's mission theology.

Those consequences are set against a background of cultures that
deprecated women and their talents. Greek and Roman societies each
displayed perjorative views of women. Aristotle thought that reasoning about moral issues was a virtue of the ruling class.[1] Women were,
of course, excluded. Aristotle, along with most philosophers of the day
believed that women were a substandard form of humanity, incomplete

---

1. Aristotle, *Ethics*, 3.4.1277b.

males.[2] Hebrew views also castigated women, although a few women rose to prominence in Jewish writings. Pagan goddesses were an exception to those views. However, both gods and goddesses had limited power in the Greek and Roman religious worlds.

The Early Church and Women

Those classical and Hebrew views contrast with Jesus' exceptional attitudes toward women. He interacted with numerous women, showing them respect as well as care. Women traveled with Jesus, supporting him in his ministry, and becoming his friends. Specific accounts of Jesus' interactions with women in the gospels show honor for women and respect for women's intelligence. He praised Mary's action of choosing to learn from him rather than help in the kitchen (Luke 10:41f.). He healed the woman with the issue of blood, announcing to the crowd that her faith had healed her (Luke 8:48). He talked theology with the Samaritan woman at the well, drawing her into conversation and revealing himself to her in a special way (John 4:1–25). He listened to the Syro-Phoenician woman's plea for a daughter's healing, allowing his own perjorative views to be corrected by her (Matt 15:21–28). He praised a woman for anointing his feet with perfume, interpreting her action as a symbol of love and forgiving her sins (Luke 7:44–48). As he died on the cross, he made provision for his own mother to be cared for by one of the disciples (John 19:27). Over and over again in accounts of Jesus' life he displayed high regard for women.

Consequently as Jesus' teachings spread and the Christian movement began, women sponsors and leaders were a common feature of this new religion. Prominent women of the New Testament supported Jesus and established churches in their homes. Women helped the Apostle Paul with teaching and spreading the gospel. Priscilla, along with her husband Aquila, took the lead in training leaders (Acts 18:26). Paul commemorated Junia's work as an apostle (Rom 16:7) and praised the many women who fostered the Christian way in those early days (Rom 16).

As the church became established, many of those gains for women were lost. Early church fathers reverted to prejorative cultural views of women. Tertullian argued that women were the cause of sin in the world. Although positive attitudes about women characterized some

---

2. Aristotle, *Generation of Animals*, 29.

of Augustine's thinking, he also espoused negative views of women. As time went on, translations of the New Testament were altered, changing feminine names to masculine ones. Paul and Peter's letters to churches correcting behavior of specific women were generalized to include all Christian women.

As a result, earlier cultural attitudes toward women, mostly negative, resurfaced in the church. Women were seen as a danger, particularly a sexual danger. Roles were circumscribed to family chores. Women were taught to obey their husbands and to be silent in the churches. Jesus' generous and respectful attitudes toward women were ignored or downplayed. Paul's gratefulness to women leaders was submerged under interpretations of Adam and Eve as unequal partners, Eve playing the weaker role and targeted as the cause of Adam's separation from God (I Tim. 2:14). As institutionalization continued and authoritarian male structures were put in place, the early church lost its liberating power to save women from degradation and utilize their gifts of intellect, commitment, and energy to further the Kingdom.

Monastic Option for Women

During the third to twelfth centuries, Christian women found another way to pursue their faith and intellectual development. Women's monasteries were formed, often independently from the formal church. Because women had no official teaching role, some claimed a special link to an immediate revelation from God. They spoke and wrote out of the authority of their own spiritual experiences, an authority sometimes accepted by the male authorities of the church.

Usually that came about if a woman found a male mentor or sponsor that would argue her case for her with church authorities. Some Church Fathers and leaders aided in the foundation of women's religious communities. Augustine encouraged women in this way and his sister, Perpetua founded an order for women in his diocese. From the fourth century on, support of a male Christian leader became essential as the male hierarchy tried to enforce a uniformity of practice and doctrine.[3] With that uniformity, by the sixth century all major cities of central France established communities for women under Bishop Caesarius.[4]

---

3. Anderson and Zinsser, *History of Their Own*, 1:75–76.

4. Wemple, *Women in Frankish Society*, cited in ibid., 75–76.

Influential women also founded monasteries. Queen Radegund (518–87) fled from her husband, Frankish king Clothar I, and founded a community for women at Poitiers. By the ninth century, women and their mentors had created an alternative to the conventional role of wife and mother for women. A new option opened up for them. They could leave their families, forbear marriage and childrearing, and devote themselves to prayer and study as "brides of Christ." By the thirteenth century not only women in religious orders but lay women were devoting themselves to religious piety and caring for the weak through associations of Beguines.[5]

Despite those developments, women's subordination in the church and society continued. They came under both the age-old traditions of male dominance and female subordination and the church injunctions for women to be "meek, quiet, gentle, sincere, free from anger, not talkative, not clamorous, not hasty of speech, not given to evil speaking, not capricious, not double-tongued, not a busybody."[6]

Medieval Christian Women in Europe

Both empowered and subordinated, women continued to do theology, often using artistic images and forms. Meththild of Magdeburg, a Beguine living in Europe in the thirteenth century wrote her book, *The Flowing Light of the Godhead*, combining ideas of courtly love with Christian bridal mysticism. Although warned against writing by her Dominican confessor, Meththild continued to write prophesies, instructions, dialogues, and poems.[7]

Women's desire to serve God through doing theology and increasing constraints by social and religious forces collided in the Middle Ages. Inquisitions grew stronger and reached a fever pitch during the witch hunts of the sixteenth and seventeenth centuries. A conservative estimate of the number of European women killed during this time is 100,000.[8] Women that wrote of the primacy of love, like Marguarite Porete were burned at the stake. Illiterate peasant women were also at risk of accusations of witchcraft and devil worship. England, France, and Germany

---

5. Ibid., 223.

6. Wemple, *Women in Frankish Society*, cited in ibid., 81–82.

7. Roberts, "Fear and Women's Writings," 21–22.

8. Anderson and Zinsser, *History of Their Own*, 1:167.

all saw massive persecution of women under charges of heresy, desecration of Christian rituals, and witchcraft during the late 1500s. Eventually the movement spread so widely that even male church officials were in danger of being declared heretics. Consequently by 1613, authorities refused to hear new accusations and by the 1730s, in England accusations were considered "fraud." But superstitions about the powers of women to cause evil in their villages persisted into the twentieth century.[9]

Women of the Reformation

As early Christianity had spawned an amazing vitality and equality of women, so too the Reformation revived notions of women's value and leadership capabilities. This was the second time in history that restrictions on female believers were questioned. The Protestant doctrine of the priesthood of all believers suggested equal status for the chosen, whether female or male. German Baptists asserted that women were the spiritual equals of men. Katherine Zell, a Protestant leader and wife of Matthew Zell, likened God to a mother who had known the pangs of childbirth and the joys of breastfeeding.[10] Reformation women, from queens to peasants responded to those ideas, speaking of their relationship with Christ and challenging state and church structures that restricted women. All of the new sects advocated literacy for women, a crucial factor in the emancipation of women in church and society in the coming centuries. Many women of the Reformation influenced their villages and countries, sometimes giving their lives for their convictions.[11]

Such changes were possible because the church was in a state of ferment. New ideas and forms of worship dominated the three wings of the Reformation as well as the counter-reformation of the Catholic Church. That fluidity in Christianity made space for special talents and voices of women. Women taught, influenced their politically powerful husbands, and sometimes changed the religion of the state itself. They founded new religious orders and became patrons of religious leaders. Some Protestant women played significant roles in the wars that arose out of the political and religious conflicts of the sixteenth and seventeenth centuries, using

9. Ibid., 171–73.

10. Ibid., 228–29.

11. See Zahl, *Five Women* and Tavard, *Women in Christian.*

their influence to help refugees, gain acceptance for religious orders, or protect sect leaders from harm.[12]

Those powerful opportunities were not to last however. With the institutionalization of Protestant churches after the Reformation, women's opportunities were again curtailed. Unfortunately, according to historians Bonnie S. Anderson and Judith P. Zinsser, the post-Reformation restrictions were more limiting than past restrictions. Although Protestant and Counter-Reformation Catholics disagreed about many doctrines, they held unanimity when it came to restricting women. Protestant denominations generalized Pauline passages about propriety in worship (1 Cor 11:3–10; 14:34) to include all women, not only the women addressed in the letters. Roman Catholic authorities emphasized wifely and motherly roles for women modeled on the Holy Family. All churches limited women's roles to the home sphere and stressed obedience to husbands, humility, and salvation through childbearing as major doctrinal points. Martin Luther declared,

> The rule remains with the husband, and the wife is compelled to obey him by God's command. He rules the home and the state, wages war, defends his possessions, tills the soil, builds, plants, etc. The woman on the other hand is like a nail driven into the wall . . . so the wife should stay at home and look after the affairs of the household, as one who has been deprived of the ability of administering those affairs that are outside and that concern the state. She does not go beyond her most personal duties.[13]

That sums up the institutional consensus of churches after the reformation. Since the authorities claimed Scriptural sources for this view, framing it as the command of God, that powerful consensus of post-reformation churches has continued to remain strong, still operating in some twenty-first century contexts.

Women in Sixteenth- to Eighteenth-Century Europe

In work, economics, and marriage, sixteenth- to eighteenth-century Europe saw women of every class defined by their relationships to men: grandfathers, fathers, brothers, and sons. Lower-class girls aged twelve or younger worked away from home on farms, in domestic service or in

---

12. Anderson and Zissner, *History of Their Own*, 229–34.

13. Luther, quoted in Tavard, *Women in Christian Tradition*, 174.

cottage industries. They earned their dowries, about fifty pounds, by the age of twenty-five, at which time they married. Middle- or upper-class women depended on their family of origin for their dowry and marriage arrangements. The Catholic Church provided orders for women that allowed some to remain celibate. Protestant women sometimes became spinsters, but the norm was marriage and motherhood.

Motherhood was fraught with difficulties as infant mortality was high and multiple pregnancies unavoidable for many women. The mother's role was to nurture the child and she was expected to hold control over the child's body and mind. If the child survived infancy, the mother's role became education. She taught her daughters cooking, needlework and all other tasks defined for girls in the home.

That training took many girls into domestic service. The 1540 Norwich census records four-fifths of girls between the ages of six and twelve working in the urban domestic industry as compared to less than one third of boys. In that situation, girls learned survival skills from their mothers. Since marriage was driven by economic considerations, mothers often set aside part of their earnings for their daughter's dowry. That "dowry bonding" cemented the mother-daughter relationship even past the early teenage years when most European parents parted with their children.

Many girls grew up without a mother, in orphanages or caring for widowed fathers and brothers. The loss of a mother presented a huge blow to any family but particularly for families of the lower classes. On the other hand, becoming a widow was sometimes a boon to an aristocratic woman as her sizable dowry sustained her in the event of her husband's death. Poorer women could depend on no such luxury and were often left in middle age with adolescent families and insufficient means to support them. The best protected women were those who ran small businesses with their husbands before they died and could carry on alone. In any class situation, however, creativity and independent action was required for widowed women. Many of the survival skills they needed were developed with the help of their own mothers during the earlier dowry-raising years.

Women outside the bonds of family and the roles of daughter, wife, and mother found life challenging indeed. It was those women who had no family or whose family could not support them that forced change toward women's independence as the eighteenth century drew to a close.[14]

Worldwide Missionary Movement

The late nineteenth- and early twentieth-century a worldwide mission movement once again opened doors for women. In the early 1800s in the United States, excitement for Christian mission work overseas began to be felt in the churches. During the early 1800s, the first American women foreign missionaries went overseas. Women went overseas with their husbands, continuing to do the work of pastor's wives in foreign settings, working alongside of their husbands to speak, heal, and nurture. The gender-based mission theories of the times constrained them to the role of wife and mother, their theological writings encapsulated in diaries and letters. Because single women missionaries were not sent by churches, some women with a call to mission married men that were headed for China, India, or other overseas destinations. During this time, women from Europe and the United States swelled the ranks of missionaries, translating scripture, writing hymns, working with the poor, teaching and preaching about the gospel.

By the late 1800s single women from the U.S. and Europe were accepted as missionaries. Maria Fearing who founded a school for girls in the Congo was among the many American Protestant women that initiated and sustained strong global and national mission programs.[15] By the early twentieth century there were more than forty women's missionary societies in the United States.[16] Both denominational and independent women's missionary societies were formed. "Women's work for women" became a major theme in women's missionary work.

By 1910 as the women's missionary movement peaked, themes of world friendship and ecumenicity dominated the movement. Both Protestant and Catholic women from the U.S. founded and continued mission work overseas and published missiological reflections in church magazines and newsletters. Mission work was the pre-eminent womens's "cause" in mainline churches before ordination became widespread.[17]

14. Davis and Farge, *History of Women*, 3:39–41.

15. Lloyd-Sidle, *Celebrating Our Call*, 86–87.

16. Robert, *Christian Mission*, 128.

17. Robert, "Influence of American Missionary Women," 59.

From the time of World War I until the mid twentieth century, two out of three Protestant missionaries were women.[18] Catholic missionary sisters organized collection boxes at schools and churches.[19]

However, by the 1930s many women's mission societies, along with the theologies they had spawned merged into male-dominated church structures. The holistic quality of women's work, addressing evangelism plus human needs, proclamation plus compassion became incorporated into the general mission agendas of churches and mission organizations. The patterns of women's mission theologies during this movement emphasized interpersonal work and concern for women and children. A connection between spiritual and physical dimensions of life led many women to focus on education and healing. Ecumenical cooperation developed easily as women were not leaders of church institutions or gatekeepers of theological orthodoxy. Many of the first ecumenical mission organizations were begun by women. Women's mission spirituality of this era also included a spirituality of self-sacrifice. The overall effects of those themes resulted in a hiddenness of women's mission theologies and a vision of church as less an institution than as a way of life. The process of incorporating those major theological themes into the general mission theory and theology of the churches proceeded without impediment.[20]

As the twentieth century went on, the merging of women's theologies into the churches and growing movement of independent mission organization had a significant impact on mission theologies and practice. Women's achievements in education and health care dominated the mission scene in the United States.

Two Waves of Women's Movements as a Global Phenomenon

Alongside of the missionary movements of the late nineteenth and early twentieth centuries, women's movements sprang up in many places in the world. Indonesia, the U.S., England, China, and some countries in Europe, are examples of places in which women's organizations began working for emancipation, equality , and social justice during this time. Many Christian women supported the first wave of feminism in the U.S.

18. Robert, *Gospel Bearers*, 59.

19. Ibid.

20. Above section indebted to Robert, *American Women in Mission*, ch. 4.

at the same time. They spoke out against slavery, joined the temperance movement, fought for women's right to vote, and worked across racial and class divisions to show the veracity of God's love for the world.

Reasons for this widespread struggle for change in women's status are many and complex. Revolutions against colonial powers utilized the talents and strengths of women. Ideals of humanism and universal suffrage spread through improved communication systems. Reason itself, the queen of the European Enlightenment seemed to demand freedom and emancipation for all. The doctrine of natural rights combined with Renaissance humanism and a Christian idea of humans created in God's image. Together those ideas formed a strong ideological base for equality and emancipation for women that Christian women could support.

The goals of this "first wave" of women's movements were clear. Women participated vigorously in the struggles for the vote, equal rights, legal status, and opportunities for education and work. By the mid-nineteenth century, women in England had gained child custody rights and divorce reform. In the United States, Susan B. Anthony and Elizabeth Cady Stanton led the battle for the ballot while Margaret Sanger fought for women's right to birth control.[21] In Indonesia Sujatin Kartowijono worked for women's education and organized the Women's Congress of Indonesia.[22] Meanwhle, Likas Tarigan of North Sumatra, along with many others, set an example by becoming a teacher and speaking out for women's rights.[23] Active throughout the century in the nationalist movement, women obtained equal political rights when the constitution of the new Republic of Indonesia was accepted in 1945. In recognition of those and other women's movements for reform, the United Nations established the Commission on the Status of Women in 1948.

In the United States a movement of religious feminism also moved boldly into male-dominated arenas of religious life. Publication of *The Woman's Bible* and women's struggle for entry into Christian theological schools brought the issue of women's rights and ability to provide church leadership into the public view. Women preachers, white and black, spoke out against the monopoly of male leadership, claiming the power of the Holy Spirit was with them as well. Although usually lacking formal education, women led churches and became leaders of new religious

21. For a brief overview of this movement and its implications worldwide, see Tooze, "Woman Suffrage" 103–12.

22. Kartowijono, *Perkembangan*, 19.

23. Katoppo, *Compassionate and Free*, 37–38.

movements. Catherine Booth, cofounder of the Salvation Army; Harriet Tubman, leader in the slave-freeing activities of the Underground Railroad; Mary Baker Eddy, founder of Christian Science; Ellen G. White, founder and educator in the movement of Seventh-Day Adventism; and Aimee Semple-McPherson, evangelist in the Pentecostal movement, changed the face of American religion.

Those religious feminists did not find support by the women scholars who were beginning to teach at that time, mainly at women's colleges.[24] Sometimes women who entered the professions did not identify with the popular base of the women's movements. A strong anti-religion bias in universities that grew up in the twentieth century also contributed to the sidelining of issues of women's spirituality in academic circles. It wasn't until the later decades of the twentieth century that a global feminist movement in women's spirituality began to gain influence.

A "second wave" of women's movements occurred during the 1960s and 1970s. Betty Friedan's book *The Feminine Mystique*, published in 1963 helped many women in the U.S. to see that social stereotypes limited women's activities and hampered their self-confidence. They began organizing and protesting, their movement rising with the wave of counter-cultural critique in universities across the nation. Christian women re-opened the struggle for ordination in the churches. Women in Indonesia actively sought status as partners in development of the nation. In China, women worked unstintingly for the common good, spending long hours away from their home and family. Equal opportunity, equal pay for equal work, and relieving the double burden of work in the home and workplace became important themes around the globe during those decades.

The Struggle for Ordination

Sometimes history surprises us. We think of women's struggle for ordination as a twentieth-century pathway. And indeed it was. What is surprising is to find that in 1872 Sarah Smiley preached to a congregation of 1400 at Lafayette Presbyterian Church in Brooklyn. In 1889 Nolin Presbytery of the Cumberland Presbyterian Church in Louisville, Kentucky, ordained Louisa Woolsey as the first woman Presbyterian minister. The backlash from those events kept women from full ecclesiastical ordination until

24. Parvey, "Re-membering," 176.

1956 when the Presbyterian Church (USA) lifted the ban and ordained Margaret E. Towner for work with Christian Education in Allentown, Pennsylvania.[25] But that those women led and were supported by congregations in the nineteenth century is certainly something to celebrate.

Before women were ordained as ministers, they sought to follow God through teaching and pastoring in positions of church leadership that might be opened to them. Jarena Lee, one of the earliest women to be recognized as a leader in the African Methodist Episcopal Church, suppressed her call to teach for years. At length, she did speak out in a church meeting. Pastor Richard Allen recognized her talent and call and supported her public ministry for many years following that incident. Lee traveled and preached as an evangelist, admonishing congregations much as a pastor would. Richard Allen paid more than lip service to Lee's calling—he even took care of her children during her ministry travels.[26] Other churches followed that liberalizing trend, ordaining women as deacons and then as elders before allowing them into equal status as ministers of congregations and leaders of churches.

Social Service and Mission

Although women were not recognized as pastors or theologians during the nineteenth and early twentieth centuries they devised ways to serve and lead in mission. At the turn of the century in the United States, Protestant women focused on "women's work for women," organizing mission projects and funding foreign missions to women. Women's mission theologies emphasized a commitment to the social and charitable side of mission work, transforming the face of American missions.[27] In England at about the same time, Catherine Booth, cofounder of the Salvation Army recruited women in London to raise money for work with the laboring class, took wealthy women into the slums with clothing and other necessities which they distributed to poor women.[28] As single women began to be accepted as missionaries, nurses were drawn to the mission field, teaching village women around the world basic hygiene and nutrition and health practices.

25. Roche, "Headlines of the Struggle," 63.

26. Lee in Andrews, *Sisters of the Spirit*.

27. Robert, *American Women in Mission*, xviii.

28. See Muck and Adeney, *Christians Encountering World Religions*, ch. 11.

Women did their social service work with a priority on getting the job done. Consequently an ecumenical spirit and a respect for third world Christians pervaded many of their social service projects. Mission historian Dana Robert concludes that "By the 1920s, women's mission theory was part of mainstream Protestant missiology, emphasizing under the concept 'World Friendship' such themes as ecumenism, peace education, higher education for women, and partnership and cooperation between first and third-world churches."[29] By the 1930s women's mission theory and their movement for social service merged into the male-dominated denominational structures.

During this time, Catholic women organized foreign missions, following the tradition of mission to the Americas. Their focus was on education and caring for children.[30] The missionaries devised ways to teach using contrasting approaches, working both with the elite classes and with the poor. They set up orphanages, drawing on a Catholic theology of woman as founder of the family and seeking converts among parents through the education of children. Mercy and compassion became central to Catholic women's missionary efforts, becoming not only a mission theory but a missionary method of service.[31]

The desire to evangelize the world drove the nineteenth-century missionary movement. As women gained access to participation in both Catholic and Protestant forms of mission, new ways of doing mission to reach non-Christian peoples developed in women's mission theory and practice. The educational focus of much of women's ministry in mission did not satisfy the desire for salvation of the peoples of the world that many women felt. Consequently many entered the ranks of nondenominational faith missions that emerged from the 1880s to the 1900s.

Robert identifies commonalities among all of those streams of missionary service by women. Holistic ministry was a strong emphasis. Serving not only the spirit but the bodies of women and children, showing compassion not only for the souls of people but for their physical and emotional wounds was part of women's missionary practice. A focus on education characterized women's missionary practice. They developed mission theory out of their gender-based experiences, working in

29. Robert, *American Women in Mission*, xviii.

30. Dries, *Missionary Movement*, 153.

31. Ibid., 138–40.

practical and ecumenical ways rather than doing a systematic theology of mission.[32]

The American missionary movement was an activist movement, focusing more on extending Christianity around the world than documenting theologies and theories of mission. Nonetheless, mission theologies of women can be inferred, and their influence on missiology can be traced. The themes outlined above serve as benchmarks for analyzing women's practices, theologies, and their impact on mission and missiology in the twenty-first century.

Education

Education was at the forefront of missionary endeavors around the world. Literacy was necessary for reading the Bible and inculcating the "universal" values of Western civilization.

It wasn't only missionaries that went abroad during the twentieth century to teach. U.S. Government sponsored schools were established in the Philippines and other countries where the U.S. had military and political interests. It was thought that common schools would bridge the chasm between other cultures and American civilization. That vision was adopted by the Peace Corps as they sent hundreds of young teachers to Asia and Africa during the American Century.

An interesting shift occurred about mid-century, however. As teachers began to appreciate the cultures of the people they were sent to teach and the human rights movement grew in the West, teachers began to question the wisdom of exporting American teaching methods and values to other countries. Cliford Geertz spoke of culture as a set of tools for meaning making.[33] The UN Declaration of Human Rights made an impact on Americans as they considered the kind of education that should be practiced in other countries. The concept of culture and the importance of respecting the cultures of others created a shift in teacher's attitudes.

By 1967, Peace Corps volunteers were wondering whether Americans "have a moral right" to design curricula for another nation's schools. Missionary teachers "flatly rejected any effort to 'impose western values

---

32. Robert, *American Women in Mission*, xviii–xix.
33. Geertz, "Ideology as a Cultural System," in *Interpretation of Cultures*, 93.

and standards."[34] The "common civilization impulse" that operated at the turn of the 20th assumed that white Americans possessed Truth and indigeneous people needed to be enlightened by that Truth. But the emerging concept of culture made Americans hesitant to impose their values on others. The concept of culture and the need to respect other cultures changed the understanding of Americans teaching abroad.

Even as respect for other cultures grew among women in mission, attention to their own situation became paramount. Christian women, including Rosa Parks, were active in the Civil Rights Movement. The 1960s and '70s saw women struggling for equal rights in the workplace. Tension among Christians regarding women's roles in society erupted in Berkeley California in 1974 when Christian women demonstrated against Maribelle Morgan's view of the "total woman." Ordination of women both as Christian educators and as pastors began in earnest.

The second wave of feminism included a strong component of Christian women, becoming a kind of mission of its own.

Spirituality, a Third Wave of the Women's Movement

During the late twentieth century, increased interest in spirituality in American society spawned a third wave of the women's movement. With the publication of Carol P. Christ and Judith Plaskow's *WomanspiritRising* in 1978, a serious challenge to male definitions of spirituality was combined with creative essays on reconstructing tradition and creating new traditions. Since then, multiple ways of understanding women's spirituality, grounded in feminist methodologies, have arisen. Judith Plaskow, Denise Carmody, Katie G. Cannon, Marianne Katoppo, Alice Walker, and Nancy S. Barnes are a few examples.

The philosophical context for those internationalist trends was the post-modern realization that all knowledge is located in communities and bounded by culture and social mores. Karl Mannheim argues that sociopolitical views and even science itself must be understood as ideologies bound up with the life and situation of the one purporting those ideas.[35] Charles Taylor describes a personal experiential connection with perceptions of truth that comprises part of the modern Western identity itself, although we tend to deny the spiritual aspects of that connection.[36]

34. Zimmerman, *Innocents Abroad*, 4.

35. Mannheim, *Ideology and Utopia*, 59–62.

36. Taylor, *Sources of the Self*, 520.

Perspectival knowledge, communal practices, and experiential under-standings fueled the women's spirituality movement. The resulting collage of writings on women's spirituality in the late twentieth century present a few salient themes that are pertinent to our study of contemporary women's theologies.[37]

Embodiment asserts that a woman's body is intertwined with every aspect of her being, including spirituality. The sacredness of everyday life is also stressed as women find their voices and name the sacred. Freedom to choose, recognizing one's agency and boldly taking action is a trend stressed by Prof. Liu Bohong of Beijing University.[38] Self-trust develops as women depend on their own resources, rediscover their ethnic traditions and create new rituals. Empowerment results from choosing and trusting one's perceptions. Relationality surfaces as an important part of this process of empowerment for women. Exploring spiritual connections becomes sustainable as an emphasis on celebrating difference grows up.

The women in the missionary movement of the nineteenth and twentieth centuries. influenced societal change as education, equality, and respect for other cultures combined with service and ecumenical cooperation. In a reciprocal manner, the three waves of feminism—for equal political rights in the early twentieth century, for economic justice in the mid-century, and for spiritual independence in the later twentieth century influenced Christian women in mission. The mission actions and reflection of the narrators in this study show the impact of those trends.

Innovation and Consolidation

Since that time, women have more and more come to realize that women's work patterns, goals, and spiritual dimensions of life cannot simply be styled on male role models. Men in industrialized societies tend to view their work as the primary focus of life. Most women, biologically and culturally, also focus on childbearing and nurturing relationships. Male spirituality can more easily separate itself from the material world and its concerns of daily life. That has become a central focus of the revived *kebatinan* movements of Indonesia.[39] Not surprisingly, those movements

---

37. See ch. 2, "Sources of Authority," for a more detailed presentation of these themes.

38. Liu, "Women's Double Burden."

39. Koentjaraningrat, *Javanese Culture*, 403.

are male-oriented. Women cannot so easily separate themselves from the concerns of daily life.

Furthermore, since so much writing about spirituality has been done by men, ideas of the domain of the sacred, and its expression, tend to be male-oriented. For example, Christian images of "the spiritual man" as a runner in a race, or as a warrior, affect one's view of the goals and activities of the spiritual person and the holy community.[40] Women today find those metaphors and their accompanying patriarchal attitudes very limiting.

More and more women are turning toward their own experiences and intuitions to redefine their spirituality and its goals and intentions. The double burden of home and work responsibilities force women to choose carefully their goals and limit wisely their activities. Male-defined spiritualites often do not fit the problems women face or provide viable alternatives to the harried pace of modern life. Women's groups for solidarity and mutual support have resulted in a focus on women's unique experiences as a basis for women's spiritualities. Dissatisfaction with male dominated religious institutions led women in the late twentieth century to form their own religious organizations, drawing from women's history and women-defined ideas of spirituality.[41]

A film that portrays the significance of this shift in consciousness came out half a century ago in 1966. *To Be Alive!* states,

> Today we are at a turning point in human history. The power to name is being claimed by Adam's silent partner. Woman for too long has been quiet, a submissive helpmate to the "naming" male, content to love and nurture, to support and assist, to give birth and care, endlessly to feed and remove dirt. For generations she has seemed content to live within the male naming of sacred reality. But no more. Women at last recognize that male "naming" always fosters male power, privilege and status, while denigrating women's. As if awakening from a long sleep, we women are slowly shaking the film of male concepts from our eyes and looking at life as if seeing it "for the first bright time."[42]

For that innovative idea to become part of the lives of individuals and societies, it must be consolidated and disseminated. Theological

---

40. See Heb 12:1; Phil 3:12–14; Eph 5:10–17.

41. For an explanation of this movement and its rationale, see Russell, *Church in the Round*, 63–66.

42. Quoted in Gray, *Sacred Dimensions*, 1.

writings by Rosemary Radford Ruether, Elizabeth Johnson and Margaret Farley, and popular books such as *A God Who Looks Like Me* by Patricia Lynn Reilly help insure that changes in perspective discovered by the third wave of the women's movement focused on spirituality in the late twentieth century continue to thrive.

Consolidation of those ideas is also aided by the realization in intellectual circles that all knowledge is located in communities and bounded by culture and social mores. The "universal truth" sought for by the Enlightenment is now understood as a cultural form itself. Perspectival knowledge, knowledge in community, and experiential knowledge are correspondingly gaining a place of importance in scholarship and community life.

As local and cultural containment of knowledge is understood by women, many feel empowered to draw on their own resources. Elisabeth Schüssler Fiorenza "reconstructs" the history of women in New Testament times.[43] Women write about the inner search for identity experienced by many older women, the unique perceptions of poor black women, and the relevance of the Bible for women in a post-modern age. Marilyn Sewell's collection of women's poetry through the ages that we looked at in the last chapter celebrates women's spirituality. Each of those women and countless others have broken new ground in defining the content of spirituality, the goals of the spiritual practices and the unique ways in which women experience the spiritual life. Those voices of the late twentieth century consolidate for women in the contemporary era, the gains of the women's spirituality movement of the late twentieth century. The narrators in this study have felt their influence and move toward doing mission theology experientially, drawing on their inner spiritual resources rather than following patterns of the past.

The missionary movement marked another third wave—a third wave of change and ferment in the church that opened doors for women in ministry. Women's innovations of each era were followed by a period of institutionalization that again limited opportunities for women. In order for the advances made in times of ferment to be lasting, the changes themselves must be institutionalized in the organizational structures of the church.[44] Sociologist of religion Max Weber outlined that process in his theory of religious change. He asserts that a prophet arises in a stable

43. See Schüssler Fiorenza, *In Memory of Her.*
44. Robert, "Innovation and Consolidation," 137.

religion, calling a corrupted institution back to the original vision of the religion. That prophetic voice instigates change. During the ensuing turmoil expanded visions are created. In order for those visions to be lasting, however, the prophetic word must be institutionalized in the structures of the religion. After that happens, the religion again gradually becomes stiff and formalized. Then a new prophet arises, again calling the people back to an original vision.[45]

As women participated in those times of ferment and change, in the early church, during the Reformation and Counter Reformation, and in the nineteenth–twentieth-century missionary movement, women's practices and ideas creatively influenced the church and the world. Women's leadership forged new directions in theology and mission practice. In order for those gains to last, they had to be institutionalized as the times of ferment settled into a new era of stability.

Many of the changes fostered by women have been incorporated into the structures of the church. We no longer identify them solely as "women's theologies." Rather they have become general theologies appropriated by the whole church. An example from the early church is the prominence of Mary, Jesus' mother in theologies throughout church history. The influence of Mary, Lazarus' sister who studied with Jesus is another. During the Reformation, the idea that each person could relate to God in an unmediated way spawned the idea that all people should be able to read the Scriptures. Women seized the opportunity for literacy that changed the structures and theologies of later generations in innumerable ways. A focus on mercy and compassion, the idea of holistic service to all in foreign missions, the respect for indigenous peoples, and the notion of the importance of education in spreading Christianity are gains from the nineteenth- and twentieth-century mission movement that women that have made. Those gains have now been institutionalized in the church around the world.

Identifying theologies of mission that are exclusively women's is difficult as it should be. The church is one. God's Spirit motivates the people, and the gains of women become the gains of the whole church. Philosopher Hans Georg Gadamer argues that when a work of art is let out in the world, it belongs to the world and can be reinterpreted and reformulated by others. It is no longer the property of the artist but belongs to everyone. Interpretation is not an occasional supplement to understand which

45. Weber, "Religion and Rationalization," 13–31.

stands apart from it. "Rather, understanding is always interpretation."[46] Women's mission theories and theologies act in a similar way. Begun in the realm of experience and practiced for the glory of God, they become the property of the whole church to benefit all.

Global Religion as a Wider Context

Throughout history in many cultures, women have been the ones to pass religion down to the next generation. As women cared for the home and educated their children in Hindu and Buddhist societies, religion was passed on. In Jewish and Christian societies women held sway in the home, teaching their children the importance of the faith of the fathers. Muslim women schooled their children in the faith, teaching a reverence and obedience to Allah to their offspring from earliest childhood. In many local religions around the world, the mother holds a prominent place in transmitting religious knowledge to her children.

The intimacy of education by mothers in the home leaves a deep impression on children. Many religious leaders credit their mothers with instilling in them the values of faith, and the courage to pursue those values in the public realm. Eleanor Roosevelt, Mahatma Gandhi, Martin Luther King, and John F. Kennedy are among modern leaders influenced by their mothers to pursue leadership based on religious values.

Mothers of founders of religion also influenced their amazing offspring that founded new religions. Tales of Buddha's mother, strong enough to give birth standing up, Jesus' mother, a poor refugee visited by God, and Muhammad's mother, show the powerful influence of women teaching religion to their children.

Missionary mothers also left a huge mark on their children. Elizabeth Elliot, wife of a martyred missionary to the Aucas in South América, left a legacy of mission outreach to those tribes that has resulted in the Christianization of the Auca people. Catherine Booth, cofounder of the Salvation Army, raised children who took over that important mission that still reaches out to people today. Edith Schaeffer, cofounder of L'Abri Fellowship in Switzerland, trained her children so well in theology that two of them now run the L'Abri centers in Huémoz-sur-Ollon, Switzerland, and London.

---

46. Gadamer, *Truth and Method*, 307.

Many of those missionary women wrote of their experiences, taught their theologies, and lived out their convictions through daily practices of service and contemplation. Their theologies can be investigated through looking at their lives, listening to the voices of their communities, and reading their writings—letters, hymns, sermons, newsletters, articles, and books. Some records have been lost. Many remain.

The wave of women's spirituality of the late twentieth century also influences religions around the world. Formal religions are being reexamined from women's perspectives. Numerous works on women in world religions describe women's traditional "place" in the religion and outline new theologies that challenge oppressive customs. Those works devise woman-affirming theologies that remain true to the spirit of the world religions.[47] In all of those works, the focus is on spirituality, the interest is in the sacred, and the theologies developed are by and about women.

Women who adhere to no religion are also exploring issues of spirituality. Emily Culpepper, who calls herself an atheist and a "free thinker" relates her journey to a sense of the sacred.[48] Black novelists Alice Walker and Toni Morrison describe their journeys in relation to spiritual roots that arose long ago in Africa. Jeanne Brooks Carritt speaks of the sacredness of women's bodies as they age in an era when both sacredness and old age are denigrated in some Western societies.[49]

Writing vs. Speaking in Women's Theology

Women writing theology has been and still is a complex endeavor fraught with contradictions and difficulties. For centuries, by definition writing theology was the domain of men—men with education and the authority of ordination. Women were excluded from those privileges for much of the Christian era. Women were barred from university education, a fact that limited their ability to write theology. Oxford University began granting degrees in 1920, but Yale University did not admit women until 1969.[50] During most of the world's history, women have been poor.

---

47. See Mayhur Amin Masruchah on world religions, Arvind Sharma on Hinduism, Rita Gross on Buddhism, Judith Plaskow on Judaism, and Rosemary Radford Ruether and Letty M. Russell on Christianity.

48. Culpepper "Spiritual, Political Journey," 146–65.

49. Carritt, "Our Bodies," 232–39.

50. Gubar, introduction to Woolf, *Room of One's Own*, xl.

Without an economic base, the luxury of even self-education, time and freedom to write have not been available to the majority of women. Until the latter part of the eighteenth century, 90 percent of women were peasants.[51] Even today, women in the world own only 1 percent of the world's property.[52] Throughout history, most women were married and without effective forms of birth control. Writing theology in the midst of a life of poverty, physical labor, and childrearing was impossible for all but a very few.

Yet some women found ways to write their mission theologies. Alternate forms of education enabled some women to write. Monastic women gained access to texts. They sought and found advocates in priests and bishops. In later centuries, women found ways to educate themselves. Times of ferment in the Church like the Reformation saw women speaking out, writing letters and treatises on the gospel, speaking their convictions publicly.[53] Literacy for women was a major step forward for women during the Reformation. The missionary movement saw women like Catherine Booth and Phoebe Palmer taking leadership, preaching, and writing mission theologies.

Many fathers throughout Christian history have seen the potential of daughters they loved and educated them in art, languages, science, and theology. Virginia Woolf, while not a mission theologian, shows how women in the early twentieth century gained access to education and the art of writing. She was granted access to her stepfather's library and later explored the British Museum for evidence of women's intellectual endeavors in history. Her view was that the best education was based on consulting historians or pulling poems and novels off shelves, meditating on the privations but also, paradoxically, on the privileges of female home-schooling.[54]

Although women were excluded from doing theology in written form, written theologies were sometimes considered secondary to the spoken word. Preaching and speaking could be limited to elite audiences. Written theologies seemed distant and less powerful to many. Paradoxically, those attitudes gave written theologies a kind of power. They could be read by anyone. They could widen the canon of acceptable theologies

51. Anderson and Zinsser, *History of Their Own*, 87.

52. Statistic from State of the World Index 2000, quoted by World Vision in Muck, *Faith in Action Study Bible*, back matter.

53. Tavard, *Women in Christian Tradition*, ch. 5.

54. Gubar, introduction to Woolf, *Room of One's Own*, xliii.

or influence people indirectly. Women wrote hymns for example. Hymnody has been spoken of as "stealth theology." Written theologies could also be read in different contexts, thus becoming subject to myriad interpretations over distance and time. When interpreted by oppressed groups, written theologies could be liberating.

Despite views that limited women's power and opportunities to do theology throughout Christian history, women have found ways to practice, reflect on, write, and preach theology. Christian women seized opportunities during the early church, the Reformation, and the nineteenth-century mission movement to do theology in public settings. They were influenced by three waves of feminism during the twentieth century. Throughout Christian history, whether alone, cloistered, surrounded by children, relegated to the home, or silenced by persecution, women have persisted in doing mission theology.

The next chapter outlines a major contribution that women doing mission theology are making to method, showing how universal values and cultural forms are linked as gender equality is fostered.

14

Contributions to Method

Contextualizing Universal Values

For in Christ all the fullness of the Deity lives in bodily form. . . . Therefore, do not let anyone judge you by what you eat or drink, or with regard to a religious festival, a New Moon celebration or a Sabbath day. These are a shadow of the things that were to come; the reality, however, is found in Christ.

—COLOSSIANS 2:9, 16–17

THIS VERSE FROM THE epistle to the Colossians shows how universal values and cultural forms relate to each other. Christ is the universal form, the fullness of Deity in bodily form. And the religious festivals practiced by people in that time and place are ways that people sought out and honored Deity. The universal value of Christ reconciling the world to God can only be expressed through cultural religious forms. Those forms attempt to apprehend Deity in more or less accurate ways. They are shadows of a reality much grander and more universal.

Christian women's mission theologies make a significant contribution to method by holding universal Christian values realizing that those values must be contextualized to fit particular situations. The value of gender equality provides an example.

Feminists advocate a universal value of women's equality and dignity. Many make "what is good for women" their critical standard. Discarding the idea of a "value free" social science, feminists unabashedly claim the value of gender equality as a basic assumption for social scientific investigations or theological reflection.

That stance provides a middle ground between an outdated "modern" approach that claims science can be value-free and a post-modern relativism that claims local knowledge as the only knowledge. In that view, incommensurability of values takes precedence making conversations across cultures virtually impossible. Christian women doing theology do more than claim a stance of gender equality. They work at communicating that universal value across cultures without imposing their own views of how gender equality must be demonstrated.

In the twenty-first century, mission scholars and practitioners are looking at Christian mission with new eyes. No longer a West to East enterprise, missionaries are now sent from Korea to Indonesia, from Japan to Thailand, from Ghana to the U.S.A. The Christian gospel takes many forms as diverse cultures meet and exchange ideas and practices. Presbyterians in Pennsylvania praise God with trumpet sounds from Latin America, seminary students in Brazil worship with African dance styles, Protestant worshippers in Indonesia sing praise songs from Christian music labels in the U.S.A.

The translatability of the gospel into various cultural forms is one of the special features of Christianity.[1] Understanding different cultures and translating the gospel into forms that are indigenous or compatible with those settings then becomes a crucial task of contemporary mission. Norman Thomas calls it "radical contextualization" and affirms it as "mission in Christ's way."[2] Contextualizing the message is one of the crucial tasks mission must embrace in the contemporary era.

The gospel message consists not only in ideas, however. It is embodied in certain universal values that need to be identified and translated into diverse cultural forms. If Christian values are not articulated and practiced in fitting ways in a particular culture, Christianity will remain a foreign religion, set apart from the life and commitments of society. And although Christian values will at some points diverge from societal mores, there needs to be enough overlap for Christianity to be experienced as part of what it means to be identified with a particular cultural group. Only then will the gospel influence social change at the level of social structures, societal mores, and political commitments.

Although the gospel is always "clothed" in culturally specific forms and cannot exist apart from particular forms, universal values of love,

---

1. The main argument of Sanneh's *Translating the Message*.
2. Thomas, "Radical Mission," 4.

human worth, and honoring the transcendent are at the heart of the gospel in any culture. How to translate those values so that they are practiced in meaningful and comfortable ways in a society becomes the task of radical contextualization. That task belongs primarily to Christian communities in a particular locale. Guests and missionaries from other cultures interact with that process of contextualization, bringing insights and theological perspectives that can aid or hinder the process of contextualization.

The women in this study offer specific ways to contextualize Christian values so that they might be re-formed in ways that are appropriate in a new setting. Missiologists in this study emphasize the unity of the human family, the importance of understanding Jesus as savior, the mercy of God, the call to follow God, and the value of following Jesus' example of humility and love for others. While recognizing the importance of honoring cultural forms, the women also understand gender equality as a universal value.

Rather that attempt an abstract description of this method, this chapter uses gender equality as an example of a universal Christian value and an Indonesian Protestant university as the setting for applying that value. I will not make a full, detailed argument that gender equality is a universal Christian value. That has been done in some detail in many other places.[3]

Problems in Communicating Universal Values across Cultures

How to facilitate cross cultural understanding and exchange has become the subject of much research, covering both processes of interaction and information about forms of communication in specific cultures.[4]

---

3. Early influences on my own study of this issue were Gundry, *Woman, Be Free* and Scanzoni and Hardesty, *All We're Meant to Be*. More recent scholarship on women in the Bible builds on the value of gender equality, developing theologies for specific groups (e.g., Van Wijk-Bos, *Reformed and Feminist*; Grant, *White Women's Christ*; and Isasi-Diaz, *En la Lucha*) and formulating new interpretations of the texts (e.g., Crysdale, *Embracing Travail*, and Frymer-Kensky, *Reading the Women*).

4. Books on understanding cultures (e.g., Geertz, *Interpretation of Cultures*), books on cross-cultural communication (e.g., Duane, *Cross-Cultural Connections*; Augsberger, *Pastoral Counseling across Cultures*), and books on Christianity and specific cultures (e.g., Donovan, *Christianity Rediscovered*; Adeney, *Christian Women in Indonesia*) are useful as guides to approaching another culture with understanding and respect.

Paul Hiebert, Daniel Shaw, and Tite Tienou's work on the church as a hermeneutical community offers excellent resources for facilitating the theological reflection recommended in this chapter.[5]

As part of their research methodology, feminists advocate a universal value of women's equality and dignity. Many make "what is good for women" their critical standard. Discarding the idea of a "value free" social science, feminists unabashedly claim the value of gender equality as a basic assumption for social scientific investigations or theological reflection.

Christian women doing theology do more than claim a stance of gender equality. They work at communicating that universal value across cultures without imposing their own views of how gender equality must be demonstrated. That work is a bit like the admonition of the letter to the Colossians quoted at the beginning of this chapter—do not judge others' ways of understanding the universal value of Christ. In this case the admonition is not to judge others' ways of expressing gender equality in their cultural settings.

That stance provides a middle ground between an outdated "modern" approach that claims science can be value-free and a post-modern relativism that claims local knowledge as the only knowledge. In that view, incommensurability of values takes precedence making conversations across cultures virtually impossible.

As a professor in Indonesia, I was careful to dress in ways that were compatible with Javanese culture and professional women colleagues. When I returned to Satya Wacana Christian University to teach after two years back in the United States, however, I was dismayed to see undergraduate women attending classes in blue jeans. Their freedom as women to attend university took on a Western tinge when they ceased wearing either traditional or modern Indonesian-style clothing and put on blue jeans.

It was clearly not my place as a visitor to laud one style of dress and condemn another. But it was important that I fit in with the society, not insisting that gender equality meant that women could dress any way they liked. It was more important to act in compatible ways. Indonesian women would find their own expressions of gender equality as I and other professors at the university spoke of that value as a universal one.

---

5. An excellent book that helps Christians think theologically about religions of other cultures is Hiebert et al., *Understanding Folk Religion*, ch. 15, especially 385–91.

Often it is difficult for women mission workers in areas where women's lives are devalued to decide how to support gender equality without imposing foreign ways on communities. One missionary found that holding cooking classes in her home demonstrated both a care for village women and a model for home life that showed self respect and value for women's work in the society.

Carrie Warren, a health worker in Africa had a more difficult issue to face. She saw the damage that multiple pregnancies was doing to women in her area. The value of women made in God's image was becoming distorted as women bore eight to twelve children and had not means to support them. She said, "I don't want to tell them whether or not to use birth control but I want them to see that women are to be valued as more than mere property."[6] Here she makes a distinction between pushing a solution onto the people and still advocating for the universal value of gender equality.

Christians hold many universal values some of which are integral to the gospel. Yet in many countries, especially in Asia, Christianity is seen as a foreign religion. The universal value of Jesus' redemptive work is discarded as a foreign idea.

The ways in which that value, gender equality, and other Christian values were presented to people in Thailand, for instance, spoke more to the people of Western ways than they did of universal values. I spoke to a Thai gentleman at a conference in Chang Mai on Christianity in Buddhist settings. He was dismayed to find that the Thai view of sin that he held was tossed out by Western missionaries. One missionary told him directly that Thai people needed to understand the concept of sin before Christianity could take hold in Thailand. Rather than attempt to understand how Thai people understood the complex concept of sin, how they made distinctions between a thief in jail and an ordinary person's behavior, for instance, the missionary rejected the Thai view at the superficial level of vocabulary.

This chapter outlines a method for getting through dilemmas like those outlined above. Bringing universal values of Christianity and also respecting the cultural forms of the society takes intentionality and care. Using gender equality as an example, here is a step-by-step method that brings a universal value to a culture while respecting its life and forms. What follows are suggestions for those outsiders who, consciously or

6. Bergner, "The Call."

unconsciously, influence the project of contextualization when they interact with Christians in another culture. The method consists of a series of suggestions for reflection, first on one's own background and culture and then, with others, on theirs.

I will outline the steps of contextualizing that value in ways that involve the community in their own theological formation, a formation that is compatible with their cultural location.[7] The same method may be used in working to contextualize other universal Christian values, following the steps illustrated below.

Six-Step Method for Communicating a Universal Value across Cultures

1. Recognize the importance and universality of the value

2. Check out the acceptability of the value in another context

3. Identify other cultural values that prevent the practice of the universal value

4. Recognize the complexities of the culture

5. Work with Christians in the culture to clarify priorities of traditional practices in light of the universal value

6. Work together to devise new patterns of behavior that demonstrate the universal value in the local context

Step 1: Recognize the Value of Gender Equality

Even before entering another cultural milieu and certainly while one is interacting with people from another culture, the universal value that one holds and wants to communicate as part of the gospel must be clearly recognized and enacted in personal and communal life. If the value is seen as relative, appropriate in one time and place but perhaps not in

7. This method was developed during a five-year period when the author, as a Presbyterian Mission Coworker, served as a professor at Satya Wacana Christian University in Salatiga, Indonesia, 1991–96, returning each summer to teach in seminaries in the U.S.A. Taking the conversation about Christian values and cross-cultural mission from Indonesia to the U.S. and back, hearing the critiques of students in both cultures about the process of intercultural exchange helped focus the process described in this chapter.

another, the universality of the value itself comes into question. Michael Polanyi argues that one cannot be committed to a value without holding that it must be good for all people at all times, in other words, universalizing that value. Charles Taylor argues that our identities as persons are shaped by the strong moral evaluations that we hold, evaluations that we apply not only to ourselves, but to others. Examining our commitment to a universal value and evaluating our practices of that value is the first step in interacting about that gospel value with those in another culture.

Christians draw values from Scripture, studying the Bible in communities that believe that God's Spirit will aid both understanding and application of the wisdom of God's word. Studying Scripture for views of gender is a logical first step. Rather than accepting without thinking past interpretations, fresh study can discover new insights from the text. The creation story in Genesis 1 that places man and woman together, charging them with care of the earth and its creatures might be a place to start. Or the wonder of the narrative of Christ's birth, a demonstration of God's love for all people and God's intention to save the world could be a beginning point for study. Jesus' dialogue with the Samaritan woman at the well and his counter-cultural interactions with women of his own culture may change traditional views of women's roles. Better translations of the New Testament may reveal Paul's praise for Lydia, Priscilla, and Phoebe as ministers of the gospel.

The past decades have brought new scholarship to bear on some of the contradictions and confusing passages of the Bible that relate to gender equality.[8] Rather than basing a theology of gender on difficult Pauline passages, an understanding of the cultural setting in which the apostle operated might illuminate those passages in a new way. A study of changes in Paul's own views of and interaction with women in the early church might also help clarify issues of gender equality and women's leadership.

Those studies are important not only for clarifying our own views of the universal value of gender equality, but as preparation for the theological study our sisters and brothers in another culture will want to do. As communities are reformed by the gospel, questions about women's worth, status, and roles will arise. Women who sense a call to become Christian leaders, will want to turn to Scripture to see if their call is in

---

8. Two general works that will direct the interested reader to further studies are Van Leeuwen, *After Eden*, and Borresen, *Image of God*.

line with the revelation of God's Word.[9] If we are to assist them with that search for God's will, we need to have our own views clarified and informed by God's word.

A second focus of study is our own cultural background and community life. "Know thyself" is an old adage that is appropriate here. We might add to that saying, "Know thy community." We will not be able to appreciate the value of gender equality as it appears in another setting if we do not understand our own cultural forms. Understanding that our own views are formed by our social location and history helps us to understand that our culture is not the center point of the world. We begin to see that our interpretations of universal values are not the only possible interpretation. By identifying the roots and patterns of the ways that we live out our Christian values , we start to see that our practices of Christian values are not the only possible ways that those values can be embodied. As we de-center our own culture, seeing that our perspectives and habits are shaped within our community, we are preparing ourselves to aid Christians in *another culture* to envision ways that universal values can become embedded in *their world*. At times it may be *our own focus* that needs to shift to begin to see the realization of a universal value in another culture.[10]

A historical look at your society and how women's roles have changed might be one place to begin. In the United States, the past one hundred years have seen amazing changes in the roles and status of women in our society. Social structures have changed, providing more educational opportunities for girls in sports, science, and higher education. Yet, inequities are still very evident in American society. The church too can be a focal point of reflection, identifying changes in theologies of gender, acceptance of women's leadership, women's public presence in worship practices, and use of gender-inclusive language. Societal changes have influenced the church and in turn, Christian values have influenced changes toward gender equality in society.

Reflection on gender equality at the present time in your own experience can also be helpful. This might include reflection on your own experiences of women's emotional strength, intellectual capabilities, or leadership qualities. Examining your community for signs of gender

9. A number of women in the graduate program in religion and society at the university wanted to center their theological study on issues of gender, beginning with Scripture and applying it to practices in their community.

10. For an example, see Walls, "Multiple Conversions."

equality might be another locus of reflection. Gender equality may be practiced in your family or church community whether or not a verbal theology of equality is in place in your community. How have women and men valued each other, worked together, fostered harmony and growth, supported each other through difficult times? How are girls valued, what co-educational activities highlight the worth of both boys and girls, how are the dreams and callings of both fostered by your community? Where are women visible in community and church leadership? That reflection may not result in a totally egalitarian picture of your culture and your community. But it gives you a realistic place to begin as you think about communicating God's valuing of women and men to others.

Finally, reflect on the humanity of women, persons made in God's image, for whom Christ died, partners in the work of family, church, and society. Given that humanity, the suffering caused by the oppression of women contravenes the values Christians uphold. Seventy-five percent of the world's poor are women and the children that they care for. The economic dilemmas of widows throughout the world are well-known, and often result in the abuse or even death of women. Infanticide in China and India have reached record levels, leading to concern about a gender-balanced society in those regions. Reflecting on the woes and oppression of women and girls throughout the world may strengthen our resolve to uphold gender equality as a value that is at the core of Christ's compassion for the world.

Step 2: Check Out the Acceptability of Gender Equality in Your New Context

Recognizing a Christian value and believing in its applicability to all cultures, seeing it supported by Scripture and enacted to some extent in your own society and church community is a first step. It does not mean that the culture that you will be working in will understand that value in the same way.

The next step is seeing how the value, in this case gender equality, is understood in the new setting. Cultural forms grow up for many reasons, weaving a web of attitudes and habits that permeates society. As you dialogue with a new culture and church community, keep an open mind toward the customs in operation, attempting to understand them as part of that web of culture.

Most societies in the world today are organized around patriarchal frames of reference. Expecting that framework to be in place to some extent, examine the church and community in your new setting. Are women visible in leadership? Do women wield power behind the scenes, working through men in public life? Are women discounted and consistently subordinated to men in all areas of church and community life? Analyzing the power relations between women and men in public life is crucial to developing the understandings necessary for instigating change toward a more egalitarian, and thus more Christian, society.

Family responsibilities and roles also contribute to practices of gender equality. Analyze the workings of the family, discovering where cooperation between husbands and wives, sisters and brothers, children and parents surfaces and how that cooperation is related to gender roles. For example, the Javanese in Indonesia cooperate around family finances, women taking a leading role in the management of financial resources.[11] Men in university housing units are often seen walking the babies and toddlers early in the morning or late in the afternoon when they return from teaching responsibilities at the university. What might those practices imply about the value of gender equality among Christians at the university?

A closer look at the employment and childcare division of labor is necessary to discover whether or not women are laboring under a "double burden," carrying heavy responsibilities for the home and care of extended family members and working outside of the home at the same time. Economic and class differences also come into play here. A look at educational institutions and opportunities presented to girls and boys for study provides another indicator of how the community views gender equality. Are girls accepted and honored as students? Are women teachers and professors active in the community?

The community environment as a whole reveals information about the value of gender equality. In Indonesia, women have enjoyed equal political rights and have been seen as partners in development since independence was declared in 1945. Yet, women are often viewed as inferior to men and encouraged to center their lives on caring for their families, while husbands take the more active public roles. That ambivalence of

11. Sullivan, *Masters and Managers,* 9.

views on gender gives Christians an opportunity to foster egalitarian values.[12]

The church shows the influence of diverse streams of culture, Christian theologies, and societal attitudes in Indonesia. In Manado, North Sulawesi, 45 percent of pastors are women as compared to 15 percent in Medan, Sumatra, and 8 percent in Java.[13] Clearly leadership roles for women are viewed differently in Christian circles in those areas. It is crucial to study the local context and congregations to discern, not only proportions of women and men in leadership, but to discern attitudes toward gender equality.

Studying the local context in a new culture can provide insights into varying attitudes and levels of openness to the Christian value of gender equality. Just as the picture was not totally clear when we reflected upon our own communities, so contradictions and complexities will appear in the culture we are working with. How can we sort out the mixed signals we get about gender equality in another culture and their church community?

Step 3: Identify Cultural Values That Prevent Gender Equality in Practice

A universal value will always be an ideal, imperfectly practiced in any community. Our understanding of another culture will also be partial and will deepen over time. Identifying cultural practices that impede the permeation of the universal value Christianity models is a next step.[14]

A number of cultural values might be evaluated to assess impediments to gender equality. The idea that women are inferior in mental capacity is a notion that has in recent years been challenged through debates in the popular press in Indonesia. Traditionally, men have been understood as the more rational of the two sexes, possessing more "akal" reason than women. This suits men for positions that involve level headed thinking, intellectual acumen, or situational discernment. Women in

12. For a further discussion of gender roles and ideologies in Indonesia, see Adeney, *Christian Women in Indonesia*, ch. 3.

13. Statistics reported by Protestant church leaders at the Lokakarya Wanita Perpendidikan Teologi di Tomohon, May 27, 1995.

14. Yayasan, *Kajian Perempuan*, is a compilation of newspaper clippings on topics of women's emancipation, work, conditions, marriage, and related issues, used to help me understand issues around gender and equality in Indonesia.

theological education at the university had to struggle both with men's attitudes in this area, but also with their own internalized sense of intellectual inferiority. Deferring to men in academic settings is common and women struggled to articulate their own ideas with confidence.

Denegration of women's work is another cultural value that prevents gender equality from being practiced in Indonesia. Working in the rice paddies, caring for children, and selling goods in the market are all activities that fall into the "informal sector" in Indonesia, that is, work that is not paid. It is low status work and not highly valued. The government in Indonesia has attempted to counter this devaluing process for women in the home by emphasizing the importance of homemaking as a partnership in development. Through training women in managerial techniques and financial management, the government has countered to some extent the lower status image of homemaking. However, educated women are also expected to work outside of the home, while also managing the home.

Despite their entrance into the marketplace, women do not often work at higher levels of corporate leadership or take on responsibilities as denominational leaders. This may be due, in part, to the responsibilities they bear at home, responsibilities that are seen as primary for women, a part of their "kodrat" or natural destiny.[15] The double burden of work in the family and social organizations along with paid work outside of the home deters women from devoting themselves to climbing corporate ladders or seeking leadership positions in the church.

Another cultural value that impedes gender equality in practice in Indonesia, a nation that purports equality of women and men as partners in development, is the glorification of the father figure in public and private life—"bapakism." That the father should be the center of the family, the community organizations, the workplace, and the nation is an idea that is deeply rooted in Indonesian culture and many indigenous religions of the region. The primordial religion of West Timor is based on the structure of the household, with the father figure at the center. This centrality of the father is not only an inter-relational premise of operation, it is pictured in the physical layout of the house itself. "Bapakism" is pictured symbolically in the arrangement of all of the rooms around a central room, the father's room.[16]

15 Tangkudung, "Mythos dan Kodrat."

16. One of the master's degree students with whom I worked while at Satya Wacana Christian University, Pak Fritz, analyzed West Timorese indigenous religion as

Reverence for the father figure is not, however, limited to family relations. At the university, it is imperative that the Rector be accorded tremendous respect. Heads of departments or schools within the university were usually men who received a similar respect. Social custom demanded that offices were positioned in ways that reflected the hierarchy of male positions of authority. Meetings were chaired by men who were older, ascribed positions of leadership often outweighing achieved status, particularly if that achievement was earned by a woman.

Limited education for girls is being overcome in many parts of Indonesia. The graduate program at the university where I taught actively sought women students for graduate level education. Stereotypes of women's intellectual or emotional inferiority were disputed and values of gender equality were upheld in many ways. But the multi-layered social strata of Javanese society sometimes cut across the best efforts of Christian Indonesian scholars to uphold the value of gender equality.

Sometimes reasons for conflict were due to a commitment in the society to other values that were also considered universal. Negotiating among values such as freedom of religious practice, care for the poor, protection of children, overcoming oppression of marginalized groups, seeking regional peace, and honoring the elderly may make seeking gender equality seem less important in some settings. Communities working with conflicting values need to take time to prioritize their efforts to practice those values in light of societal norms and their Christian commitments.

Step 4: Recognize the Complexity of Culture

A further step must be taken. Recognizing the complexity of culture is crucial to influencing change in cultural values. The full import of practices that seem to hamper equality in another setting may not be readily apparent. Hastily criticizing or rejecting a practice before it is fully understood as part of a set of behaviors with complicated meanings and implications can work against the goal of showing the importance of gender equality. Throughout the process described in this article, we, as guests, need to be open listeners not judges and evaluators of other

---

a factor that impeded economic development. Fritz, "Pemperbangan Economi dan Agama di Timor Barat."

cultural forms. At this stage of recognizing the complexity of customs that bear on gender equality, this open attitude is especially important.[17]

For example, as the head of a doctoral committee for a student at the university, I had the responsibility of summarizing and evaluating faculty input to the student. As chair, I held the responsibility of deciding which suggested revisions to the proposal were to be required and which should be seen as suggestions. When the meeting was held, however, the head of the graduate school ended the session before I had a chance to make this evaluation. Rather than take affront, I realized that the director could not ask a woman to evaluate the input of Indonesian male faculty colleagues. He was caught in a bind between the demands of university protocol and the requirements of ascribed status traditions of the utmost importance. The issue was resolved amicably for all when I asked permission to say a few words at the close of the formal meeting. In this way, the student was publicly informed of his responsibilities on the thesis and the male faculty members were not dishonored by the head of the department asking a woman to make formal recommendations that disagreed with some of their statements.

In this situation everyone wanted the head of the committee to make those decisions although it was a woman doing it. But finessing that decision to fit with cultural norms of *bapakism* and collegial respect in Indonesian terms took some effort by all parties.

Recognizing the complexities and interconnections of cultural forms that bear on the universal value in question requires social and cultural analysis. It may be a religious expectation brought to the culture by former missionaries whose theology opposes gender equality, for instance. Or, it may be deeply held cultural values related to respect of men as leaders or father figures as in the case of Indonesian *bapakism* or Chinese reverence for ancestors. A question of ethics and the etiquette required in social situations may also be at work in situations that may prevent women from speaking in a public or formal way, while allowing her voice in a more informal setting.

The importance of learning the multi-layered reasons that certain practices occur cannot be overstated. Showing respect for those complexities will enable people in that culture to find their own way in

17. Attention to that openness is stressed in the hermeneutic circle developed in Adeney, *Christian Women in Indonesia*, 185–89. Based on the work of Hans-Georg Gadamer, the circle emphasizes the need to lay aside one's own prejudices, becoming open to the "foreign text," in this case another culture, as a way to acquire knowledge.

sorting out the practices, finding ways to affirm the universal value that Christianity may bring to them. It may also be the case, that the universal value is already being practiced in ways that the outsider does not yet understand.

Step 5: Working Together to Clarify Priorities of Traditional Practices in Light of the Universal Value of Gender Equality

As one works with the people of another culture, the information and wisdom to navigate between traditional practices and new forms that honor equality of men and women can develop. This step can only be taken in dialogue with Christians in another culture. They are the ones who will do theological reflection from within their culture and articulate changes in practices that can reflect gender equality in fitting ways in that society.

The dialogue about values is greatly enhanced as the people articulate what makes a traditional practice meaningful to them and what is at stake in changing it. In the case of honoring men over women in Indonesia, the importance of the practice varies from culture to culture within Indonesia. Cultural groups like the Minahasans and the Torajans have had women leaders in their indigenous religious background. Patterns of showing respect for men may be different in those groups. Or, patterns of behavior may appear similar on the surface but hold differing meanings at a deeper level. An outsider cannot presume meanings for a group but must explore *with them* the importance of certain practices and their links to concepts of gender power and equality.

As this exploration goes on, men and women in the culture will identify the deeper meanings and interconnectedness of their traditional practices. It may be a sense of belonging that keeps the practice in place. It may be that gender roles are weighted with spiritual or societal meanings that the people themselves are reluctant to change. Alternatively, the power of men to control and govern may not be something that they wish to share. In that case, Christian theological reflection can soften attitudes and change thinking.

One older male church leader in the doctoral program in Indonesia came with the strong idea that although women were equal and should be given opportunity to study, they should not hold positions of authority in the church. After three years of study he stated that he was now totally committed to using the "other half of the church" in leadership. That change came about through dialogue with women and men from other parts of Indonesia, studies in gender and ethics, and theological reflection on the biblical text as well as with experience of women in leadership at the university.

Step 6: Working Together to Devise New Patterns of Behavior That Demonstrate Gender Equality

Working with Christians in the culture to clarify values and foster theological reflection on the meanings of practices sets Christian communities in a new direction. As traditional practices are evaluated theologically, discussion can focus on how women and men in that culture think a practice could be reformed to reflect gender equality. Can small changes in a practice engender equality? Are there practices that must be discarded? Can a shift in meaning of a practice encourage a more egalitarian interpretation? What can work in one setting may fail in another. Certain roles may not be possible for women within traditional structures. Should those structures be changed? If so, how?[18]

The final step, then, is to devise practices that respect traditional practices while creating changes that stimulate gender equality. New ways of relating to one another, modified forms of respecting age and status, expanded roles for both women and men in home and public life can result from this praxis approach.

For example, a new interpretation of the practice of husbands walking young children in the mornings and evenings can be made. Rather than see this as "helping" the woman with *her* task of childcare, Christians can interpret this practice as a way of balancing time spent at work and at home for both spouses.

Women entering professions at the university and in the church find themselves changing not only their lifestyles but their way of dress, offering another example of cultural change toward gender equality. Professors and pastors face the problem of dress on at least two levels. On the physical level, traditional clothing constricts movement and limits activity. On the symbolic level, traditional clothing sets women apart as objects of beauty or workers at the "back of the house."[19] Rather than give

18. I explore some of these questions in the Indonesian context in Adeney, "From the Inside Out," 171–84.

19. In the Javanese language, the meaning of the word *wife* is "the one at the back of

up the custom of wearing traditional clothing many women teaching at universities have modified traditional dress to fit more active lifestyles or limited the wearing of traditional clothing to special occasions.

Whatever steps are taken toward gender equality will spring from within the culture, directed by the reflection of Christians on Scripture, tradition, and the culture itself. Those changes will, therefore, be compatible with cultural forms and values of the society even as they change the forms and values of the culture from within.

Cultures are never static. They change constantly. The power of the gospel to change cultures, shifting values, reorganizing structures, and modifying traditional practices has been evident since the church began. The Holy Spirit continues to work in Christian communities around the world as Christian communities wrestle with universal values and cultural forms.

Women in mission have utilized this method without necessarily articulating it in a step-by-step format. Roberta Rose King's "dialogue of listening," Miriam Adeney's focus on unity, Sherron George's model of partnership, Elaine Heath's focus on contemplation, Antonia van der Meer's emphasis on listening, Kim Lamberty's understanding of accompaniment and Carrie Warren's work in health care and human rights for women each exemplify in various ways parts of this method.

Utilizing this method can stimulate value changes in societies as Christians cross cultural boundaries. Outsiders can become more aware of their influence and adjust their role in the process of contextualization. Insiders can interpret the meanings of their practices in Christian ways. Dialogue across cultures can foster practices of universal values in culturally appropriate ways as Christians in many contexts work to embody universal values in their communities and societies. Those benefits result from this method of fostering universal values across cultures, comprising an important contribution of women in mission to contemporary methods in mission theology.

The next chapter sums up general contributions of this study of women in Christian mission—practices, values, and character traits of women knowing and doing mission theology.[20]

---

the house." The kitchen is traditionally placed at the back, outside of the house, under a separate roof. Throughout Java, women in traditional dress work in such kitchens.

20. A version of this chapter was published in the International Bulletin of Missionary Research, Vol. 31, No. 1, Jan. 2007.

15

Contributions of Women to Mission Theology

In the last days, God says, I will pour out my Spirit on all people.
Your sons and daughters will prophesy, your young men will see visions,
and your old men will dream dreams.
Even on my servants, both men and women, I will pour out my Spirit in
those days and they will prophesy.

—ACTS 2:17–19

THIS EXTENDED STUDY OFFERS many contributions of women to mission theology. The last chapter outlined a method women use to communicate universal values across cultures. In this chapter we will summarize other contributions of women to mission theology—contributions of both method and content. As those contributions become understood and integrated in mission studies, stronger mission theologies will result.

Women often do theology "feet first." I have done that in my own life. Many experiences in my life have led me to ask, "What contribution is my life making to what God is doing in the world?" I could ask what drove me as a young person during the 1970s to teach English speaking children at L'Abri Fellowship in Switzerland, to travel with five "spiritual seekers" for four months in Europe, to engage newly initiated Druids in all night conversation about life's meaning and walk their sunrise ritual with them at the spring equinox at Stonehenge? I could ask why during the 1980s I walked the conflict line of the Contra war in Northern Nicaragua with a National Delegation of Women from the U.S., to share bread and water with a group of village women studying the Bible together, to plant a cross at the site of the death of a twelve-year-old girl killed while she slept in her bed? I could question my participation in anti-nuclear demonstrations at the Lockheed plant near Oakland, California. I could search for reasons for living in Indonesia for six years during the 1990s helping to develop a graduate program in religion and society at Satya Wacana Christian University in Java and working with the graduate women's group on domestic violence issues. I could ask why, sixteen years ago, I took a position to teach evangelism and mission at Louisville Presbyterian Theological Seminary when my formal training was in sociology of religion and social ethics? I could ask those questions and more. What I would be asking is, "What is my mission theology?"

And I would start by looking at my feet. Where have I been walking during the last forty years? I would find the answers in my practices, in my spirituality, and in my community. Perhaps that is what Cardinal Cajetan of the sixteenth century meant when he said the woman who did his laundry was not just a better believer, but a better theologian than he was. Steve Bevans and Roger Schroeder tell this story in their book *Prophetic Dialogue*. They aren't so sure that the "theologizing" of the woman surpassed that of the Cardinal. But what they *are* sure of is that "To be a Christian at all is to be a theologian."[1]

Theologizing about what one does for God in life differs from *showing* one's mission theology in one's acts. The action side demonstrates one's mission theology. The reflection side may or may not be expressed. It may not even be thought of. Through the centuries of Christian history, it is mainly men that have taken on the task of theologizing about mission action. They have had the privilege of time and resources to speak and write theology. They have enjoyed the status of authority to speak about matters of the *Missio Dei*. And they have done it well.

Christian women, on the other hand, have practiced the *Missio Dei*, usually *without* the privilege of time and resources or the status of authority to speak and write about those matters. Some women did break through that barrier and we are grateful to them for the insights that they have given the Church. But many more women have *practiced* a theology of mission without writing about it. Some may have reflected deeply on the reasons that they followed God in a particular way. Others may have

---

1. Bevans and Schroeder, *Prophetic Dialogue*, 95.

simply taken up tasks that they were given, doing them with care and grace. Tasks like doing the laundry.

The last century has seen many more women speaking and writing about mission theology. Women took the opportunities offered by the nineteenth–twentieth-century missionary movement to do mission. They traveled as evangelists, they set up monasteries, they engaged in teaching, health care, and political work in many countries. More opportunities surfaced during the twentieth century as women became more active in church affairs and theological education, writing theologies and seeking positions of leadership. During the last fifty years many more written theologies by Christian women have enriched the church and society.

But the contributions Christian women have made and are making to mission theology are not always self-evident. Many women in mission today practice their theologies much more than they write about them. Some do write: Chun Chae Ok, Dana Robert, Angela Dries and Kirsten Kim are narrators in this study that articulate their theologies of mission. Others must be searched out by looking at their feet. Identifying those theologies and the methods used to develop them has been the task of this study.

Method

Analysis of interviews and written works of contemporary women reveal a common methodology. Women work and think contextually. Whereas some begin articles with abstract theological themes, most of the creative theology analyzed in this project is firmly located in the contexts and experiences of the narrators. Evangelical theologian Antonia Leonaora van der Meer, a contributor to the Protestant Evangelical Iguassu Affirmation of 1999 for example, begins her article on mission with the concept of *Missio Dei*. She works from South African missiologist David Bosch as she describes the role of mission in the world. But the creative part of her essay speaks of emotions and their place in mission theology. In a similar manner, Rose Uchem, a Roman Catholic religious from Nigeria who led the women's track at the International Association of Mission Studies Quadrennial Meeting in Toronto in 2012, spoke of obstacles faced by women doing mission in Africa. Chun Chae Ok, a Presbyterian theologian from Ewha Women's University in Seoul, South Korea describes a ministry of suffering as women's main mission method in a country where women have suffered tremendously over the last century. My own work in Indonesia helped me develop a method for applying universal values to cultural forms as described in the last chapter.

Experience thus becomes a major source for theological method and content. Some of that experience is located in a woman's setting, some of it is located in their emotions and bodily experiences—that is in their person. That those sources can be primary in doing mission theology is significant both for women's mission theology and for the field of mission theology as a whole. Aristotle argued that forming habits, repeating actions with one's mind and body, led to the formation of character.[2] Augustine spoke of the importance of intentions in making moral decisions.[3] In paying attention to both of those dimensions, the women in this study stand in that tradition.

They also participate in the theological methods of liberation theologies, locating theology in spirituality and practices. Theology is not simply what one *thinks* but what one *does*. It is the combination of the two in *praxis* that comprises one's theology. Gustavo Gutierrez noted that theology of liberation is first of all a spirituality.[4] Martin Luther King's insight that he must stand unwaveringly against injustice came to him late one night as he sat praying at his kitchen table. Catholic women in the 1940s and contemporary African American missiologist exemplify the use of liberation theologies in this study.

The interpretive framework for this study suits that praxis model. The study assumes that knowledge is local and developed in community. Whereas the God we serve is ever present and universal, our knowledge of God and everything else we know is located in our experience, informed by our family, our village, and our world as we perceive it. To do theology "from above" assuming that we can know God's intentions is certainly part of our journey. We long to be illuminated by the Holy Spirit. We want to know fully. Our faith leads us in this direction. Yet certainly *how we know* brings us back to our bodies, our experiences, and our place and time. We know in part and not fully.[5] And the part that we know is situ-

2. Aristotle, *Ethics*, 2.1.1103b (24f.).

3. Augustine, *City of God*, 19.21 (Dods, 524). For an explanation of how Augustine's ideas about intention in moral action apply to public theology, see Adeney, "Citizenship Ethics," 113–17.

4. Gutiérrez, cited in Dries, *Missionary Movement*, 325 n. 18.

5. 1 Cor 13:12.

ated and limited. Women narrators in this study work from that premise. The findings show that women doing mission theology, whether or not they analyze the framework and limits of their knowledge, also find truth in their experience, in their communities, and in their bodies.

As women told their stories in the interviews, most did not identify themselves as theologians, even though some developed theological curricula and others taught theology in educational institutions. Franciscan Sister Gretchen Berg from Minnesota started Regina Mundi in 1963, a university center in Lima Peru. In addition to teaching courses, the center sponsored weekly seminars on liturgy, ecclesiology, Scripture, and the church in the modern world. According to historian Angelyn Dries, that program for superiors and novice directors "carried the impetus of Vatican II as it was occurring."[6] Missiologist Bonnie Sue Lewis considers herself a teacher rather than a theologian. Missionaries in the study also follow an active praxis model, engaging in teaching or service in areas that are open to them. It is *what they do* that defines them. They teach, they make friends, they meet needs of the people they are called to serve. They receive gifts from them. Much of their work centers on women and children, following the tradition established during the early twentieth century of women working with women.[7]

Gender

Open-ended questions about a woman's journey into mission, mentors, obstacles, and how gender influences her life in mission yielded multiple theologies but many *similar experiences*. More than a few mentioned mentoring by their fathers or male pastors and teachers. Most focused not on obstacles that they faced but on how they overcame or circumvented those obstacles.

Other experiences differed widely. A question about gender as an influence on their lives brought up areas of concern for many. Others stated that gender had no influence at all on their work. Differing contexts and personal gifts has much to do with that variation of responses. In many mission settings, teaching is part of a woman missionary's role, especially teaching children and women. Teaching alongside a husband is also accepted by many mission organizations. Developing curricula or

6. Dries, *Missionary Movement*, 207.

7. Robert, *American Women in Mission*, 130.

informal teaching can be part of ministry for many. For those women, gender did not dominate as a differentiating factor.

Sometimes issues of authority or "proper roles" does prevent women from fully exercising their gifts and calling to teach theology. In those cases, identity confusion or resentment against institutional structures breaks out. One narrator and and her husband both taught theology as well as health courses at Kijabi hospital in Kenya until her husband was named Field Director for the mission. At that point, she was barred from teaching or having any formal role in the mission although she continues to work in medicine. She spoke of the identity confusion that resulted.[8] One cannot be someone in a role that the community does not accept. The narrator's identity confusion was related to the contextual methods she used in doing theology. Women practice the mission that they are convinced God has led them to. When gender issues interfere with that call in the midst of one's ministry, trouble follows.

Working Together

Relationships took precedence over denominational hierarchies and formal job descriptions for many. Others developed relationships with those above them in the church hierarchy to further their work. In some societies women and men live separate daily lives. Friendships among women offer an entrée into communication, identifying felt needs, and developing the trust necessary to work with women to fill those needs. In some conservative Protestant and Catholic settings, women's leadership in the congregation is curtailed and their institutional authority severely limited. In those settings particularly, friendships could break through barriers. In the middle ages, women in Europe found sponsors in bishops to form their monasteries. In contemporary global contexts, friendships with male leaders can open the way for women to lead and influence their organizations along the lines of the values listed above. Friendships with women also break down walls between the local people and what is often considered in Asia to be a "foreign religion."

Some narrators stressed *listening* as a vehicle of developing friendships. Rather than come into the mission situation with an agenda, or even a conviction of what is needed, women in this study listened to

---

8. Interview December 2012 and email correspondence with research assistant Kim Okessen, January 23, 2013.

other women in formal and informal settings. Listening builds the trust that presented narrators with the opportunity to hear views that they might not have imagined, ideas that originated from the culture, taboos and insights that a missioner could not have imagined. Listening served not only as a way to find out what needs were paramount for women but also as a way of showing respect for the value of equality. The women they heard from are as valuable and human as the missionaries, Listening also opened the way for community cooperation on important issues. One result is what Claude Marie Barbour and Eleanor Doidge call "mission in reverse."[9] Locals teach missionaries, bringing them the good news as it is embodied in their life and community."[10]

Not surprisingly, *cooperation and teamwork* led the way as methods of working in mission contexts. Sometimes help came from unexpected sources. Mother Theresa found aid for her work with the dying from a Hindu organization in Calcutta.[11] On the ground teamwork also functioned to highlight local leadership. Missioners could come alongside, work ecumenically and inter-religiously to fill needs expressed by the community. Theologically, that de-centered methodology is expressed in Latin American liberation theologies. The base community becomes the source of theologies that connect with the local community, that express justice in areas of suffering, that allow missioners to accompany the people in their efforts rather than direct ministries.

In evangelical Protestant circles, it was the women that directed attention to both the listening and the community cooperation methods in mission. Women contributors to the Iguassu Affirmation repeatedly stressed the importance of listening to locals and working alongside of them, respecting them as equals and honoring them as leaders. When that happens, teamwork takes on a different tone, generating energy and appreciation for others.

Contributions of Obstacles

This study reveals that many obstacles women encounter in their mission work and academic study of mission contribute to both their methods of

9. Bevans et al., *Healing Circle*, 4–5.

10. Bevans and Schroeder, *Prophetic Dialogue*, 59.

11. See Muck and Adeney, "Charity," ch. 13 in *Christianity Encountering World Religions.*

doing mission and their mission theologies. A particular obstacle may consciously or unconsciously influence a woman's way of doing mission theology.

The Body

Negative influences of women's body image presented obstacles in a number of ways. Traditionally in Western societies the female body has not been considered normative. That makes it difficult for men to relate to women as academics or theologians. Nancey Murphy deals with this by trying "make my body disappear" when she is presenting a paper or finds herself in a formal academic setting.[12] She tries to neutralize her femaleness, but allows it to resurface in less formal settings, e.g. receptions after academic sessions. "I'll put on a scarf and let my hair down, do a little flirting and get into the boy-girl thing."[13]

How does this influence her theology? Since she deals with gender issues in her ways of acting, gender disappears from her theology. Murphy's *kenotic* ethic is a case in point. She does not make gender distinctions in the self-sacrifice that ethic requires. But that self-sacrifice can be damaging to a woman that already gives too much because of a low self-esteem. When confronted on this possibility, Murphy responded by saying that it is not self-sacrifice unless it is a choice. But choices are related to socialization. So the ethic isn't helpful for a woman who may be emeshed in relationships in a way that limits her range of choices to what will please other people.

Embodiment can also have a positive influence on a woman's theology. Nancey Murphy has a very clear idea of herself as an embodied woman. She is a physicalist, so her body is integral to all that she thinks, feels, and does. That plays out in her attitude of self-confidence and also in how she does theology and the content of her theology. Murphy's outstanding work in science and theology results in part from her positive and embodied view of herself as a woman.

Other women in the study spoke of their bodies as an integral part of the practices that sustained them in their work. Exercise, sports, healthful ways of eating, gardening, and other physical activities provided nurture and sustenance to women doing mission or academic work.

12. Interview, Pasadena, California, February 4, 2006.
13. Ibid.

Socialization and Status

Narrator and psychologist Dr. Margaret Singer sees being a woman as a disadvantage from the beginning. Early childhood socialization teaches women passivity that is not conducive to women doing theology. Moreover, "It didn't take long to figure out that being female was a disadvantage. The boys got to do all of the fun stuff." The influence on her theology seems to be that she ignores gender completely. She insists that her method has nothing to do with her being a woman. Many people expect her to deal with women's studies, especially since she worked with Paul Jewett but that is not her interest.[14]

This could be read as a negative influence on women's theology in that any aspect of theology that has to do with gender is not only ignored but avoided. The positive influence might be that a woman who does theology with the methods used by men may find more support for her ideas and be able to move in male circles more freely.

Obstacles presented by negative socialization of others can also be used intentionally to shape a mission theology. For example, while working in a conservative Christian setting Professor Judy Lingenfelter found many distressing aspects of social life at her university. She was expected to be seen with her husband on campus, to keep his calendar, and to find her identity in being his wife. Students wanted to study with her husband, who was also on the faculty, and made it clear that they didn't expect her to be as good a scholar as he. Although she found these stereotypes upsetting, she decided that in order not to become bitter about gender obstacles she would focus on doing what she could do. She would not worry about opportunities that were denied her. Nor would she take it personally when she was criticized or excluded. That decision may have had an unconscious effect on her theology of mission in that gender difficulties are not addressed. However, a conscious and positive influence that this obstacle provided was the unfettered opportunity to focus on issues of language, learning styles, and the importance of mentoring women without the negativity of obstacle issues getting in the way of her work.[15]

---

14. Margaret Singer Interview, Pasadena, California, February 3, 2006.

15. Interview, Pasadena, California, February 3, 2006.

Exclusion

Being barred from doing the tasks one is trained to do can produce anger and distress. When Dr. Roberta Rose King was told she could not preach because she was a woman when working in Kenya, she countered by taking every opportunity to stand in the pulpit. Leading hymns, and eventually doing liturgy from the pulpit prepared the congregation for the eventual break down of women's exclusion from preaching.[16]

That exclusion influences women's mission theology, particularly if they are called to a preaching ministry. They need to study the Scriptures to find warrants for their call. The autobiographies of three nineteen century women evangelists, compiled in *Sisters of the Spirit*, shows women with a calling to preach developing a theology of evangelism that included their own ministry of preaching. Rather than keep them from following their call, exclusion from the pulpit pushed them to develop a theology of mission that included them.

It has been common for women to be intentionally excluded from doing mission theology in a public way. One African professor, after earning both the Mdiv and the PhD in theology was kept from teaching mission theology at the seminary where she taught. When asked what drew her to teach spirituality, her first response was, "I'm barred from teaching mission theology, and spirituality is a way to indirectly address the theological issues that I want to address."[17] This has had a great influence on her theology of mission because she intentionally includes the dimension of spiritual formation in her work. She brings to the discussion of spiritual practices the HIV/AIDS crisis in Africa, for example. That interdisciplinary effort combines spiritual practices, contextual issues of HIV/AIDS, and ways doing mission.

Another biblical scholar in Africa, describes how the crisis of HIV/AIDS shapes her teaching. "I looked over my class and realized that in ten years time, half of the students would be dead from AIDS. How could I teach New Testament without addressing that crisis?"[18] Her story shows another type of exclusion, not on the basis of gender, but on the basis of academic discipline. New Testament scholars are to teach about the New Testament. The current HIV/AIDS crisis is not part of that text. A silencing of contemporary issues because of academic specialization hampers

16. Roberta Rose King Interview, Pasadena, California, February 4, 2006.

17. Interview, IAMS Conference, Malaysia, 2012.

18. Interview, IAMS Conference, Malaysia, 2012.

scholars from applying biblical texts to current issues. This scholar broke through that boundary, creating a theology of mission grounded in the New Testament and applicable to the HIV/AIDS crisis.

Resistance

Sometimes there is a resistance due not to exclusion but to inclusion in the theological collegium. Women can resist listening to their own experience, developing theologies that do not blindly follow the norms, and opposing discipline separations of traditions theological methods that may not be helpful in their context. Professor of anthropology Miriam Adeney cautioned the scholars at the Iguassu conference about the separations in missiology that preserve a limited status quo and hamper development of new ideas.[19]

Resisting gender distinctions and issues can also hamper women in the task of doing theology. As we saw in the chapter on overcoming obstacles, ignoring problems caused by gender discrimination does not foster creative solutions to those issues.

Some women theologians said that other women were the biggest obstacle to their development as theologians. Margaret Singer said that they are jealous because you are doing what they have told themselves they cannot do. My mother resisted my becoming a theologian and writing about women in the church. Yet she periodically contributed to the Plymouth Brethren newsletter, a curious contradiction that was hard to understand.

Nancey Murphy recounts an incident of resistance from her doctoral study at the University of California Berkeley. Male professors were ignoring women or relating to them in inappropriate ways. The women got together and confronted one of the worst offenders. He admitted to not knowing how to relate to intellectual women and confessed that his behavior was inappropriate. The tenor of the department changed after that, becoming more woman-friendly. Nancey speaks of the anger engendered by such discrimination. Anger, she says, is a biological response that readies one to fight. The approach she takes is to cool down, and then make a plan that will change the situation.[20] The women at UCB did that quite effectively. This story documents a theology of assertion

19. Adeney, "Telling Stories," 384.
20. Interview, Pasadena, California, February 4, 2006.

that can change attitudes and improve conditions for women working in academic settings.

Women that ignore the gender issue in doing theology, or women that are very negative toward other women may be unconsciously influenced to see gender as negative, or as a non-issue. Margaret Singer has male mentors that she greatly admires. She sees the influence of women in her life as negative. How does that affect how she does theology? She does not learn from women theologians or take their work into account in her own creative endeavors. She does not see issues that may be gender related. That leads to a conflation of attitudes and actions in ethics, mission, and other topics in theological reflection.

Attitudes toward obstacles can be crucial in developing mission theology. A negativity toward obstacles can entrench them or lead to bitterness or exclusion of women in the academy or church life. Ignoring obstacles, or denying their reality can also influence theologies of mission to become blind to the gender discrimination that could inform churches and academics in their study of mission.

On the positive side, gender-related obstacles can help women theologians develop new directions in theologies of mission. The use of anger for positive change, the wisdom of taking small steps to overcome gender barriers, a focus on what God is calling a woman to do rather than on what she is excluded from doing, the ability to appreciate embodiment while not letting it detract from getting the job done—each of these examples displays a theology that grows out of dealing with gender obstacles revealed in this study.

Values

The women interviewed held *differing theologies of mission*. Many articulated received theologies from their denominations or mission organizations. Some shared differences with those received theologies particularly in the areas of women's spiritual authority and leadership. None of that is surprising. Yet despite differing theologies, from evangelical, African American, or charismatic Protestant, to liberal Protestant, from conservative to liberation Catholic theologies, certain core values were stated again and again. This is perhaps the most significant finding of this study.

The values of *spirituality, equality, justice, and compassion* ran through the interviews like a crimson thread on a dark background.

Women spoke of the practices that sustained them, including a priority on *spiritual practices*. They prayed, alone and together, they studied the Bible and read Christian authors, they sought the wisdom of the Holy Spirit in their everyday life and in their relationships.

Many spoke of *equality* across gender, race, and class lines. Some spoke of the human family, others of how every person is created in the image of God. They stressed the importance of listening and receiving from those they served. Not one offered a hierarchical view of human worth on any scale.

Justice, especially for the poor was an important theme. However, the language of justice as used in liberal Protestant and Roman Catholic circles did not dominate interviews of those with a conservative received theology. Justice was expressed more in the language of anti-racism, honoring local leaders, and working for rights of women and children in oppressive contexts.

The stereotypical justice vs. charity dichotomy did not appear in the interviews. No one saw acts of service as "charity" to the helpless or less deserving. *Compassion* instead, a compassion for equals, was frequently voiced. Service without love was not an option. Nor was placing denominational doctrines above meeting needs.

Character

Who we are becoming as people and theologians offers another contribution of women to mission theologies. The narrators in this study exhibited three qualities of character that marked their ministries and theologies: *perseverance, flexibility, and creativity*. Growth in their character mattered to each interviewee. Many told stories of perseverance in the face of obstacles. The stories focused not so much on what the problem was but how they pursued a solution or way out of the problem that would benefit others. One Brazilian spoke of her calling to become a missionary and how it was put on hold for years as she raised her children. In the meantime she supported a missionary in Peru. After her children were grown she went to Peru to visit this missionary through whom she had fostered her own vision for mission work. She wrote and published a book about that missionary. When I met her in 2009 she was in training to become a missionary herself.[21] Perseverance . . .

21. Interview, Tereolpolis, Brazil, July 2009.

At a recent meeting of the American Society of Missiologists, mission historian Angela Dries spoke about the *flexibility* exhibited by Catholic women religious. She said that when the Church is in a state of flux, women find a niche to do crucial work. When institutionalization takes over that area, women sometimes find themselves excluded. But in that window of time, flexibility marks their work and much can be accomplished.[22] For example, although racial problems plagued the United States during the 1940s, Catholics worked to establish school curricula that would overcome ignorance and distain for others. Sister Roslia Walsh of the Missionary Helpers of the Holy Souls developed course outlines for grade schools addressing racism and Maryknoll Sister Mary Just David became the best spokesperson for a positive appreciation of world cultures and people.[23] Before Latin American liberation theologies became accepted by the Vatican, teams of priests, Sisters, and laity went among the people in Latin America demonstrating the observe, listen to the Word, and then act methodology of liberation theology.[24] That required an amazing and assertive flexibility.

Flexibility rests on a deeper virtue, that of *humility*. Flexibility is incompatible with pride because pride demands a place, a role, an authority, a recognition. To be flexible one must fit in, find the place where the work can be done, usually without recognition. Jesus' mother Mary provides a model here. Her song in Luke describes the attitude women narrators often expressed. They were lowly but exalted in God's eyes.[25] Narrators expressed gratitude for the ability and opportunity to do the work of God, regardless of any recognition they may or may not have received. Flexiblity . . .

Those attitudes show a *creativity* in theological interpretation and personal interpretation of life's meaning. Women showed creativity in working with local communities, in devising paths through difficulties, in using the arts to express theologies and develop ministries, in making a way out of no way. When I shared this quality exhibited in so many interviews in the Women's Track at the Quadrennial Meeting of the International Association of Mission Studies in 2012, women latched onto it. Creativity of women in theology and mission became a theme for the

22. Discussion after Panel Presentation, ASM Annual Meeting, June 17, 2012.

23. Dries, *Missionary Movement*, 171.

24. Ibid., 219.

25. Luke 1:52

week. Participants highlighted the creativity of women in their contexts and in their ministries. They shared stories of creative ways to accomplish their God-given work.

One described the difficulty of doing AIDS education among African pastors at regional meetings. She was consistently turned down. Her creative solution? To refocus the seminar description to keeping healthy, something the pastors were interested in. Her presentation to gain access to seminars became more general. But the seminar itself didn't change much. She began with a few comments about general health. The rest of the seminar focused on HIV and AIDS.[26] Creativity . . .

Women and Men as Co-Workers

It has been a privilege to work with women doing the research for this project. The project is small but I hope gives a glimpse into a larger movement of women doing mission theology. By listening, I discovered that women work contextually, using their own experiences as a source for theological reflection. They tell their stories and honor the stories of others. By listening, I learned that women build theologies from their practices and community involvement. They hear others into speech. By listening I learned that women use obstacles as avenues to develop new pathways and theologies of mission. I learned that women value spirituality, equality, justice, and compassion. They care about their character, humbly developing habits of perseverance, flexibility, and creativity. Without holding a single mission theology, women are contributing to mission studies, to communities, and to the *missio Dei* in very significant ways.

The significance of the study lies in the praxis methodology and the ways of dealing with obstacles. The women put their feet first. Interviews also reveal crucial themes that show the values and methods of women doing mission theology and the qualities of character that drive their efforts.

The process of discerning how those contributions influence the church and broader society and how they can be integrated with existing theologies of mission is a task only just begun. A number of questions may be helpful in that discernment process:

26. Discussion after presentation, IAMS Quadrennial Meeting, Toronto, 2012.

- Which contributions are locally or denominationally contained and which can be universally applied?

- How do the values and practices women exhibit in this study relate to Scripture and church tradition?

- Are the findings of this study consistent with the methods and values of women doing ministry in other religious traditions?

- How can these contributions be integrated into mission theologies of churches, denominations, and mainstream mission theologies?

Perhaps those questions can help us initiate a conversation among mission workers and theologians of mission, both women and men.

Our task as women and as men called to leadership in the church is to think about and discuss in the presence of the Holy Spirit our lives and experiences with God, the calling we have each have received in our communities, and the actions we are taking to fulfill those callings. For some, resistance may be necessary in order to follow the visions that God has given. For others, supporting the new ways that God is calling women to leadership may be required. Leaders in the church can become Acts 2 Christians, dreaming dreams and seeing visions, developing practices that develop competences and nurture Christians in following the call that turned us around and set us upon this journey. We need to write and speak about these things so that in our communities and in our mission work as a church we can more fully understand for our own time the depth and riches of the wisdom and love of God, who has been revealed to us in Jesus Christ.[27]

---

27. This chapter was first presented as the Annual Lecture in Mission at the Chicago Theological Union, March, 2012.

Appendix on Method

THIS STUDY FORMALLY BEGAN in 2006 at the American Society of Missiology women's luncheon in Techny, Illinois. About twenty women attended—Christian workers, wives of missionaries or academics, and a few women missiologists. The following questionnaire was used for seventy-five one-hour personal interviews and fifteen email interviews.

Using this tool, interviews garnered the narratives of women as they articulated their journey into mission. I attempted to keep myself and my own opinions out of the interview, focusing on their stories. They became narrators, rather than interviewees, taking the subject of their own lives and mission work as the central focus of the study.

Interview Tool

Name:
Email:
Age:
Ethnicity:
Origin:
Family:
Education:
Work:
Address:
Phone:

1. When and how did you first become interested in Christian Mission? Influences? Call?

2. What experiences have you had in mission experiences? Where? What?

3. How has being a woman influenced your identity, experience and work?

4. What is mission all about for you?
   Theology: What is God doing?
   Ecclesiology: How church involved?

5. What ways can Christian mission best be accomplished?
   Methods?
   Contexts?
   Groups/Individuals?

6. What goals do you have for Christianity Mission?
   Personal?
   Community?
   Global?

7. Anything Else?

8. Permission to use material from this interview in book? With name or anonymous?

The theoretical framework for this study is an interpretive, socially constructed world that is value laden and contextually oriented. Actions and stories reveal theologies of mission that were sometimes but not always articulated by the narrators. Using grounded theory, I collated the results, discovering themes and issues that crossed cultural lines and differences in received theologies and denominational stances.

Narrative studies contribute to mission theories and mission theologies as described in my article "Why Biography?" I hope this study makes contributions in those areas.

Bibliography

Adeney, Frances S. *Christian Women in Indonesia: A Narrative Study of Gender and Religion.* Syracuse: Syracuse University Press, 2003.

———. "Citizenship Ethics: Contributions of Classical Virtue Theory and Responsibility Ethics." PhD diss., Graduate Theological Union, 1989.

———. "Desert Blooms: Nicaraguan Women in the '80s." *Radix Magazine* 16.5 (April–May 1985).

———. "Factors in the Rise of Women Leaders in the Sulawesi Protestant Churches." In *Een vakkracht in het Koninkrijk: Kerk-en zendingshistorische opstellen*, edited by Chr. G. F. de Jong. Netherlands: Uitgeverij Groen, 2005.

———. "Feet First: How Practices Have Shaped My Theology of Evangelism and Mission." In *Teaching Mission in a Global Context*, edited by Patricia Lloyd-Sidle and Bonnie Sue Lewis, 8–22. Louisville: Geneva, 2001.

———. "A Framework for Knowledge, a Source for Ethics and a Vision of Justice." In *The Unique Christ in Our Pluralist World*, edited by Bruce J. Nicholls, 119–27. Carlisle: Paternoster, 1994.

———. "From the Inside Out: Gender Ideologies and Christian Mission in Indonesia." In *Gospel Bearers, Gender Barriers: Missionary Women in the Twentieth Century*, edited by Dana L. Robert, 172–84. Maryknoll, NY: Orbis, 2002.

———. *Graceful Evangelism: Christian Witness in a Complex World.* Grand Rapids: Baker Academic, 2009.

———. "How I, a Christian, Have Learned from Buddhist Practice." In *Christians Talk about Buddhist Meditation, Buddhists Talk about Christian Prayer*, edited by Rita M. Gross and Terry C. Muck, 15–19. New York: Continuum, 2003.

———. "Human Rights and Responsibilities: Christian Perspectives." In *Christianity and Human Rights: Influences and Issues*, edited by Frances S. Adeney and Arvind Sharma. Albany: State University of New York Press, 2007.

———. "Insights from Women's Spirituality: An Argument for Embodiment." *Radix Magazine* 23.3 (Fall 1995).

———. "Strategies of Resistance." In *Christian Women in Indonesia: A Narrative Study of Gender and Religion*, 76–103. Syracuse: Syracuse University Press, 2003.

———. "Universal Values and Cultural Forms." *Dialog* 34 (1995) 297–300.

————. "Why Biography? Contributions of Narrative Studies to Mission Theology and Mission Theory." *Mission Studies* 26 (2009) 153–72.

Adeney, Miriam. *Daughters of Islam: Building Bridges with Muslim Women.* Downers Grove, IL: InterVarsity, 2002.

————. *Kingdom Without Borders: The Untold Story of Global Christianity.* Downers Grove, IL: InterVarsity, 2009.

————. "Telling Stories: Contextualization and American Missiology." In *Global Missiology for the 21st Century: The Iguassu Dialogue,* edited by William D. Taylor, 377–88. Grand Rapids: Baker Academic, 2000.

Allen, Catherine B. "Shifting Sands for Southern Baptist Women in Missions." In *Gospel Bearers, Gender Barriers: Missionary Women in the Twentieth Century,* edited by Dana L. Robert, 113–26. Maryknoll, NY: Orbis, 2002.

Ammerman, Nancy. "North American Fundamentalism." In *Media, Culture, and the Religious Right,* edited by Linda Kintz and Julia Lesage, 90–101. Minneapolis: University of Minnesota Press, 1998.

Anderson, Bonnie S., and Judith P. Zinsser, eds. *A History of Their Own: Women in Europe from Prehistory to the Present.* 2 vols. New York: Harper & Row, 1988.

Andrews, William L., ed. *Sisters of the Spirit: Three Black Women's Autobiographies of the Nineteenth Century.* Bloomington: Indiana University Press, 1986.

Aquinas, Thomas. *Summa Theologica.* Translated by Fathers of the English Dominican Province. Revised by Daniel J. Sullivan. 2 vols. Great Books of the Western World 19–20. Chicago: Encyclopedia Britannica, 1952.

Aristotle. *Generation of Animals.* Translated by A. L. Peck. Cambridge: Harvard University Press, 1962.

————. *Nicomachean Ethics.* In vol. 2 of *The Works of Aristotle.* Translated into English under the editorship of W. D. Ross. Great Books of the Western World 9. Chicago: Encyclopedia Britannica, 1952.

Augsberger, David. *Pastoral Counseling across Cultures.* Philadelphia: Westminster, 1986.

Augustine. *The City of God.* Translated by Marcus Dods. Great Books of the Western World 18. Chicago: Encyclopedia Britannica, 1952.

Aycock, Jennifer. "At the Crossroads of Narratives: Identity Formation among Second Generation *Maghrébin* Women in France and Christian Mission." Paper submitted to the International Association of Mission Studies, Toronto, Ontario, August, 2012.

Bacon, Margaret Hope. *Mothers of Feminism: The Story of Quaker Women in America.* San Francisco: Harper & Row, 1986.

Barfoot, Chas H. *Aimee Semple McPherson and the Making of Modern Pentecostalism, 1890–1926.* London: Equinox, 2011.

Bauman, Zygmunt. *Liquid Times: Living in an Age of Uncertainty.* Cambridge: Polity, 2007.

————. *Postmodern Ethics.* Cambridge: Blackwell, 1993.

Bednarowski, Mary. *The Religious Imagination of American Women.* Bloomington: Indiana University Press, 1999.

Belenky, Mary Field, et al., eds. *Women's Ways of Knowing: The Development of Self, Voice, and Mind.* New York: Basic Books, 1986.

Bellagamba, Anthony. *Mission and Ministry in the Global Church.* Maryknoll, NY: Orbis, 1992.

Bellah, Robert N., et al. *Habits of the Heart: Individualism and Commitment in American Life*. Berkeley: University of California Press, 1985.

Bendroth, Margaret Lamberts, and Virginia Lieson Brereton, eds. *Women and Twentieth-Century Protestantism*. Urbana: University of Illinois Press, 2002.

Berger, Peter. *The Sacred Canopy: The Elements of a Sociological Theory of Religion*. Garden City, NY: Doubleday, 1967.

Bergner, Daniel. "The Call." *New York Times Magazine*, January 29, 2006. http://www. nytimes.com/2006/01/29/magazine/29missionaries.html?pagewanted=all&_r=0.

Bevans, Stephen B., and Roger P. Schroeder. *Prophetic Dialogue: Reflections on Christian Mission Today*. Maryknoll, NY: Orbis, 2011.

Bevans, Stephen B., et al., eds. *The Healing Circle: Essays in Cross-Cultural Mission*. 2000. Reprint, Eugene, OR: Wipf & Stock, 2004.

Bolton, John Robert Glorney, and Julia Bolton Holloway, eds. *Aurora Leigh, and Other Poems*. New York: Penguin, 1995.

Borresen, Kari Elisabeth, ed. *The Image of God: Gender Models in Judaeo-Christian Tradition*. Minneapolis: Fortress, 1995.

Brasher, Brenda. *Godly Women: Fundamentalism and Female Power*. New Brunswick, NJ: Rutgers University Press, 1998.

Burke, Mary P. "Women's Rights Movement" and "Women's Status." In *Encyclopedia Americana*, 29:103–10. Danbury, CT: Grolier, 1991.

Capra, Fritjof. *The Web of Life: A New Scientific Understanding of Living Systems*. New York: Anchor, 1997.

Carritt, Jeanne Brooks. "Our Bodies Are Still Ourselves as We Age, and They Are Still Sacred." In *Sacred Dimensions of Women's Experience*, edited by Elizabeth Dodson Gray, 232–39. Wellesley, MA: Roundtable, 1988.

Chadwick, Whitney. *Women, Art and Society*. 4th ed. New York: Thames & Hudson, 2007.

Chilcote, Paul W., and Laceye C. Warner, eds. *The Study of Evangelism: Exploring a Missional Practice of the Church*. Grand Rapids: Eerdmans, 2008.

Christ, Carol P., and Judith Plaskow. *Womanspirit Rising: A Feminist Reader in Religion*. San Francisco: HarperOne, 1992.

Chun, Chae Ok. "Integrity of Mission in the Light of the Gospel: Bearing Witness of the Spirit; An Asian Perspective." Paper presented at the 11th International Conference of the International Association for Mission Studies, Port Dixon, Malaysia, August 4, 2004.

Chung, Hyun Kyung. *Struggle to Be the Sun Again: Introducing Asian Women's Theology*. Maryknoll, NY: Orbis, 1991.

Coles, Robert. *Dorothy Day: A Radical Devotion*. Reading, MA: Addison-Wesley, 1987.

Cooey, Paula M. "The Redemption of the Body: Post Patriarchal Reconstruction of the Inherited Christian Doctrine." In *After Patriarchy: Feminist Transformations of the World Religions*, edited by Paula M. Cooey et al., 106–30. Maryknoll, NY: Orbis, 1991.

Creegan, Nicola Hoggard, and Christine D. Pohl. *Living on the Boundaries: Evangelical Women, Feminism and the Theological Academy*. Downers Grove, IL: InterVarsity, 2005.

Crysdale, Cynthia S. W. *Embracing Travail: Retrieving the Cross Today*. New York: Continuum, 1999.

Culpepper, Emily. "The Spiritual, Political Journey of a Feminist Freethinker." In *After Patriarchy: Feminist Transformations of the World Religions*, edited by Paula M. Cooey et al., 146–65. Maryknoll, NY: Orbis, 1991.

Cummings, Kathleen Sprows. *New Women of the Old Faith: Gender and American Catholicism in the Progressive Era*. Chapel Hill: University of North Carolina Press, 2010.

Davis, Natalie Zemon, and Arlette Farge, eds. *A History of Women in the West*. Vol. 3, *Renaissance and Enlightenment Paradoxes*. Cambridge: Harvard University Press, 1993.

Day, Dorothy. *From Union Square to Rome*. 1938 Reprint, New York: Arno, 1978.

———. *Loaves and Fishes: The Inspiring Story of the Catholic Worker Movement*. New York: Harper & Row, 1963.

———. *The Long Loneliness: The Autobiography of Dorothy Day*. New York: Harper, 1952.

Devi, Swarnalatha. "The Struggle of *Dalit* Christian Women in India." In *Feminist Theology from the Third World: A Reader*, edited by Ursula King, 135–37. Maryknoll, NY: SPCK, 1994.

Dickinson, Emily. *The Poems of Emily Dickinson: Reading Edition*. Edited by R. W. Franklin. Cambridge: Belknap Press of Harvard University Press, 1998.

Donovan, Vincent J. *Cristianity Rediscovered*. 2nd ed. Maryknoll, NY: Orbis, 2001.

Dowling, Collette. *The Cinderella Complex: Women's Hidden Fear of Independence*. New York: Summit, 1981.

Dowsett, Rose. "Dry Bones in the West." In *Global Missiology for the 21st Century: The Iguassu Dialogue*, edited by William D. Taylor, 447–62. Grand Rapids: Baker Academic, 2000.

Dries, Angelyn. *The Missionary Movement in American Catholic History*. Maryknoll, NY: Orbis, 1998.

Duane, Elmer. *Cross-Cultural Connections: Stepping Out and Fitting In around the World*. Downers Grove, IL: InterVarsity, 2002.

Dube, Musa W. "Methods of Integrating HIV/AIDS in Biblical Studies." In *HIV/AIDS and the Curriculum: Methods of Integrating HIV/AIDS in Theological Programmes*, edited by Musa W. Dube. Geneva: WCC, 2003.

Dube, Musa W., and Musimbi R. A. Kanyoro, eds. *Grant Me Justice! HIV/AIDS and Gender Readings of the Bible*. Pietermaritzburg, South Africa: Cluster, 2004.

Elaw, Zilpha. "Memoirs of the Life, Religious Experience, Ministerial Travels and Labors of Mrs. Zilpha Elaw." In *Sisters of the Spirit: Three Black Women's Autobiographies of the Nineteenth Century*, edited by William L. Andrews, 49–160. Bloomington: Indiana University Press, 1986.

Elshtain, Jean Bethke. *Public Man, Private Woman: Women in Social and Political Thought*. Princeton: Princeton University Press, 1993.

English, Leona M. "Feminist Identities: Negotiations in the Third Space." *Feminist Theology* 13 (2004) 97–125.

Espinosa, Gastón. "'Your Daughters Shall Prophesy': A History of Women in Ministry in the Latino Pentecostal Movement in the United States." In *Women and Twentieth-Century Protestantism*, edited by Margaret Lamberts Bendroth and Virginia Lieson Brereton, 25–48. Urbana: University of Illinois Press, 2002.

Estés, Clarissa Pinkola. *Women Who Run With the Wolves: Myths and Stories of the Wild Woman Archetype*. New York: Ballantine, 1992.

Fiorenza, Elisabeth Schüssler. *In Memory of Her: A Feminist Theological Reconstruction of Christian Origins.* New York: Crossroad, 1985.

———. "Word, Spirit and Power: Women in Early Christian Communities." In *Women of Spirit: Female Leadership in the Jewish and Christian Traditions,* edited by Rosemary Radford Ruether and Eleanor McLaughlin, 29–70. New York: Simon & Schuster, 1979.

Foote, Julia A. J. "A Brand Plucked from the Fire: An Autobiographical Sketch by Mrs. Julia A. J. Foote." In *Sisters of the Spirit: Black Women's Autobiographies of the Nineteenth Century,* edited by William L. Andrews, 161–234. Bloomington: Indiana University Press, 1986.

Fritz, Pak. "Pemperbangan Economi dan Agama di Timor Barat." Master's thesis, Satya Wacana Christian University, 1994.

Frymer-Kensky, Tikva. *Reading the Women of the Bible: A New Interpretation of Their Stories.* New York: Schocken, 2002.

Fulkerson, Mary McClintock. *Changing the Subject: Women's Discourses and Feminist Theology.* Minneapolis: Fortress, 1944.

Furfey, Paul Hanly. *Love and the Urban Ghetto.* Maryknoll, NY: Orbis, 1978.

Gadamer, Hans-Georg. *Reason in the Age of Science.* Translated by Frederick G. Lawrence. Cambridge: MIT Press, 1981.

———. *Truth and Method.* 2nd rev. ed. New York: Continuum, 1996.

Gateley, Edwina. *Psalms of a Laywoman.* Franklin, WI: Sheed & Ward, 1999.

Gaustad, Edwin S., ed. *Memoirs of the Spirit.* Grand Rapids: Eerdmans, 1999.

Geertz, Clifford. *The Interpretation of Cultures.* New York: Basic Books, 1974.

George, Sherron Kay. *Better Together: The Future of Presbyterian Mission.* Louisville: Geneva, 2010.

———. *Called as Partners in Christ's Service: The Practice of God's Mission.* Louisville: Geneva, 2004.

———. "From Missionary to Missiologist at the Margins: Three Decades of Transforming Mission." In *Teaching Mission in a Global Context,* edited by Patricia Lloyd-Sidle and Bonnie Sue Lewis, 40–53. Louisville: Geneva, 2001.

Gilligan, Carol. *In a Different Voice: Psychological Theory and Women's Development.* Cambridge: Harvard University Press, 1993.

Gladwell, Malcolm. *Outliers: The Story of Success.* New York: Little, Brown, 2008.

Glanville, Elizabeth. "Breaking the Dividing Walls: A Theological Reflection." Paper for the IAMS Quadrennial Assembly, Malaysia, 2004.

———. "Leadership Development for Women in Christian Ministry." PhD diss., Fuller Theological Seminary, 2000.

Grant, Jacquelyn. *White Women's Christ and Black Women's Jesus: Feminist Christology and Womanist Response.* Atlanta: Scholars, 1989.

Gray, Elizabeth Dodson, ed. *Sacred Dimensions of Women's Experience.* Wellesley, MA: Roundtable, 1988.

Grogan, Sarah, *Body Image: Understanding Body Dissatisfaction in Men, Women and Children.* London: Routledge, 1999.

Gross, Rita. *Feminism and Religion: An Introduction.* Boston: Beacon, 1996.

Gubar, Susan. "Introduction." In *A Room of One's Own,* by Virginia Wolf. Orlando, FL: Houghton Mifflin Harcourt, 2005.

Gum, Florence J. "A Designing Woman." *Horizons* (January/February 1995) 14.

Gundry, Patricia. *Woman, Be Free!* Grand Rapids: Zondervan, 1977.

Habermas, Jürgen. *The Theory of Communicative Action.* Vol. 1, *Reason and the Rationalization of Society.* Translated by Thomas McCarthy. Boston: Beacon, 1984.

Haney, Marsha Snulligan. "Africentricity: A Missiological Pathway toward Christian Transformation." In *Africentric Approaches to Christian Ministry: Strengthening Urban Congregations in African American Communites,* edited by Ronald Edward Peters and Marsha Haney Snulligan, 151–65. Lanham, MD: University Press of America, 2006.

———. "Development of a New Christian Missiological Identity." In *Teaching Mission in a Global Context,* edited by Patricia Lloyd-Sidle and Bonnie Sue Lewis, 79–92. Louisville: Geneva, 2001.

Haney, Marsha Snulligan, and Ronald Edward Peters, eds. *Africentric Approaches to Christian Ministry: Strengthening Urban Congregations in African American Communites.* Lanham, MD: University Press of America, 2006.

Hardesty, Nancy A. *Women Called to Witness: Evangelical Feminism in the Nineteenth Century.* Nashville: Abingdon, 1984.

Harris, Paula. "Nestorian Community, Spirituality, and Mission." In *Global Missiology for the 21st Century: The Iguassu Dialogue,* edited by William D. Taylor, 495–502. Grand Rapids: Baker Academic, 2000.

Harrison, Beverly Wildung. *Making the Connections: Essays in Feminist Social Ethics.* Edited by Carol S. Robb. Boston: Beacon, 1985.

Harvey, Paul. "Saints but Not Subordinates: The Woman's Missionary Union of the Southern Baptist Convention." In *Women and Twentieth-Century Protestantism,* edited by Margaret Lamberts Bendroth and Virginia Lieson Brereton, 4–24. Urbana: University of Illinois Press, 2002.

Hatch, Edwin. "Breathe on Me, Breath of God." In *The Hymnal 1982,* 508. New York: Church Publishing, 1982.

Heath, Elaine A. *The Mystic Way of Evangelism: A Contemplative Vision for Christian Outreach.* Grand Rapids: Baker Academic, 2008.

———. "The Quest for Holiness." In *The Oxford Handbook of Methodist Studies,* edited by William J. Abraham and James E. Kirby. Oxford: Oxford University Press, 2011.

———. "The *Via Negativa* in the Life and Writing of Phoebe Palmer." *Wesleyan Theological Journal* 41 (2006) 87–111.

Heath, Elaine A., and Larry Duggins. *Missional, Monastic, Mainline: A Guide to Starting Missional Micro-Communities in Historically Mainline Traditions.* Eugene, OR: Cascade, 2014.

Heath, Elaine A., and Scott T. Kisker. *Longing for Spring: A New Vision for Wesleyan Community.* Eugene, OR: Cascade, 2010.

Heim, Melissa Lewis. "Standing Behind the Looms." In *Gospel Bearers, Gender Barriers: Missionary Women in the Twentieth Century,* edited by Dana L. Robert. Maryknoll, NY: Orbis, 2002.

Henry, Carl F. H. *God, Revelation, and Authority.* Vol. 1, *God Who Speaks and Shows: Preliminary Considerations.* Waco, TX: Word, 1976.

Hiebert, Paul G., et al. *Understanding Folk Religion: A Christian Response to Popular Beliefs and Practices.* Grand Rapids: Baker, 1999.

Holmes, Emily A., and Wendy Farley, eds. *Women, Writing, Theology: Transforming a Tradition of Exclusion.* Waco, TX: Baylor University Press, 2011.

Hunt, Mary E. "Priests, Priests Everywhere and Not a One Ordained." *Horizons* 21 (1989) 10–12.

Isasi-Díaz, Ada María. *En la Lucha: Elaborating a* Mujerista *Theology*. Minneapolis: Fortress, 2004.

Johnson, Elizabeth A. *She Who Is: The Mystery of God in Feminist Theological Discourse*. New York: Crossroad, 1992.

Kartowijono, Ny Sujatin. *Perkembangan Pergerakan Wanita Indonesia*. Jakarta: PT Inti Idayu, 1980.

Katoppo, Marianne. *Compassionate and Free: An Asian Woman's Theology*. Maryknoll, NY: Orbis, 1980.

Kenyon, Jane. *Collected Poems*. St. Paul, MN: Graywolf, 2005.

Kim, Kirsteen. *The Holy Spirit in the World: A Global Conversation*. Maryknoll, NY: Orbis, 2007.

King, Roberta Rose, et al. *Music in the Life of the African Church*. Waco, TX: Baylor University Press, 2008.

King, Ursula, ed. *Feminist Theology from the Third World: A Reader*. Maryknoll, NY: Orbis, 1994.

Kintz, Linda, and Julia Lesage, eds. *Media, Culture, and the Religious Right*. Minneapolis: University of Minnesota Press, 1998.

Koentjaraningrat. *Javanese Culture*. Singapore: Oxford University Press/Institute of Southeast Asian Studies, 1985.

LaCugna, Catherine Mowry. "The Practical Trinity." In *Exploring Christian Spirituality: An Ecumenical Reader*, edited by Kenneth J. Collins, 273–82. Grand Rapids: Baker, 2000.

Lamberty, Kim. "Christian Mission in Zones of Violent Conflict: Accompaniment as Prophetic Dialogue." Paper presented at the annual meeting of the American Society of Missiology, Techny, IL, June 16, 2012.

Lee, Jarena. "The Life and Religious Experience of Jarena Lee." In *Sisters of the Spirit: Black Women's Autobiographies of the Nineteenth Century*, edited by William D. Andrews, 25–48. Bloomington: Indiana University Press, 1986.

Lewis, Bonnie Sue. *Creating Christian Indians: Native Clergy in the Presbyterian Church*. Norman: University of Oklahoma Press, 2003.

Liu, Bohong. "Women's Double Burden." Lecture given at the International Conference on Role Conflicts of Contemporary Career Women, Hangzhou University, Zhejiang Province, People's Republic of China, October 26, 1993.

Lloyd-Sidle, Patricia, ed. *Celebrating Our Call: Stories of Women's Ordination*. Louisville: Westminster John Knox, 2001.

Lloyd-Sidle, Patricia, and Bonnie Sue Lewis, eds. *Teaching Mission in a Global Context*. Louisville: Geneva, 2001.

Maddux, Kristy. *The Faithful Citizen: Popular Christian Media and Gendered Civic Identities*. Waco, TX: Baylor University Press, 2010.

Mannheim, Karl. *Ideology and Utopia*. New York: Harcourt, Brace, & World, Harvest edition, n.d.

McAvoy, Jane, ed. *Kitchen Talk: Sharing Our Stories of Faith*. St. Louis: Chalice, 2003.

McClure, Marion. "In the Picture, in the Halls, in the Home." In *Celebrating Our Call: Stories of Women's Ordination*, edited by Patricia Lloyd-Sidle, 101–9. Louisville: Westminster John Knox, 2001.

McCoy, Charles S. *When Gods Change: Hope for Theology*. Nashville: Abingdon, 1980.

McDade, Carol. "Prayer to Friends." In *Celebrating Our Call: Stories of Women's Ordination*, edited by Patricia Lloyd-Sidle, 56. Louisville: Westminster John Knox, 2001.

McFague, Sallie. *Abundant Life: Rethinking Theology and Economy for a Planet in Peril*. Minneapolis: Fortress, 2001.

Mead, George Herbert. *Mind, Self & Society from the Standpoint of a Social Behaviorist*. Edited by Charles W. Morris. Chicago: University of Chicago Press, 1962.

Miller, William D. *Dorothy Day: A Biography*. New York: HarperCollins, 1984.

Miller-McLemore, Bonnie J. "Work and Family: Can Anyone 'Have It All'?" *Horizons* 12 (1999) 4–6.

Moltmann-Wendel, Elisabeth. *Rediscovering Friendship: Awakening to the Power and Promise of Women's Friendships*. Minneapolis: Fortress, 2001.

Moraga, Cherrie, and Gloria Anzaldúa, eds. *This Bridge Called My Back: Writings by Radical Women of Color*. New York: Kitchen Table, 1981.

Muck, Terry C. "Dynamic Identity, Christian Conversion, and Missiological Praxis." Paper presented at the annual meeting of the American Society of Missiology, Techny, IL, June 18, 2011.

———, ed. *Faith in Action Study Bible: Living God's Word in a Changing World*. Grand Rapids: Zondervan, 2005.

Muck, Terry C., and Frances S. Adeney. *Christianity Encountering World Religions*. Grand Rapids: Baker Academic, 2009.

The Mudflower Collective. *God's Fierce Whimsy: Christian Feminism and Theological Education*. New York: Pilgrim, 1985.

Niebuhr, H. Richard. *The Meaning of Revelation*. New York: Macmillan, 1960.

Njoroge, Nyambura J. "Groaning and Languishing in Labor Pains." In *Groaning in Faith: African Women in the Household of God*, edited by Musimbi R. A. Kanyoro and Nyambura J. Njoroge, 3–15. Nairobi: Acton, 1996.

———. *Kiama Kia Ngo: An African Christian Feminist Ethic of Resistance and Transformation*. Legon, Ghana: Legon Theological Studies Series, 2000.

Nussbaum, Martha C. *Upheavals of Thought: The Intelligence of Emotions*. Cambridge University Press, 2003.

O'Connor, June E. *The Moral Vision of Dorothy Day: A Feminist Perspective*. New York: Crossroad, 1991.

Parvey, Constance F. "Re-membering: A Global Perspective on Women." In *Christian Feminism: Visions of a New Humanity*, edited by Judith L. Weidman, 158–79. San Francisco: Harper & Row, 1984.

Polanyi, Michael. *Personal Knowledge: Towards a Post-Critical Philosophy*. Chicago: University of Chicago Press, 1958.

Pope-Levison, Priscilla, and John R. Levison. *Jesus in Global Contexts*. Louisville: Westminster John Knox, 1992.

Putnam, Robert D., and David E. Campbell. *American Grace*. New York: Simon & Schuster, 2012. Kindle Edition.

Rabinow, Paul. "Humanism as Nihilism." In *Social Science as Moral Inquiry*, edited by Norma Haan, 52–75. New York: Columbia University Press, 1983.

Reilly, Patricia Lynn. *A God Who Looks Like Me: Discovering a Woman-Affirming Spirituality*. New York: Ballantine, 1995.

Riegle, Rosalie G. *Dorothy Day: Portraits by Those Who Knew Her*. Maryknoll, NY: Orbis, 2006.

Ripley, Dorothy. *The Bank of Faith and Works United*. Philadelphia: J. H Cunningham, 1819.

Robert, Dana L. *American Women in Mission: A Social History of Their Thought and Practice*. Macon, GA: Mercer University Press, 1997.

———. *Christian Mission: How Christianity Became a World Religion*. West Sussex, UK: Wiley-Blackwell, 2009.

———. *Converting Colonialism: Visions and Realities in Mission History, 1706–1914*. Grand Rapids: Eerdmans, 2008.

———. "Evangelist or Homemaker?" In *North American Foreign Missions, 1810–1914: Theology, Theory, and Policy*, edited by Wilbur R. Shenk, 116–32. Grand Rapids: Eerdmans, 2004.

———, ed. *Gospel Bearers, Gender Barriers: Missionary Women in the Twentieth Century*. Maryknoll, NY: Orbis, 2002.

———. "The Influence of American Missionary Women on the World Back Home." *Religion and American Culture: A Journal of Interpretation* 12 (2002) 59–89.

———. "Innovation and Consolidation in Methodist Mission History." In *World Mission in the Wesleyan Spirit*, edited by Darrell L. Whiteman and Gerald H. Anderson, 127–37. Franklin, TN: Providence, 2009.

Roberts, Michelle Voss. "Fear and Women's Writings: Choosing the Better Part." In *Women, Writing, Theology: Transforming a Tradition of Exclusion*, 11–32. Waco, TX: Baylor University Press, 2011.

Roche, Barbara A. "Headlines of the Struggle." In *Celebrating Our Call: Stories of Women's Ordination*, edited by Patricia Lloyd-Sidle. Louisville: Westminster John Knox, 2001.

Ross, Cathy, et al. "The Iguassu Affirmation: A Commentary by Eight Reflective Practitioners." In *Global Missiology for the 21st Century: The Iguassu Dialogue*, edited by William D. Taylor, 521–48. Grand Rapids: Baker Academic, 2000.

Ruether, Rosemary Radford. *Sexism and God-Talk: Toward a Feminist Theology*. 2nd ed. Boston: Beacon, 1993.

———. *Women-Church: Theology and Practice of Feminist Liturgical Communities*. San Francisco: Harper & Row, 1985.

Ruether, Rosemary Radford, and Eleanor McLaughlin, eds. *Women of Spirit: Female Leadership in the Jewish and Christian Traditions*. New York: Simon & Schuster, 1979.

Russell, Letty. *Church in the Round: Feminist Interpretation of the Church*. Louisville: Westminster John Knox, 1993.

Sabuni, Nyamko. "Q&A." *Monocle: A Briefing on Global Affairs, Business, Culture,& Design* 6 (2012) 58.

Sandberg, Sheryl. *Leaning In: Women, Work and the Will to Lead*. New York: Knopf, 2013. Kindle Edition.

Sanneh, Lamin. *Translating the Message: The Missionary Impact on Culture*. Maryknoll, NY: Orbis, 1989.

Savage, Barbara Dianne. *Your Spirits Walk Beside Us: The Politics of Black Religion*. Cambridge: Harvard University Press, 2008.

Scanzoni, Letha Dawson, and Nancy A. Hardesty. *All We're Meant to Be: Biblical Feminism for Today*. Waco, TX: Word, 1974.

Schneiders, Sandra. "Does the Bible Have a Post-Modern Message?" In *Post-Modern Theology: Christian Faith in a Pluralist World*, edited by Frederic B. Burnham. New York: HarperSanFrancisco,1989.

Sedmak, Clemens. *Doing Local Theology: A Guide for Artisans of a New Humanity*. Maryknoll, NY: Orbis, 2002.

Sewell, Marilyn, ed. *Cries of the Spirit: A Celebration of Women's Spirituality*. Boston: Beacon, 1991.

Shapiro, Judith. *Sources of the Spring: Mothers Through the Eyes of Women Writers*. Berkeley: Conari, 1998.

Sharma, Arvind, and Katherine K. Young. *Fundamentalism and Women in World Religions*. New York: T. & T. Clark, 2008.

Smith, J. Alfred, Sr. *Speak Until Justice Wakes: Prophetic Reflections from J. Alfred Smith, Sr.* Edited by Jini M. Kilgore. Valley Forge, PA: Judson, 2006.

Smith, Susan. *Women in Mission: From the New Testament to Today*. Maryknoll, NY: Orbis, 2007.

Stott, John. "The Bible in World Evangelization." In *Perspectives on the World Christian Movement: A Reader*, edited by Ralph D. Winter and Stephen C. Hawthorne. Rev. ed. Pasadena, CA: William Carey Library, 1992.

Sullivan, Norma. *Masters and Managers: A Study of Gender Relations in Urban Java*. St. Leonards, NSW: Allen & Unwin, 1995.

Tangkudung, Magdelena H. "Mitos dan Kodrat: Suatu Kajian Mengenai Kedudukan dan Peranan Wanita Kristen di Minahasa" [Myth and Fate: An Analysis of the Position and Role of Christian Women in Minahasa]. Master's thesis, Satya Wacana Christian University, 1994.

Tavard, George H. *Women in Christian Tradition*. Notre Dame: University of Notre Dame Press, 1973.

Taylor, Charles. *The Ethics of Authenticity*. Cambridge: Harvard University Press, 1991.

———. *Sources of the Self: The Making of the Modern Identity*. Cambridge: Harvard University Press,1989.

Taylor, William D., ed. *Global Missiology for the 21st Century: The Iguassu Dialogue*. Grand Rapids: Baker Academic, 2000.

Thomas, Norman. "Radical Mission in a Post-9/11 World: Creative Dissonances." *International Bulletin of Missionary Research* 29 (2005) 2–8.

Tooze, Ruth E. "Woman Suffrage." In *Encyclopedia Americana*, 29:110–12. Danbury, CT: Grolier, 1982.

Torrey, R. A., et al., eds. *The Fundamentals: A Testimony to the Truth*. 1917. Reprint, Grand Rapids: Baker, 1972.

Uchem, Rose. "Gender Inequality as an Enduring Obstacle to Mission." Paper presented at International Association for Mission Studies 2004, Malaysia, August 6, 2009.

———. "Overcoming Women's Subordination: An Igbo African and Christian Perspective: Envisioning an Inclusive Theology with reference to Women." Parkland FL: Dissertation.com, 2001.

Valian, Virginia. *Why So Slow? The Advancement of Women*. Cambridge: MIT Press, 1998.

Van der Meer, Antonia Leonara. "The Scriptures, the Church, and Humanity: Who Should Do Mission and Why?" In *Gobal Missiology for the 21st Century: The Iguassu Dialogue*, edited by William D. Taylor, 149–62. Grand Rapids: Baker Academic, 2000.

Van Leeuwen, Mary Stewart, ed. *After Eden: Facing the Challenge of Gender Reconciliation.* Grand Rapids: Eerdmans, 1993.

————."A Bit of Evangelical Evasion." *New York Times,* October 4, 1997, 15.

————. *Gender and Grace: Love, Work and Parenting in a Changing World.* Downers Grove, IL: InterVarsity, 1990.

Van Wijk-Bos, Johanna W. H. *Reformed and Feminist.* Louisville: Westminster John Knox, 1997.

————. *Reimagining God: The Case for Scriptural Diversity.* Louisville: Westminster John Knox, 1995.

Walker, Alice. *The Color Purple.* New York: Washington Square, 1983.

————, ed. *In Search of Our Mothers' Gardens: Womanist Prose.* San Diego: Harcourt Brace Jovanovich, 2003.

Walls, Andrew F. "The Multiple Conversions of Timothy Richard: A Paradigm of Missionary Experience." In *The Cross-Cultural Process in Christian History,* 236–58. Maryknoll, NY: Orbis, 2002.

Warner, Laceye C. *Saving Women: Retrieving Evangelistic Theology and Practice.* Waco, TX: Baylor University Press, 2007.

Weber, Max. *From Max Weber: Essays in Sociology.* Translated and edited by H. H. Gerth and C. Wright Mills. New York: Oxford University Press, 1958.

————. "The Meaning of Discipline." In *From Max Weber: Essays in Sociology,* translated and edited by H. H. Gerth and C. Wright Mills, 253–64. New York: Oxford University Press, 1958.

————. "Religion and Rationalization." Author's introduction to *Sociology of Religion.* In *The Protestant Ethic and the Spirit of Capitalism,* edited by Robert N. Bellah, 13–31. New York: Scribner's, 1958.

————. "The Sociology of Charismatic Authority." In *From Max Weber: Essays in Sociology,* translated and edited by H. H. Gerth and C. Wright Mills, 245–52. New York: Oxford University Press, 1958.

Weidman, Judith L., ed. *Christian Feminism: Visions of a New Humanity.* San Francisco: Harper & Row, 1984.

Welch, Sharon. *A Feminist Ethic of Risk.* Minneapolis: Fortress, 1990.

Wemple, Suzanne Foray. *Women in Frankish Society: Marriage and the Cloister, 500–900.* Philadelphia: University of Pennsylvania Press, 1981.

Williams, Delores S. *Sisters in the Wilderness: The Challenge of Womanist God-Talk.* Maryknoll, NY: Orbis, 1992.

Wilson, Edward O. *On Human Nature.* Cambridge: Harvard University Press, 1994.

Woolf, Virginia. *A Room of One's Own.* Annotated and with an introduction by Susan Gubar. Orlando, FL: Houghton Mifflin Harcourt, 2005.

Yayasan Bina Darma. *Kajian Perempuan: Dari Kodrat Hinqqa Ipteck* [*Women's Philosophy: From Fate to Independence*]. Salatiga, Indonesia: Universitas Kristen Satya Wacana, 1992.

Young, Barbara A. "Moderator? Who Me?" *Horizons* (July/August 1994) 34.

Zahl, Paul F. M. *Five Women of the English Reformation.* Grand Rapids: Eerdmans, 2001.

Zimmerman, Jonathan. *Innocents Abroad: American Teachers in the American Century.* Cambridge: Harvard University Press, 2006.

Websites

Christians for Biblical Equality (CBE). http://www.cbeinternational.org/.

Films

The Curse of the Jade Scorpion. Directed by Woody Allen. Paramount, 2004.

Fried Green Tomatoes. Directed by Jon Avnet. Universal Studios, 1991.

A League of Their Own. Directed by Penny Marshall. Columbia Pictures, 1992.

Out of Africa. Directed by Sydney Pollack. NBC Universal, 1985.

To Be Alive! Codirected by Francis Thompson and Alexander Hammid. Produced by S. C. Johnson & Co. 1964.

Index

abundant life, theology of, 204
academic positions
  for women, 70
  women's exclusion from, 192
accompaniment, mission practice of,
  169
Adam and Eve, 215
Adeney, Miriam, 72, 80–81, 92, 106,
  252, 263
Africa, 14
  Christians' view of, 71
  HIV/AIDS crisis, 262–63
  hymns in, 189
  restrictions for Catholic women,
    102
  traditional music, 188–89
Africa Inland Mission, 165
African American Protestant women,
  opposition, 164
African Methodist Episcopal Church,
  18, 22–23, 224
  ordination of women as deacons,
    41, 43–44
aging process, 29
alienation, 154–155
Allen, Richard, 22–23, 41, 224
Allen, Woody, *The Curse of the Jade
  Scorpion*, 200, 202
Althaus, Terry, 160
ambition, 161
American Academy of Religion, 54
American Grace, 167
American Society of Missiologists,
  xiii–xvi, 76–81

meeting, 266
  meeting in 2012, 96
  women's luncheon, 2006, 269
American Women in Mission (Robert),
  77
Anabaptist theology, 150
Anderson, Bonnie S., 218
Andrews, William, *Sisters of the Spirit*,
  17, 174, 262
anger, 96, 116, 263
Anglican church in Rwanda, 22
Anthony, Susan B., 222
anthropological insights, 80
Apostles' Creed, 95
Aquila, 36*n*
Aquinas, Thomas, 38, 56
Archer, Doreen, 137
Aristotle, 51, 104, 143, 197–98, 213,
  256
Arregrei, Josune (sister), 90
art resources, 187–209
  historical perspective, 192–194
  hymns, 188–190
  poetry, 194–205
Asbury Theological Seminary, 92
Askew, Anne, 37
associations of Beguines, 216
atomic bomb, as act of love, 199
attributes of God, 38
Auca people, 232
Augustine, 215, 256
  on sin, 199
authenticity, 107–8
authority sources, 11, 15–34, 35

285